Rehab

Your Way

(to)

Riches

Christmas 1996

Dear Maire and Luiz —

Merry Reading
and
Happy "Habilitating!"

With love,
Susan, David
Eamon & Aisling Hegarty

Other books by R. Dodge Woodson:

Get the Most for Your Remodeling Dollar
The Complete Guide to Buying Your First Home
The Complete Guide to Home Plumbing Repair and Replacement

Rehab Your Way to Riches

Guide to High Profit/Low Risk Renovation of Residential Property

R. Dodge Woodson

BETTERWAY BOOKS
Cincinnati, Ohio

Cover design by Rick Britton
Cover photograph by Newlight Studios
Typography by Park Lane Associates

97 96 95 94 93   5 4 3

Library of Congress Cataloging-in-Publication Data

Woodson, R. Dodge (Roger Dodge)
    Rehab your way to riches : guide to high profit/low risk renovation
of residential property / R. Dodge Woodson.
       p. cm.
    Includes index.
    ISBN 1-55870-247-4 (paperback)
    1. Housing rehabilitation. 2. Real estate investment. I. Title.
HD1390.5.W66 1992
332.63'243--dc20   92-17177
                                                    CIP

*This book is dedicated to my daughter, Afton Amber Woodson,
and my wife, Kimberley Woodson who provided suggestions and many hours
of patience in the production of this book.
I also thank my parents, Woody and Maralou Woodson, for many years
of attention and support.*

CONTENTS

INTRODUCTION: CREATE YOUR OWN WEALTH

You have seen the television advertisements and read the books; can you really get rich with real estate? Absolutely! You can build a respectable fortune recycling real estate. You don't have to be a carpenter or a plumber to renovate rundown houses for a living. Even if you have never worked around construction, you can make money in the rehab business. If you are already a real estate investor, getting involved with rehab projects will open a world of new opportunities.

The secret is in what you buy, the price you pay, and what you do with the property after you own it. Real estate is the foundation for the fortunes of scores of millionaires. Historically, this commodity has been safe and profitable for experienced investors. I started as a rental tenant, and after less than four years I controlled real estate assets in excess of $4,000,000.

My real estate wealth was not a product of luck —I worked hard to reach my goals. If you think you can stroll into the real estate business and with no effort emerge a millionaire, you're wrong. Investing in real estate does not require a college degree, but it does demand intelligence and good judgment. Jumping on the no-money-down bandwagon and hoping for a free ride to financial independence is more likely to drive you into bankruptcy. You must know the rules of this competitive game to win.

Quick profits are normally associated with dangerous risks. With the right knowledge and preparation, you can limit the dangers and maximize your profits. Real estate offers many ways for building a profitable income. This book is dedicated to one of the quickest ways to amass a fortune with limited risk and minimal time. Buying rundown properties and renovating them creates an outstanding opportunity to make serious money. Risks are always present, but they can be neutralized with the proper procedures.

WHAT MAKES A REAL ESTATE INVESTOR?

The most important qualities of a triumphant investor are a creative mind and an awareness of the real estate market. These two qualities can produce wealth beyond belief. Market awareness is essential in making decisions. Using the creative mind is how you get the most from your investment. Combining these two will result in a winning investment portfolio.

When investors look at a property, each sees a different opportunity. Some will see the chance for a quick turnover with a satisfactory profit. Others will recognize the long-term holding appeal of the property. Many consider the risks and ultimately talk themselves out of making a purchase offer. How you view a potential property has much to do with your final decision.

What would you see if you were inspecting a neglected triplex? Is your attention riveted by the ugly kitchen and the outdated bathroom? Maybe you concentrate on the income potential of the property. Seeing an opportunity to make interior renovations, to allow for an extra bedroom, might influence your thoughts. The extra bedroom will provide the basis for a higher rental income or sale price. Can you visualize the dwelling's appearance after cosmetic improvements? Do you have the ability to look beyond the present condition and envision a comfortable place to live, with a healthy rental income? If you can, you are on the right track.

When you examine the building, can you estimate the fair market value of the investment? There is more to consider than just the asking price of surrounding properties and rental incomes. You must learn to analyze a property's merit using a variety of methods. Will you assess the value through an income approach or a comparable sales approach? With a small multi-family building, the comparable sales approach is the most reliable appraisal method. Using an income approach does not work well on buildings with fewer than six apartments. These are only a few of the considerations pertinent to the purchase of the property.

Before you can become a prosperous rehab investor, you must learn the techniques required to sway the odds. A low sale price alone does not make a building worth buying. Good investments are the result of research and careful evaluation. This is where using your brain power is critical. You must spend the time to learn how and what to buy before you purchase real estate. The methods are complex, but they are not unduly difficult. There are numerous ways to begin rehabbing your way to riches.

When done properly, renovating real estate will produce more profit than any other easily accessible real estate venture. Rehabbing real estate is open to anyone with average intelligence and good credit. You don't need large sums of reserve capital, and you need not be a mechanical engineer. The skills needed to be successful are easily defined and quickly learned. If you are enterprising, you can mastermind some major deals.

HOW MUCH CAN YOU MAKE?

How much money can you make recycling real estate? The earnings are limited only by your imagination and effort. On an average single-family house, your walk-away profit could be more than $12,000. Rehabbing an eight-unit apartment building could produce a profit exceeding $50,000. Working with office and commercial space can send the profits over $100,000.

How long does it take to achieve these earnings? Renovating a single family home can be accomplished in less than sixty days. An eight-unit apartment building could be substantially improved in less than four months. Commercial projects vary in nature and in the time needed to complete them. Are you willing to work part-time for four months to earn $50,000? This type of project is not beyond the reach of most potential rehab investors.

What do you have to do to make this kind of money? The answer to this question is formidable. It would require an entire book to explain all the requirements of being a successful rehabber. Fortunately, you have that book in your hands. This book teaches you everything you need to know to get into the rehab business. To make the money we will talk about here, you will have to use your head, not your hands. If you decide to participate in the physical work of the project, your profits will grow even larger.

I based the profit potential of the examples above assuming an experienced real estate investor acting as his own general contractor. The skills needed for such a project are completely detailed throughout this book. Many of the other books available on this subject assume the readers are going to be do-it-yourself tradesmen. I have written this book to benefit the individual who does not have the time, skills, or inclination to do the actual work. If your personality allows you to be well-organized and a good manager, these income figures are possible.

Don't think the profit figures are the most you can make. The profit numbers are based on average conditions, not some fantasy deal you will never find. It would be misleading only to present the best case scenarios. I have seen such percentages realized on a regular basis. I have done it myself, and I have helped scores of other investors do it. By writing this book, I am helping *you* to do it.

Why is the rehab business so lucrative? The profit potential from rehab deals is high due to the type of work being done. In some cases, you are changing the function of a property to a more valuable use. In other cases, you might be turning a rundown home into a highly desirable showplace. It could be as simple as modernizing a property by replacing outdated siding and installing new kitchen cabinets. The profit possible from real estate is good if all you do is buy and sell. When you add the rehab dimension, the profit potential multiplies rapidly.

Acting as your own general contractor can be worth 20% of the total rehab expenses. On an apartment building, the general contractor's portion of the profit is significant. If you renovate eight apartments, with a retail cost of $30,000 per unit, the general contractor's gross profit should be $48,000. On a job this large, the contractor may bid the work with a lower profit margin. The general contractor may only charge 15% for his services. This is still $36,000. As an added profit incentive, there are special improvement loans available for neighborhood revitalization. It is possible to obtain these loans in amounts up to $33,500 for each apartment renovated. You can use these below-market loans to save additional money, while making up to $48,000 for your time.

There is nothing preventing you from capturing most of this money for your personal bank account. The general contractor does have many responsibilities, but you can learn to manage your own projects. If you get into technical difficulty, you can consult with professionals on an hourly basis. This will be expensive, but not nearly as expensive as hiring a general contractor.

Learning how to sell your own property effectively is a major factor in your search for higher profits. Brokerage fees vary greatly. For residential properties, expect to pay between 5% and 7%. For commercial property, don't be surprised when asked to commit to a 10% commission. Saving 10% on the sale of a $500,000 apartment building is a noticeable addition to your financial statement. There will be some cost of sale expense incurred to sell your own property, but it will not come close to $50,000.

As an investor who plans strategically, you can profit from your investment. This profit is in addition to the money you can save by being your own general contractor and broker. Awareness and understanding of creative financing concepts will yield an even higher return on your investment. Once you learn to structure a combination acquisition and rehab loan, you will only be responsible for up-front loan fees and closing costs. Some lenders will even allow these charges to be paid from the loan proceeds. With this type of financing, you can do this $500,000 deal with very little of your own money.

In this example, assume the renovations will be complete in four months. It will take three months to sell the building. Your investment is locked up for seven months. Now run the numbers and see how much money you could make for seven months of part-time work. Depending on how much of the expediting work you do, you could walk away with over $100,000. This is not a bad return on your time or your investment.

Deals like this are done regularly by investors with an aptitude for recycling real estate. As you can see from this example, my earlier forecast for a $50,000 profit is not just a dream. Rehab projects give you the opportunity literally to build your own wealth. Can you think of another way you could make $100,000 per year on a part-time basis? To achieve this goal, you will have to learn to think with an open mind.

CAN ANYONE BECOME A REHABBER?

Are you asking yourself, if it's this easy, why isn't everyone else doing it? They are! Look around your area, do you see houses being remodeled? Are apartment buildings being improved in sections of your city? If you live in an area capable of supporting human habitation, you can bet there are rehab professionals working around you. In small towns, the projects may be concentrated on homes and business space. In cities, multi-family properties are a prime target for experienced rehab investors. Even retailers use rehab techniques to overhaul a property and unveil the improvements with a grand reopening sale.

One reason more real estate investors are not involved in rehabilitation work is the fear of failure. They look at decrepit properties and have no idea what is required to convert them to profitable investments. On the surface, the job looks enormous. The average person does not feel qualified to assess the extent of damage to a rundown property. Most people don't know how to measure a building's improved value against the cost to fix it. They are afraid the improvement costs will push the properties above their market value. It is natural for people to be afraid of the unknown. With this book and the appropriate research, you do not have to remain ignorant of the rehab business.

It is not reasonable to assume you can perfect the needed rehab skills in a week or two. It will take time, exposure to the process, and study to maximize your money-making abilities. Consider the money you can make as a rehab investor. Then, after reading this book, evaluate the time you will need to prepare for the task. I believe you will conclude the requirements of the job are obtainable and will produce hitherto undreamed of wealth.

This book is intended to make you money. By reading it, you will gain the advantage of my years of experience in real estate investing and rehabilitation.

As books take time to publish and have long shelf lives, the information contained in them can become outdated. At the time of this writing, all the information is current and accurate to the best of my knowledge. The examples may be rounded off to make them easier to understand, but the principles are sound. Before you rely on potentially dated programs, confirm their present existence and conformity.

WHITE-COLLAR REHAB PROJECTS 1

Finding the right path to travel is one of the most important elements in winning the real estate game. As a professional broker and consultant, I have witnessed many investors entering the real estate business. One of the first questions typically asked is, "Do I have to do the rehab work myself to make the investment profitable?" There are many ways to make money rehabbing real estate without ever picking up a hammer. Although there is a place for the hands-on investor, an analytical mind and good credit will produce as many, if not more, profitable results.

Unfortunately, lack of information seems to lump most white-collar investors into limited categories. They base their decisions on the common misconception that smaller is better. Most of these new investors plan to buy single-family homes and small multi-family properties. After reading the many books on no-money-down deals, these novice investors get pumped up. Typically, they are ready to sign any no-money-down contract to purchase property.

Amazingly enough, they are willing to buy any property, in any place, as long as it is a no-money-down deal. Price is not a prime consideration for these investors. Their focal point is to build a rental portfolio without investing their own cash. There are times when this type of strategy is effective, but tax reform laws have reduced the advantages of highly-leveraged rental properties. Many of the books written prior to the tax changes are still being sold. Inexperienced investors read those books and believe the procedures will work in today's market.

In reality, the deals carried a high risk *before* the tax changes, and now they can result in catastrophe. Another misconception many new investors have pertains to small multi-family properties. The investors believe they can buy these properties and retire on the rental income. On average, it is very difficult for a residential-grade small multi-family property to produce a positive cash flow. These buildings, containing four apartments or fewer, are a common target for new investors.

The sale prices are low when compared to commercial-grade buildings, with more than four rental units. Down payment requirements are less, and interest rates on the loans for smaller buildings are lower. For the non-owner occupant investor, the small properties are not very profitable on a monthly income basis. Some investors plan to live in one of the apartments and rent the others. Under these conditions, the smaller units can be a viable consideration.

When first-time investors move to buy multi-family property, they are concerned with the wrong qualities. If the investor plans to owner-occupy one of the units, he tends to concentrate on the aesthetics and amenities of the property. Often these investors end up over-improving a property and never recovering their costs. The definition of an investment is the act of putting money into a venture in order to make a profit. You can't allow your personal desires to cloud your judgment. Many investors see duplexes as a way of having their tenant pay the mortgage payment. They don't take financing requirements or vacancy ratios into consideration.

Due to loan underwriting requirements on residential-grade loans, you are limited in your financing options. Commercial-grade buildings require larger down payments, but these down payments can be made in many ways, without using cash. The interest rates are higher on commercial loans, but the income from larger buildings is greater. A vacancy in a triplex could be critical to your cash flow; the same vacancy in an eight-unit is easier to float. Prices on big buildings are higher, but the rate of return on the investment improves significantly. In general, for the off-site investor, a building with six to eight apartments offers the most potential.

Determining the best types of projects to tackle is an important step in setting your rehab goals. What works well for one investor can be a terrible disappointment for another. There are many factors to influence your decision on what properties to work with. There are also questions to be answered about your intended use for completed projects. Before you embark on the rehab trail, you must have some idea of where you want to go.

PICKING YOUR PATH

There are three basic paths to choose from in the real estate rehabilitation business. All three paths are profitable but require different actions and adjustments. Ask yourself why you want to become a rehab investor and how long you want to keep the property. Are you trying to generate quick cash? Do you want to limit your exposure to a few years, or do you want to retain the properties as retirement income? When generating fast money is your goal, you should follow the quick-flip route. The mechanics of this involve selling the property immediately upon completion of the rehab work.

The Quick-Flip

This practice has the advantage of producing cash profits in a relatively short time. The quick-flip procedure is the most difficult avenue to follow. Finding properties with potential to support a quick turnaround takes time and creative thought. Real estate for this purpose must be bought at a low enough price to accommodate your improvements and profit. You will not have the advantage of annual appreciation to increase your income. The property must be ideally suited for renovations, and the market demand must support your plans.

All your profit will come from the improvements made. If a change in use is possible, the profits from the quick-flip deal improve. If the economy sags, you could be left out on a limb. You are committed to the project, and if it doesn't sell, you could have a serious problem on your hands. Most experienced investors use the quick-flip concept in conjunction with one of the other rehab paths.

Limited Exposure

The second path requires you to be prepared to become a landlord. In this mode, you keep the building as a rental property for a specific period of time before selling. The holding time is generally three to five years. This approach provides a safety-net for quick-flip investors and a stronger profit for most rehab investors. You derive all the profit from the quick-flip deal, plus you enjoy annual appreciation and some tax advantages.

You lose the immediate cash income, but there are ways to extract cash from the improved property. When you do a quick-flip, you must pay taxes on the profits. Learning to pluck your profit from completed projects, through refinancing for example, you get the use of your money without paying taxes until the property is sold. This can amount to thousands of dollars.

As a quick-flip investor, this second method will provide added protection from risks. If you are willing and able to hold your completed project, you are not at the mercy of the market. This requires forethought. The improvements you make must be both economical and attractive to appeal to both purchasers and tenants. If economic conditions are good, once the improvements are made, you may decide to sell the property immediately for a quick profit. However, if your completed property hits the market during a slump, you can still use it as rental property, instead of selling for a minimal profit. If your costs run overboard, you can hedge your losses by renting the property. As time passes, annual appreciation will lift your property's value. At some point, you will be able to sell and recover your initial investment. This is a much better option than selling fast at a loss.

Retirement Portfolio

The third option is meant to carry you into your retirement years. With this approach, the rehabber has no intention of selling the completed property. He plans to keep all rehabbed property as a long-term investment. This technique is popular among settled investors. While the properties are not sold, you can still get to use a percentage of your rehab profits. The more property you hold, the stronger your net worth becomes. The increased net worth enables you to continue building your retirement portfolio.

Strategies for each method differ. There is enough difference between the three methods to require distinct types of property and financing. All pertinent information for each method is covered in this book. Your rehab business will do best when you combine the paths to success.

RESIDENTIAL PROJECTS

Residential rehab projects are where most investors launch their career. The potential profit from small residential properties is limited, but so is the risk. Most people have some concept of how the residential market works. They have been tenants or homeowners. Following the For Sale and For Rent ads in your newspaper can give you a good feel for the prices of residential property in your area. There is usually a large supply of buyers for residential property. The purchasers are not hard-nosed business professionals who judge the property on numbers alone. Residential purchasers buy based on emotions and affordability.

This can be reason enough to start with residential property. If you have little or no experience with income property, trying to jump directly into it could be a mistake. Residential deals are relatively tame, and risk factors are kept at a minimum. If the deal goes bad, you should be able to bail out of it with limited losses. There is money to be made with single-family properties, but mid-range multi-family buildings offer some of the best rehab deals. Even though people reside in apartment buildings, if the building has more than four units, it is considered commercial property, not residential. There is much more on this subject later in the book, but we will go over the generalities here.

COMMERCIAL PROJECTS

For novice rehabbers, most commercial projects should be avoided. With large commercial deals, the players are heavyweights. There is a lot of money on the table, and these professionals will often go to any extreme to win. Unless you are uniquely qualified, rich, or clairvoyant, don't compete with the big boys of the commercial arena. After you have gained experience, you may wish to try your hand, but be careful. There are no rules in the commercial arena, and the gladiators of this game can be ruthless.

The exception to the commercial rule is office space and mid-range multi-family projects. Both of these opportunities are open to the average investor and offer very prosperous returns. For most investors, this level of the business is a desirable and attainable goal. The profits are high, the risks are moderate, and almost anyone can learn to meet the criteria of these light commercial deals.

MINIMUM QUALIFICATIONS

You won't need a pickup truck and a tool belt. The primary requirement for becoming a rehab investor is a sharp mind. Ideally, you should be an entrepreneur with a strong desire to succeed. Good organizational skills are another valuable asset for the rehab investor. Good credit makes the job easier, but you won't need a lot of cash. Having or developing a knowledge of financing and business principles will make your projects more effective and profitable.

If you can manage the execution of the rehab work yourself, you will see your profits pile up. Sales skills are always helpful, but they are not a requirement. You can start at ground zero, with nothing more than a desire to make money. The more you learn to do, the more money you can make. There is no limit to what you could do to increase your profits. The remainder of the book points out specific ways to maximize your earnings. If you have the ability to learn, you can get into the real estate recycling business.

Do You Have to Be a Carpenter?

Many investors would say they are at a loss in

the rehab market because they lack remodeling skills. Since they are not able to perform the physical work, they believe they are not suited to rehab projects. This belief is ridiculous. It is understandable that they might feel that way, but there is no merit to such an assessment of the situation. We are not talking about performing brain surgery or splitting the atom. You don't have to have years of experience in the field of construction to consider rehab projects. Are full-time carpenters better qualified for the rehab business than you are? Sure, they are.

Without question, the full-time carpenter has some advantages over the office professional when it comes to rehab projects. A carpenter has the knowledge to perform much of the work himself, but the tradesman and the office manager have one thing in common. They will both have to work with subcontractors to complete work in specific areas of the job. There will be plumbing, heating, and electrical contractors needed in most improvements. Carpenters are not accustomed to working with drywall, paint, or carpet. While a carpenter may be able to do the job, it is doubtful he can do it cost effectively. Outside of the hammer and nails portion of the job, the carpenter will have to depend on numerous people to put his deal together. Both the experienced tradesman and the inexperienced bookkeeper will have to rely on a variety of contractors to yield a good rehab project.

Real Estate Experience

What advantages does a real estate broker have? A professional broker benefits from a current knowledge of market conditions. The broker should know how to buy and sell her rehab projects. She should understand financing and have a feel for what investments market demands will support. Does she have any advantages with the construction process? She may know a few people in the trade, but being a broker does not automatically qualify her to be a general contractor.

A good broker possesses negotiating skills to use in the rehab business, but she is not usually accustomed to playing with her own money. It is easy for brokers to advise other people how to spend money, but spending their own is a different story. As a commissioned salesperson, the broker may have trouble obtaining financing for the project.

Brokers have undependable incomes, therefore making it difficult to meet qualifying ratios and standards.

The list of potential rehabbers could go on indefinitely. Everyone who has ever been associated with real estate in some way could itemize his or her edge as a real estate investor. If this is true, then why should you feel at a disadvantage? If you are a banker, you have financing experience and money connections. If you are a surveyor, you know people in related trades and are not a stranger to real estate transactions. You also have a feel for the future of different areas from surveying properties being sold.

A doctor knows all types of people. Clients and associates can be parlayed into players for the rehab game. Almost any business contacts can become beneficial to your rehab strategy. Clients with trade skills can be recruited for the hands-on work. Clients with tax consequences could be approached as buyers for your completed project. Don't feel as though you are taking advantage of your professional position by mentioning investment opportunities to these people. In fact, you are opening the door for them to make money. This is a symbiotic relationship; everyone wins when they put profits in their pockets.

The fact that you are not an expert in every aspect of a rehab endeavor is no reason to scrap the idea of becoming a rehab investor. The full-time carpenter can do his own carpentry work, but can he organize and manage the entire project? Does he have the ability to structure creative financing? What sales skills does the carpenter possess? It is rare to find an individual with *all* the skills used in the renovation business. After years of working in the business, you may become competent to handle a majority of the tasks, but it is unlikely you will be able to do everything yourself.

Even if you could do the whole job without help, it would not be cost effective. A good manager has developed the ability to delegate duties to other team players. The ability to allocate allows the manager to make the best use of his or her time. It is no different with rehab projects. As you define what you do best, those are the areas for you to tackle personally. Leave the aspects you struggle with to better qualified talent. Concentrate on your strong points, and assemble a squadron of experienced professionals to enable you to make more deals. If you can learn enough about each phase to understand what is going on, you can administer a profitable venture.

As a white-collar rehabber, you have the advantage of developing a volume business. By delegating duties instead of hammering nails, you can work several projects at the same time. With the right team, you can do every deal you find. By having time away from the job, you are free to ferret out hidden rehab treasures. If you were stuck on the job doing the work, you would not be able to find new deals until the current job was done. There is a lot to be said for having the freedom to move around finding new projects.

Another advantage to the volume business is its ability to spread your risks. If you have one job going and it turns bad, your income could be severely strangled. If you have four projects going simultaneously and one goes bad, you still have three successful projects to pull from. The three good ones will help keep the bad one floating until you can recover your investment. There is no reason you should feel disadvantaged.

THE END RESULT

When you get past your fears and into the business, you are headed for financial freedom. When done correctly, white-collar rehab deals can provide a very comfortable income. You can maintain your present job while building your rehab business. When the investments start paying off, you have an option. You can pursue rehabbing full-time, or you can continue working the deals on a part-time basis. You have the dual advantage of drawing on your contacts to benefit your rehab business and reaping large profits on top of your regular salary.

As you gain experience, you can move up to larger projects. When you get into rehabbing for professional office space and mid-range multi-family buildings, your income will be envied by top professionals. When people go to college, they spend years earning a degree. When they enter the workplace, they are placed in entry-level or junior positions with modest salaries. Spending half the amount of time required to get your degree, you can become a seasoned rehabber with an annual income in excess of $75,000.

The future for rehab investors is rosy. Undeveloped land is disappearing, and new-construction prices are pushing real estate out of reach for many people. These two factors combine to put more emphasis on making use of existing resources. In the next ten years, the demand for recycled real estate will be even stronger. Many investors recognized this pattern years ago, and have already benefited from the first wave of investment profits. Although it is too late to get in on the ground floor of the rehab industry, it is never too late to join the ranks of real estate millionaires.

WHAT'S NEXT?

You now know what the rehab business is about; you will learn how to become a part of it. The following chapters are filled with invaluable information, capable of putting you in touch with rehab riches. The information compiled here is the result of more than seventeen years' experience in the businesses surrounding rehab investments. The suggestions and advice are produced from firsthand training.

Let me tell you about my credentials for guiding you through the rehab business. I am a licensed, designated real estate broker. I hold a master plumber's license and a general contractor's license. I have owned a remodeling company and held a Class A builder's license. I have dealt with people from all walks of life, from first-time home buyers, to tradesmen, to millionaires. My daily activities put me in touch with people from all venues of the business world. As a consultant, I work with investors on a regular basis. I have amassed large real estate holdings and have rehabbed many properties.

As a remodeling contractor, I know what to expect from old buildings. As a general contractor, I am well aware of the challenges you will face in that role. I can teach you how to complete a rehab project effectively and efficiently. During my career, I have made mistakes, some of them very costly. You will have the advantage of learning from my mistakes for just the cost of this book.

I have dealt with land development, shopping center development, single-family homes, multi-family properties, and light commercial projects. For my skills and personality, single-family homes and mid-sized apartment buildings have produced the most consistent profits. Some of my associates have had their best luck with commercial projects. I believe you will have a good feel for your personal preference by the end of this book.

Turning fear into respect is the most important step you can take. By expanding your knowledge, fear will subside as it is replaced with understanding. You will be able to appreciate the requirements and benefits of investment endeavors. Most people work long and hard at their jobs to be able to afford a good life for their families. Yet there never seems to be enough money to alleviate the pressures of bills and everyday life. The rehab business is much more than a means for the other guy to get rich. It can be your ticket to a rewarding future.

WHAT TO LOOK FOR IN HIGH-PROFIT, LOW-RISK VENTURES

2

Rehab profits come in many forms and fashions. Sharp negotiating skills can provide above-average profits. Acting as your own general contractor offers the opportunity to pocket 20% of the total renovation cost. Selling your property without involving a broker can save another 5% to 10%. Structuring a tight financing package adds to your overall profit. Learning to stretch an appraisal will have a positive effect on your earnings. All of these are viable methods to increase your income from the rehab business.

These variables should all be considered in your improvement plans. When you are able to combine them, your profits will multiply. While all these methods are effective in theory, their implemented value depends on acquiring the right property. Having the knowledge and proper tools makes any job easier. Creative financing and self-supervision of the improvements and sale are the tools. Knowledge comes with experience. To realize maximum profits, you must start with the right properties.

PROPERTY SELECTION

Regardless of your experience and tools, if you are building on a bad foundation, your achievement will collapse like a house of cards. While your rehab project may not physically fall, your profit percentage will. Developing skills to choose the best properties takes time, but the effort is worthwhile. Starting with the appropriate property allows you

two luxuries. First, you should make more money. Second, if you make some miscalculations in your cost factors, the cushion provided by prime properties will soften your loss.

If you begin your project with a poor property selection, your trip through the renovations will be uphill all the way. With research and legwork, you can turn up some excellent opportunities. Chapter 4 tells you which properties to avoid. This chapter instructs you in the types of properties to pursue.

What makes one property more valuable as a rehab project than a similar property on the next street corner? How do a property's characteristics raise the risk level? The answers to these questions are complex and numerous. Throughout this chapter, you will find vital information to answer both questions. The examples given can be applied to different types of property. In each example, you will be told what types of properties suit the mold for the advice given. The potential for profit exists in almost any real estate transaction. The distinguishing difference is the degree of risk required to achieve the profit.

ZONING

A property's zoning status can have a tremendous impact on its future value. Zoning values apply to all types of real estate. For the sake of this example, assume you have found two houses with basically identical physical characteristics. They are large homes, with multiple levels and numerous rooms. The cost to put each house into marketable condition is the same. Both houses are located in the same town, but in areas that are zoned differently. Except for the zoning status, all other factors are equal. The asking price for each property is the same.

The first house is zoned for residential use only. The second house is zoned residential, but its zoning also allows professional services and office space. Often these will be termed commercial development districts or mixed use zones. The result of this decision should be obvious. If you rehab the first house, you have a nice home to sell. If you rehab the second house, you have a lucrative investment property to sell. Which would you prefer to own?

There will be additional rehab costs incurred to convert the second house to professional space. These costs will be insignificant when compared to the difference in the sale price of each completed property. Working the zoning angle enables you to seek the highest and best use of a property. This is one of the best ways to watch your profits grow.

Change of Use

Another good example of using the zoning advantage involves small multi-family properties. In this example, you have found two duplexes. They are both acceptable rehab projects. The two duplexes are priced about the same, but one duplex is in a different zoning grid. The first duplex offers good profit potential as a duplex rehab job. The second duplex promises a much higher rate of return. While the first property can be renovated into a very desirable duplex, the second building provides a more prosperous potential for expanding your investment dollars.

The first duplex does not allow for any change of use. It can be dressed up, but it must remain a duplex. The second building's zoning allows four apartments. With creative interior remodeling or simple exterior additions, you can own a handsome four-unit income property. The improvement cost will be more on the second duplex, but the sale price will be much higher.

The sale price will increase for several reasons. The first reason is the cost of improvements and conversion. The second way the value escalates is

through the change of use. This profit is a direct result of your research and purchasing skills. When you convert the duplex into a quadruplex, your profit potential mounts. This type of profit is a result of brain power. Zoning can mean much more to your project's value than physical improvements.

Present Use vs. Zoning Restrictions

Whether you are buying residential, multi-family, or commercial space, zoning can be your quickest track to unparalleled profits. Zoning can also turn your dreams into nightmares. Imagine finding a property being used as a triplex, with strong rehab potential. You run the numbers and jump on the deal. After closing, you apply for the required permits to refurbish the place. You believe that, once the place is fixed up, the rents can be raised and your profit will be very attractive.

When the permits are applied for, you are informed the property is zoned for single-family use. The previous owner converted the property into apartments without approval from the local jurisdiction. You bought what you thought was a triplex, but it is only legal as a single-family home. All your projections and cost estimates were based on the present use of the property. Since the property was converted without the proper authorization, you must return the building to single-family use as the new owner. What does this do to your anticipated earnings? It drives your investment into the red and forces you to take heavy financial losses.

This type of situation is not rare. Many property owners convert their homes into rental property without the proper approvals. Confirm that what you believe you are buying is factual and functional. Never take anything for granted. If you have any recourse against the seller, the cost and time to pursue it may be extensive. In the time it takes you to go after the seller, you may lose the property and your credit rating. Real estate is a serious business; you must protect yourself at all times.

LOCATION

Location is much of the value of real estate. Among real estate brokers, there are three things affecting a property's value. The three things are said to be location, location, and location. The saying may be a cliché, but there is truth in the phrase. How many times have you found the perfect property, except for its location? Have you ever wished you could pick up the property and move it to another location? If you have been in the business for a while, you know what I'm talking about.

It is always better to buy the worst house in the best location than the best house in the worst neighborhood. The same principle applies to business property. How valuable would an apartment complex be forty miles from the nearest town? What could you sell a newly renovated motel for, if it was located on a remote county road? These questions are blatantly obvious, but many investors make mistakes producing similar quandaries.

The Right House in the Wrong Location

My initial attempt at the rehab business was embarrassing, but it's worth telling you about. My first rehab project was an old home I intended to convert to a duplex. I bought it cheap and thought I had the first piece to my retirement puzzle. I planned to live in the house while I did the rehab and conversion work. During this rehab, I found another deal I couldn't resist. It was in the same neighborhood, about four streets away from the first job.

This investment looked like a house with potential to produce a quick profit. I figured it could be updated, cleaned up, and sold in less than a month. On paper, the numbers worked and promised a net gain of 30% for the quick-flip house. I worked on both properties simultaneously. It was my intention to sell the quick-flip house and keep the one being converted to a duplex.

To jump to the end of the story, neither deal worked out. I did sell the quick-flip, but I didn't make much money. It was more like a bail-out then a quick profit. The duplex conversion was rented, but the neighborhood attracted low-quality tenants. These tenants had a tendency to pay late and leave without notice. Each consecutive occupant seemed to do more damage to the property than the previous tenant. During my ownership, the property produced more problems than money. I tried to sell the converted property but couldn't recover my investment. My first two rehab deals were mistakes.

I had read all the books on no-money-down deals. I thought my decisions were in line with the

advice in the retire-into-riches books about rental property. What had I done wrong? At the time, I had no idea why my ventures failed. The real estate broker said the deals were solid investments. He also raved about how good the financing was. When I dissected the situation, I discovered what had ruined my plans. The cause of my grief was *me*.

Research the Area

My first mistake was acting on emotions. I did not know the area very well, and the low sale prices influenced me. I didn't do a market study for demand and comparable sales. The neighborhood was in a declining cycle, but I didn't know it. Crime rates for the area were above average. The broker was persuasive and incredibly encouraging. His great financing turned out to have negative amortization. Two years after buying the first property, I owed more on it than I bought it for.

The depressed location attracted a less than desirable tenant element. To ride through the streets, the location appeared to have potential. After being there for a while, it was obvious the neighborhood was not being improved, it was deteriorating. I had made a snap decision, without evidence to support my decision. The lack of research cost me money and months of frustration. This was a no-profit, high-risk venture. My first rehab experience is a great example of what *not* to do. In Chapter 3, you will discover effective ways to avoid this problem by properly evaluating a property. You can't let appearances fool you.

PHYSICAL CONDITIONS

The physical condition of a property has much to do with its rehab potential. In order to buy the property at a good rehab price, it must need work. The pivotal point of the property's potential is the cost of the work needed. You must buy the property at a price that allows for the cost of repairs and your profit. To do this, you have to assess the amount and the cost of the work needed to make the property marketable. This can be a demanding task.

Until you have been involved with the rehab process for an extended time, you will have to rely on other people to evaluate your projects. Anytime you must depend on other people, you are at risk. The best choice you have in this situation is to develop trusted contacts. You will need a professional property inspector and competent contractors. The property inspector is the first assistant you need in making this part of your purchasing decision.

INSPECT THE PROPERTY

To have a clear understanding of how important an accurate property inspection is, consider the following example. Assume you have found a single-family home, seeming to offer a good investment value. However, there are underlying physical problems.

When you tour the property, you find it to be acceptable. The work you envision is primarily cosmetic work. It includes replacing paneling with drywall, to lighten up the family room. You plan to reface the ugly fireplace hearth. New paint is needed inside and out. New cabinets and a new sink in the kitchen will transform the room into a valuable showplace. Replacing the scarred interior doors with six-panel doors will produce winning results at a low cost. The list of intended repairs goes on, but all the repairs are of this nature.

After viewing the property, you sit down to work up the numbers. Your market research is strong, and you know what your completed project will be worth. With this type of work, you are capable of estimating the cost of labor and material for the job. After pulling all your information together, you arrive at the price you can afford to pay for the property. Then you make an offer to purchase.

With minor negotiations, you arrive at agreeable terms for the purchase of the home. After closing on the property, you bring in your tradespeople. The work begins and problems develop. When the painter is consulted, he tells you the paint is peeling because of a moisture problem. When the paneling is removed in the family room, the carpenter discovers termite damage. Your plumber finds several problems with the plumbing system when he begins the kitchen sink replacement.

The wall cabinets in the kitchen are difficult to hang properly. The wall is out of plumb, and one corner is lower than the other. Upon further investigation, your contractor finds the corner of the foundation is sagging. The foundation fault is due to poor foundation construction. Your profits are quickly being depleted with these unexpected costs.

To make matters worse, the heating system has a cracked heat exchanger. Everywhere you turn, there are more expensive repairs needed. Your budget is blown, and your profits are turning to losses. You begin to cut corners in order to minimize your losses. By the end of the job, you cannot sell the property for enough to recover your investment. Your only option is to retain the house as a rental property. In time, the house should appreciate enough to get your money out of it, but this certainly was not a wise investment.

If you had consulted a professional property inspector prior to purchasing the home, you could have avoided these unknown expenses. Your decision to save a few hundred dollars, by forgoing the professional inspection, has cost you thousands of dollars. The inspector would have done a detailed examination of the property. He would have provided an itemized report on the condition of the house. With this summary, you could have accurately estimated the costs to correct the problems.

Using Inspection Results to Project Costs

Competent contractors could have been a big help with the estimates. They could have reviewed the inspection report and provided proposals for the work to be done. With this supporting evidence, you could have negotiated for a lower sale price on the home. Your cost for this type of protection would have been small compared to the security received. Professional property inspections rarely exceed $300. The contractors would provide their professional expertise without a fee. Most contractors gladly give free estimates to obtain work.

The physical attributes of a property can make or break your rehab deal. The risk of wading in without a comprehensive understanding of the work to be done is just not worth taking. You should inspect potential properties very closely. After exhausting your abilities to inspect the real estate, call in a professional. Professional inspectors are some of the best insurance you can buy. Their reports keep you on budget and out of trouble.

INVESTIGATING THE POSSIBILITIES

It is unwise to assume that because a property seems to meet your rehab criteria, it can be transformed easily. It is important to research every possible glitch or restriction on your proposed changes. The area may have appropriate zoning to allow you to change a property's use, but you may have to go through months or years of town approvals before obtaining the use. A neighborhood may look nice on your initial ride, but police records on the area may show a darker picture. Although the building may appear to be in good condition, you must take the time to inspect for damage. You need time for market research to determine the value of a property. All this investigation requires legwork and a lot of questions.

Controlling the Property

Be careful not to ask questions about ways to increase a property's value and potential unless you have the property tied up. Once the real estate broker, or town clerk, or tax assessor gets wind of what you have in mind, word will spread like wildfire. If you don't control the property, you may do a lot of investigative work only to lose the property to a higher offer.

THE POWER OF A CONTRACT

Remember, we are concentrating on low-risk propositions in this chapter. One of the most effective methods of reducing your exposure to potential problems is an airtight contract, full of escape clauses. If you believe the profit potential can be increased due to factors such as zoning, you can make your offer based on several assumptions. First, determine the value of the property, presuming you can make your desired alterations.

Let's say the house you are interested in has an asking price of $128,000. You calculate your rehab costs to be $30,000, forecast the potential rental income, and estimate your cost of sale. Assuming you can in fact change this house to office space, at a cost of $30,000, and if you can then sell it for a profit of $35,000, you determine you are willing to pay $120,000 for the house. You have used the process of supposition to determine your offer amount. But I told you never take anything for granted. Why then are you making an offer based on assumptions? Because, with the proper wording in your contract, you will not be at risk.

Using Contingencies to Your Advantage

A contract contingency form is shown on the next page, so you can see examples of such protective clauses.

Notice how the purchaser uses the word "satisfactory" as a means of escape. If your research reveals the property cannot be converted to office space, or that the costs to do so exceed your anticipated $30,000, items 3 and 5 give you a way of voiding the contract and getting your earnest money back. You have not risked anything. You have simply tied up your earnest money long enough to determine whether the property is feasible and profitable. Not only have you ascertained the practicality of the project, you are the only one who has benefited from your efforts.

Option to Buy

Don't confuse the benefits of a contingency contract with the requirements of an option to buy. These two forms of offers are similar in many ways. Both require the seller to honor your offer for a specific period of time. With a contingency contract, the time frame can be spelled out, as in the example above, but it does not have to be. If no deadlines are included, the seller has to honor your offer until you tell him the contingencies have been met. If the contingencies are not resolved to your satisfaction, you get your deposit money back. You are not even required to give a deposit with the offer, although an earnest money deposit indicates the seriousness of your interest.

The Disadvantage of the Option

With the option, you agree to give the seller a specific sum to keep the offer open. Although this still gives you time to do your research, the period of the option is always defined. Moreover, even if you are not pleased with the results of your investigation, the seller retains the option money. Essentially, an option is a contract in which the seller agrees to give you the opportunity to buy a property, but for a set option fee and set time frame. Options do not effectively reduce your risk, because they cost you money. If an option is the only way you can tie up a property, limit your exposure as much as possible. Try to maintain some leverage over the seller by requesting a substantial option period, such as sixty

CONTRACT CONTINGENCY FORM

This contract is contingent on the following items and shall be voidable by the Purchaser if contingencies are not removed. For contingencies to be removed, the Purchaser must remove them by providing a written statement to the Seller. This statement will detail the contingencies being removed and any conditions pertaining to the removal of said contingencies.

(1) Purchaser must be granted financing from a commercial lender for eighty percent of the sales price. This loan shall be for a term of twenty years with an interest rate not to exceed twelve percent. Payments will be amortized for twenty years. Purchaser will pay no more than two discount points. Purchaser will pay all closing costs required of the Purchaser. Purchaser will apply for financing within fourteen days of this date.

(2) Purchaser shall obtain a satisfactory title search on the property showing the property to be free of any liens or encumbrances. The cost for this title search will be paid by the Purchaser.

(3) Purchaser shall have ten days from this date to enter the property for inspections of the property and buildings. Purchaser shall have fourteen days from this date to report the findings of these inspections and may void the contract if the inspection results are not satisfactory to the Purchaser. The cost of these inspections will be paid by the Purchaser.

(4) Purchaser shall be entitled to a full survey of the real estate. If said survey reveals facts different than those represented to the Purchaser, Purchaser may void this contract. The cost of the survey will be paid by the Purchaser.

(5) Purchaser shall be able to obtain all necessary permits and permissions for the Purchaser's intended use of the property. These permits will be applied for within fourteen days from this date and all costs will be incurred by the Purchaser.

(6) Building and fire code inspections will be ordered within five days of this date. If the building is found in violation of local or state ordinances, the Seller shall correct the violations, at his expense, prior to the closing date.

Until all of these contingencies are removed by the Purchaser, the Purchaser may void this contract without loss of the earnest-money deposit and without risk or recourse from the Seller.

days, or by limiting your option payment to $100.

MOTIVATED SELLERS

Sellers are as diverse as the properties being sold. Some sellers are selling to make a profit, without having a need to sell. These are the worst sellers to work with. They can afford to wait for their price. This type of seller is under no pressure and will only sell when the price is right. The right price for the seller is the wrong price for you. Unless you find a hidden angle to increase the property's value, dealing with these sellers is fruitless.

Many sellers are liquidating their real estate to settle tax liens or other debts. This type of seller can provide opportunity, but don't count on it. Logic tells you these sellers should be willing to sell for a lower price to obtain a quick sale. In many cases, they are willing to sell below market value, but they may not be able to. They may owe too much on the building to sell it for a price suitable to a rehabber. If there are liens on the property, selling for less than the lien amount will not solve the seller's problems.

Motivated vs. Desperate

Consider this example of a real estate investor trying to sell a rundown six-unit multi-family building. The investor bought the building two years ago. He convinced the seller to hold a 20% second mortgage, in lieu of a down payment for the first mortgage. His first mortgage was issued for 80% of the sale price. The loan is an adjustable-rate loan without a conversion feature. This is the investor's first rental property. When the investor bought the building, he had no landlording experience.

During the first year of ownership, the investor had many difficulties with the property. Vacancies were common, and the apartments were damaged by the tenants. The property's physical condition has deteriorated steadily since its acquisition. In the second year of ownership, the investor's interest rate on the first mortgage jumped 2%. Cash flow was negative before this increase, and the higher rate forced the investor to try to sell the property. The building has been on the market for four months. The owner is desperate to sell.

During this time, the real estate taxes have become delinquent. You have been tracking the investor's classified ads in the "For Sale" column of the local paper. Over the months, you have seen the price drop progressively. You decide to look into buying the property. After a close look at the property, you see it as a good rehab project. Inspecting the profit and loss statements, you are able to determine why the property failed. With your rehab abilities, you can make the property desirable again.

Why Desperate Sellers Refuse Low Offers

The problems caused by the tenants were the result of poor management. The location will support the building and produce good tenants for a knowledgeable landlord. After days of thought, you make an offer on the building. At the asking price of $199,000, there is not enough spread to cover your desired profit. You offer the distraught investor $175,000 for the building. Expecting a counter-offer, you are surprised when your offer is countered at the full price of $199,000. Why wouldn't this unfortunate investor negotiate to make a sale?

The original asking price of the property was $249,000. In the last four months, the price has been dropped to $199,000. Now the investor will not budge from the asking price. What could be the logic behind the investor's actions? This investor is in a box, with nowhere left to go. Two years ago, he bought the building with no down payment. The building was 100% financed with the first and second mortgage. On top of this leverage, there is an outstanding real estate tax bill of $2,800.

The other factor is the condition of the property. When it was purchased, it was an average multi-family building. Now it is beat up and ready for rehab. The economy has been stable, without much property appreciation. This investor cannot sell for less than $199,000, and the building is not worth more than $180,000. To sell the property, the seller will have to satisfy the liens against the building. These include two mortgages and the tax lien.

In this type of situation, your best negotiation skills will be useless. This investor is headed for bankruptcy and you will have to wait and deal with the bank, after the bankruptcy. This type of situation is common with commercial-grade multi-family properties.

LOCATING MOTIVATED SELLERS

The type of seller you need to find is a highly motivated one, with the ability to sell cheap. These sellers can be found in many places. Banks attempting to sell property they foreclosed on are a good source. The bank is only trying to recover its loan amount and handling costs. Many of these foreclosed properties, especially rundown properties, can be bought cheap. The banks are also in a position to help you with attractive financing. These are some of the best deals available.

People getting divorced are another good source of below-market deals. They will frequently be willing to sell at attractive prices to expedite the divorce settlement. Elderly people are another viable source for good deals. If they want to move into smaller accommodations, they will consider selling on your terms. Please don't abuse this opportunity. The elderly are often not aware of fair market values. If you abuse the opportunity and take advantage of their lack of market knowledge, you will have to live with it for a long time. There is plenty of money to be made in the business without abusing senior citizens.

Seek out sellers with strong motivation and limited time to make their sale. When you find this type of situation, you are on the track to a very profitable deal. As a rehabber, you will be interested in properties the public would never consider buying. This is a convincing advantage when you open negotiations.

ASSUMABLE FINANCING

Whether you are buying property to keep or to resell, assumable financing can increase your profits. Many residential loans made before the mid '80s were assumable. If you can find these deals, they will save you closing costs and may make the property easier to resell. Many of the older loans will have low interest rates. Rehabbing to build a stable of rental property will become much more profitable with these low interest rates.

Commercial-grade multi-family buildings are still available with assumable second mortgages. Most of the first mortgages on these properties are not worth assuming. An assumable loan for multi-family property is usually an adjustable rate type. If you can find a fixed-rate, low-interest assumable loan, it can have dramatic effects on the value of the property. Income property values are heavily based on the net income of the building. Low interest rates mean lower monthly payments and higher net income.

With any assumable loan, you will have to pay the difference between the assumable loan amount and the sale price. This can be done in several ways. Chapter 7 will explain how you can use blend mortgages and other financing tools to accomplish this. When you are looking for high-profit, low-risk investments, don't overlook assumable financing.

SPECIAL IMPROVEMENT FINANCING PLANS

When you are shopping for a new rehab project, inquire about special financing plans for the improvements. The local housing authority will be able to answer your questions on this subject. It is possible to obtain grants and very low-interest loans for neighborhood revitalization. The areas supporting these funds are targeted, and the locations are on file with the local housing authority. See Chapter 13 for full details on this profit-increasing advantage.

SUMMARY

Six ways to increase your profit while reducing your risk have been discussed here. They are: zoning, location, physical condition, motivated sellers, financing, and special-term improvement money. A contingency contract with strong wording can reduce your risks considerably. As you continue through the book, you will see how these tips can be developed into well-honed skills. An essential weapon in every rehabber's arsenal is the ability to choose the best property for his or her needs. These suggestions are an excellent place to start, but you will need to expand on them to reach your full potential. The following chapters are filled with valuable information to enable you to broaden your knowledge.

FINDING AND EVALUATING POTENTIAL PROPERTIES

3

To be successful in recycling real estate, you must be able to determine which property to purchase. For an inexperienced investor, this may initially appear an easy task. Many budding entrepreneurs consider the purchase price the deciding factor in a good deal. Price alone is not sufficient reason to purchase a building. This fact is amplified when the property is being acquired for renovation. Rehabbing real estate is a business surrounded by profits and pitfalls. Before you can hope to make money, you have to understand the principles of the venture.

Renovation techniques and negotiation techniques are discussed throughout this book. Before these techniques can be used, you must find the best properties to refurbish. If you use logic in your remodeling efforts, capitalize on creative financing, and start with a suitable property, you will prosper. The final decision of which property to buy will be the result of extensive research. This chapter is dedicated to describing the various types of properties and how to find them.

TYPES OF PROPERTY

The first consideration should be determining the type of property you are interested in buying. There are twelve basic groups of real estate for most investors to evaluate. For entrepreneurs just entering the business, there are six primary categories to consider. They are:

- ☐ single-family dwellings
- ☐ townhouses and condos
- ☐ duplexes
- ☐ triplexes
- ☐ quadruplexes
- ☐ seasonal property

Single-family homes are the most popular choice for novices. Townhouses and condominiums are also frequent targets for beginners. The remainder of the group includes small multi-family units, which frequently offer the best value. Each of these projects offers different challenges and rewards.

Single-Family Homes

I am going to show you how to rate each type of property for your investment portfolio. The first investment to be explained is the single-family home. Single-family homes make up the largest portion of the residential real estate market. They are the most sought after form of shelter and historically have proven to be solid investments. When used as a primary residence, houses are a good tax shelter and traditionally increase in value. If a single-family home is used as rental property, there are some areas for concern. When you consider buying a single-family home for renovation, you must establish your motivation. Will you live in the house, sell it, or rent it to others?

This question has significant bearing on your buying decision. When buying a detached home to rehab, you must have a plan for the finished product. One approach is buying a house and living in it during and after the remodeling. This is cost effective, but it requires a special personality. You must be willing to live out of boxes and with dust and noise your constant companions. Your home life will be constantly disrupted, and you can quickly become disenchanted with the rehab business. If you don't mind the inconvenience, this approach can be very lucrative. When buying your first home, it is an excellent strategy.

When the intent is to sell the completed property, single-family homes are one of the best places for a beginner to enter the rehab enterprise. There is a large sector of the population seeking housing at all times. Before buying a home to remodel, assess the strength of the real estate market. Invest in a before and after appraisal. Certified appraisers will be able to project the completed value of your project from plans and specifications. A residential appraisal will cost between $200 and $400, but it is money well spent.

By obtaining an appraisal before you purchase a property, you will know whether your plans are justified. Use a bank-approved appraiser for the job. If you seek financing for your project, the bank will require an appraisal. If the appraisal you buy in the preliminary stage is done by an approved appraiser, the bank can use it for your loan application. Engaging a certified appraiser in the beginning eliminates the need to pay for a second appraisal at the time of loan application.

Building a rental portfolio is another solution to the question of the finished product. Single-family homes are in high demand by tenants, but there are obstacles to overcome. Rental property requires different rehab techniques than property you plan to sell. Single-family homes are not usually the best investment for rental property. Their acquisition cost makes it difficult to realize a positive cash flow from rental income. This deficiency can sometimes be overcome through the rehab process. If you buy a home well below market value, it can produce an acceptable rate of return. If your objective is to become a landlord, single-family homes are probably not the best place to start.

One of the best reasons for buying and renovating homes is to sell them for a profit. This stratagem provides the opportunity to recover your investment and your profits quickly. Master this procedure, and you are well on your way to becoming wealthy. Competition in the real estate market is strong, but the proper renovation techniques will sell your property fast. There are many factors to consider in buying houses to sell. Location is always a key element in the sale of a house. Other factors include size, design, market conditions, and the ability to make payments until the house sells.

Townhouses and Condos

The opportunities offered by townhouses and condominiums are similar to those of detached houses. The same basic evaluation principles apply to these types of housing. In general, there is a stronger market demand for detached homes. In some cases, condos and townhomes are preferred, because of their minimal exterior maintenance needs. The rental aspects are parallel between these single-family dwellings. All three types of housing are difficult to rent for a cash profit. There is high demand for single-family rentals, but the numbers rarely work. If you are interested in rehabbing your way to a rental portfolio, consider small multi-family dwellings.

Multi-Family Units

The next group of residential properties to consider is multi-family units. Multi-family units, up to four units, are an excellent investment opportunity. They make dependable owner-occupied rental properties, and there are always buyers seeking them for investment. The initial purchase price of these buildings is higher than that for detached homes, but they offer more flexibility. The question of what you will do with the property after it is renovated must still be answered. You have the same three options. You can live in it and rent the additional units, sell it, or use it as a rental investment.

Duplexes are very desirable for owner-occupants, but they are restricted in their ability to pay for themselves. As a straight investment property, duplexes cannot be considered a worthy investment. If you are buying with the intent of selling upon completion, duplexes are worth a look. Many people like the idea of having part of their home mortgage paid by a tenant. These people don't want the responsibility of landlording for numerous tenants. They are only interested in having a good tenant next door, to help make their loan payments.

Duplexes are also a viable contender if you are looking for a place to live. You can purchase the property and rehab it for occupancy and rental income. The rental unit can be filled to produce income, while you renovate the other unit for your own habitation. Later, if you want to move, simply rent your unit to tenants and move on to another project. If you bought the property right and made wise improvements, the property should be worth maintaining for a rental investment.

When your intent is to buy and renovate for rental investment, consider a larger building. Duplexes rarely produce enough net income to be considered a wise non-owner-occupied rental investment.

One advantage to buying small multi-family buildings is the financing available. The interest rates and loans available for buildings with fewer than four units are enticing. Typically, buildings with four units or fewer can be bought with less money down and lower interest rates. These loans are designed for people planning to live in one of the units. The difference in down payment and interest rates is substantial. The down payment can be up to 20% less than it would be on properties with five or more units. The interest rates can be up to 3% below the rates of larger buildings. All of this helps to make the smaller units more financially feasible.

Triplexes are similar to duplexes; the same fundamental principles should be used in your evaluation. The primary difference is the third rental unit. This extra apartment can make the rental numbers more positive and the building more alluring to prospective purchasers. The only disadvantage is the initial acquisition cost. You will have to use cost analysis spreadsheets to evaluate the benefits of the third unit.

Quadruplexes, or four-unit buildings, are the most sought after of all the small multi-family dwellings. They maximize all the benefits of rental proper-ty, without the expenses involved in buildings having five or more apartments. When you are looking for a property to start a rental portfolio, these are the ones to study. If you plan to live in one of the units, you can benefit from a low down payment and reduced interest rates. If you are planning to sell the building, there will be a large audience of potential purchasers.

Buildings with four units can produce enough income to support themselves. The ideal approach is to live in one of the units while you are renovating, and then move on to another building. This meets the criteria for the low rate, low down payment loans and allows you to amass a profitable rental portfolio. Once your stable of rental property appreciates, you can refinance the building to extract your rehabbing profits. If you bought the property with a 10% or less down payment, refinancing will not be feasible for a long time. As a non-owner-occupied building, you will only be able to borrow 80% of the appraised value on a refinancing loan.

A popular strategy involves keeping the property for three to five years and then selling it. You enjoy a break-even or slightly positive cash flow during ownership and receive a cash reward at the time of sale. The building and its improvements should appreciate in the coming years. This increases the profit on your improvements and allows you to take full advantage of a healthy real estate market. When you sell, your investment should be returned, along with a superb profit.

Seasonal Property

Seasonal cottages can be considered in certain circumstances. This type of property is limited in options and carries a higher risk factor for the investor. Seasonal cottages offer the lure of enjoyment and relaxation, but financing can be difficult to obtain. This can be reason enough to disqualify them from serious consideration.

Depending on their acceptance in the area, cottages do offer some advantages. Cottages are in demand for recreational purposes. They can be looked at as resale property or rental property. In some cases, they provide excellent rental income. If the property is in a desirable location, it can rent for over a hundred dollars per day. If you are able to obtain satisfactory financing, cottages can provide an often overlooked opportunity. Another potential advantage to cottages is their relative ease of renovation.

Most cottages are small and don't require a lot of money to renovate. A few well-placed improvements and decorations can be all it takes to turn a profit. I do not recommend cottages to inexperienced investors, as there are many hidden risks. Often with cottages, the transfer of ownership on a cottage or seasonal property will trigger compliance with modern zoning or town regulations. Many properties are granted variances or grandfather status for their existing use. These latitudes may only protect the current property owner. This means you may have to install a septic field, tie into town water, or bring the cottage up to current code standards. Some states allow variances for private camps or cottages, which do not apply to properties if you elect to live in them year round. You need to do thorough homework before considering a seasonal property for rehab.

Stick with conventional dwellings until you gain experience. If you make a mistake with conventional units, you are much more likely to be able to salvage your investment. The wrong moves with cottages can haunt you for a very long time.

Commercial and Liquidated Properties

The next group of investments to consider is commercial grade and liquidated properties. This category rounds out the twelve types of endeavors and is composed of the following:

❑ buildings of five to twelve units

❑ buildings of thirteen or more units

❑ mixed-use property

❑ full commercial property

❑ damaged and abandoned property

❑ repossessions and actions

When a building contains more than four residential apartments, it is considered commercial real estate. This is significant for many reasons. Loan qualification requirements change, and so do the terms and interest rates of the loans for these properties. Some of these changes are advantageous to the investor. It is much easier to use creative financing methods with commercial loans. Lenders' rules are dramatically different between residential and commercial loans.

Buildings having six to eight units are the ones most often sought by average real estate investors. They are large enough to produce a positive cash flow, and small enough for an individual investor to manage effectively. Any building with six to twelve units is attractive to small and medium-size investors. These buildings frequently provide outstanding rehab possibilities. You will often find low interest loan money available for neighborhood revitalization in the areas supporting these larger units. Grant money is sometimes offered to improve the buildings, and this money may never have to be repaid.

Making the proper improvements may allow the rents to be raised. Higher rents mean increased value and more profit. Obtaining financing for the improvements can be accomplished easily with a good rental increase prospectus. All in all, if you are looking to build a rental empire, these are the buildings to make it happen.

If you venture into buildings with more than twelve units, you are approaching deep water. Only the strongest investors can handle such large buildings. Trying to sell these apartment buildings can be very difficult. Investors qualified to buy complex-style buildings are street smart and sometimes ruthless. Vacancy is a common word in larger units. With twelve apartments, the odds increase for tenant turnover. This demands a strong knowledge of leasing laws and techniques or the use of a professional management firm. Unless you are used to playing in the big leagues, avoid property with more than twelve apartments.

The cash reserve required to operate a large building is staggering. Down payments can reach into the hundreds of thousands of dollars, and the closing costs alone can strain the average investor. These buildings are for pros only. You have to be a heavyweight in the real estate world even to consider these complex-style buildings.

Mixed-use buildings sometimes allow for exciting opportunities. These are properties that house residential tenants and commercial or retail tenants. Generally, the businesses are located on street level and the residential tenants inhabit apartments above the businesses. These buildings depend on a healthy economy and a strong location for success. The new or average investor will do better with straight residential properties. Mixed-use buildings can be plagued with zoning and building code problems. These are problems rarely encountered in straight residential structures.

Full commercial properties are best left to investors specializing in them. Finding suitable tenants can be very difficult, and the competition is fierce. Most of these properties are owned or controlled by corporations or realty groups. This is not a good place to begin your rehab occupation. Unless you have an impressive financial statement and large amounts of liquid assets, don't waste your time looking for commercial projects. The players in this game are full-time professionals. Inexperienced participants won't last long in the battle for commercial dominance.

The last collection of properties to consider is unique. These are the ugly stepsisters of the rehab society. They include properties damaged by fire, wind, or water. Some properties are simply abandoned and left for the lender to worry about. Many of these buildings can be bought cheap, but they may require extensive work and money to bring them back to life. Fire damage is probably the most common in this category. Even when buildings are adequately insured, they are sometimes sold as is.

Fire jobs are the most difficult rehab projects to undertake. It is nearly impossible for the average person to evaluate the extent of damage caused by a fire. What appears to be minor damage can turn into serious problems. Charred structural members and unknown plumbing and wiring conditions are only part of the challenge. As attractive as these deals may appear, I strongly recommend you avoid them. Unless you are a seasoned remodeling contractor, with heavy experience in fire jobs, you stand to lose large sums of money. There is plenty of money to be made in lower level rehab projects. Start with cosmetic improvements and work your way up to more complicated jobs. It will take years for you to learn enough to consider fire jobs.

Abandoned buildings come available for many reasons. Their owners can't make the payments and disappear, or the properties are tied up in litigation and become empty. Empty buildings are sometimes very difficult to finance and may have clouded titles. If they are income properties, how will you verify their rental history without records from the owner? Income properties are the holdings most frequently abandoned. Single-family homes are seldom left by their owners. Empty and unclaimed properties do show up and they can be excellent investments, but you have to find them. Any building offering a high profit potential requires some extra effort to locate.

HOW TO FIND PROPERTIES

Now that you know the types of properties to consider, you must learn how to uncover them. Sure, you can read the "For Sale" ads in the local paper, but everybody is doing that. You will be competing with large numbers of potential buyers for every desirable property. You could call a real estate company and inquire about their listings, but again, you are going after the same properties everyone else is interested in. To make money rehabbing real estate, you must buy the right property at the right price. This can be accomplished by reading the paper or calling real estate brokers, but not in the traditional way.

Knowing where and how to look for potential rehab properties is half the battle. Some investors go through their entire career without ever discovering the ways to maximize their efforts. The methods for finding the best properties are not common knowledge. Savvy investors and brokers are not going to share their trade secrets. They earn handsome incomes from these well-honed skills. I am going to share some ideas with you now that would take years of trial and error to learn on your own.

I learned these techniques in many ways. Some were learned from mistakes—those were the most expensive lessons learned. Many of the ideas were developed by expanding on ideas found in books and magazines. The remainder were learned from working as a full-time real estate investment broker. At the peak of my activity, I owned more than fifty properties and controlled many more rentals for clients. As a selling broker, I was known for my investment strategies and creative financing maneuvers. I have rehabbed numerous properties and know what to look for and where to find it. If you pay attention to the following suggestions, you will be years ahead of the competition in your quest for quality renovation projects.

The unconventional ways for finding real estate deals are nearly unlimited. We are going to explore, in detail, many of the best ways to find hidden treasures in the real estate market. Auctions are one way to buy properties below market value. Real estate is sold at auction for a variety of reasons. Some of the reasons include foreclosures, bankruptcy, tax liens, divorces, and estate settlements.

AUCTIONS

Auctions are typically conducted in two ways. In the first method, the selling party retains the right to reject any offer. This type of auction can produce good values, but the property is rarely sold for a song. The second type of auction is an absolute auction. In these auctions, the property must be sold to the highest bidder, regardless of the bid amount. It is possible to buy desirable homes for less than the appraised value of an empty lot. A home with an appraised value of $100,000 might be sold for $25,000 at this type of auction.

Typically, bidders are allowed to inspect the property prior to the auction. This gives you the chance to decide what the property is worth to you. When the bidding begins, you compete until the offers exceed the maximum amount you are willing to pay. You hope to be awarded the sale of the house before it reaches your price cap. The disadvantage to auctions is the demand to perform quickly. Most auctions require the property to be paid for on very short notice. You must give a substantial deposit at the time of the auction, and follow up with the remainder of the sale price in just a few days. This criterion does not allow time for the average person to arrange financing. You must either have cash or an established credit line to take advantage of auction sales.

BROKERS

Real estate brokers can line up properties for you, but they may be competing against you. If the broker is also an investor, the broker will take the best properties for his own portfolio. Brokers frequently gobble up good properties before they are officially listed. This is easy for the real estate professional. Brokers are called to establish the market price of a property, and once they see the value they often buy it on the spot. To get the most from real estate brokers, you must play the numbers game.

Send a letter to all brokers regularly advertising the types of property you are interested in. The letter should advise the brokers of your interest in buying specific types of property. Explain your desire to have an ongoing relationship and that this is not a one-time shot for the broker. Ideally, purchase stationery identifying yourself as a real estate investor. Presenting the image of a successful and active investor will attract the attention of experienced brokers. Ask the brokers to send you information on their best properties.

When the information arrives, study it closely. Did the broker send top-shelf properties, or did he make copies of everything in the multiple listing service book and use the shotgun method? If the property data sheets are edited to include only the best properties, pursue a relationship with the broker. If you receive information on any and all properties on the market, scratch the broker off your list. You are seeking a specialist: a broker with insight and experience in the types of properties for which you are searching. When you find such a broker, let him work for you.

Once you establish a solid relationship, a good broker will inform you of all pertinent information on new listings before they are advertised to the public. Getting a jump on the public gives you the advantage of picking from prime properties without competition. Brokers can be an excellent source of leads when you know how to utilize them. Good brokers get return business from satisfied clients. They will know when a property they sold is about to go on the market, because the previous buyer now becomes the seller.

Rental properties seldom have a "For Sale" sign posted. The owner does not want to frighten tenants into moving. This causes the cash flow of a building to plummet, making it less desirable. Brokers often know about unadvertised properties. Advance notice, concealed properties, and distress sales are all areas to pursue to find strong rehab projects.

OBITUARIES

As morbid as it sounds, obituaries can be good leads for rehab properties. Keeping an eye on the obituaries column in your local paper will alert you to possible opportunities. When people die, their property is frequently sold. A quick trip to the tax assessor's office will tell you what property the deceased owned and the tax value of that property. A letter to the decedent's address, informing the recipient of your willingness to buy property in his or her area, may bring fast results.

So as not to appear a vulture, make the letter a form letter. Don't mention the recent loss; rather, emphasize your interest in purchasing property in the neighborhood. Mail the form letters to the deceased's address and the surrounding homes. This approach will not be construed as tactless, and it can expose terrific acquisition opportunities.

You should not view this method as a means to take advantage of people during a time of loss. Realize that many people in this situation are faced with estate taxes and related expenses that cause financial hardship. By supplying quick cash flow with minimal difficulty, you can provide a beneficial conclusion to a stressful situation. Don't expect immediate results, as the family will need some time to adjust to their grief. When they are ready to make a disposition of the property, they may remember your letter and give you the first opportunity to purchase the property. By knowing the tax value in advance, you can often structure an immediate deal for the assessed price. You get the property with a favorable savings, and the sellers get instant cash flow when they need it most.

BACK TAXES

While you are at the tax office investigating estate properties, inquire about properties with delinquent tax bills. These holdings will ultimately have liens placed against them and may be sold. A letter to the current owner can result in an exciting deal. You may be able to buy the property for little more than the taxes owed on it. These situations are rare, but the opportunities do exist. More likely, you will have to pay more than just the tax amount for the properties, but they can often be bought well below

their market value.

A letter to the owner of the property can get you into negotiations. There are many possibilities for acquiring the property. You do not have to buy the house in the next few months to realize a major profit. There are ways to structure life estates, reverse mortgages, and other appealing bail-out plans for the owners. These methods are discussed in Chapter 6.

ADVERTISING

Placing a classified ad in the newspaper might bring sellers to you. If you are able to make quick commitments and have access to fast financing, these ads can work wonders. Distressed people will call and sell you their property for a fraction of its street value. When individuals lose their jobs, get divorced, or are facing bankruptcy, they will sell cheap if they can sell fast. These ads can be placed in the "Money to Loan" section of the classified ads or the "For Sale" or "Wanted to Buy" sections.

People on the edge will be searching for any way to avoid their financial woes. They read the "Money to Loan" column for loans. When they see your ad, you have got their attention and may soon have their property. People preparing to sell their property read the "For Sale" ads to formulate a price and strategy for selling their property. If they are already advertising their home, they will read the ads to be sure their ad is worded correctly. These sellers are often under pressure to sell and are apt to make any deal, as long as it is a fast deal.

There is nothing wrong with buying this way; you are not an unethical opportunist. You are getting what you want, and the sellers are getting what they want. Before you try this procedure, be sure you can close on the property quickly. Your ability to convert their real estate into cash, fast, is your bargaining chip. Without the ability to close quickly on the sale, the seller will not be motivated to sell at wholesale prices.

DIRECT MAIL

Direct mail is an excellent way to target your assault on the real estate market. Find areas with the type of properties you desire and mail to each of the owners. You can get their names and addresses from the tax office or from a cross-reference directory. A simple letter making owners aware of your interest in purchasing property in their area can result in multiple responses. There is a sample letter at the end of the chapter. Getting to these people before brokers do will better your odds of buying at a lower price.

Direct mail can also be effective when used with professionals. A well-written letter to the right people can have your phone ringing in a matter of days. Mail to banks, attorneys, appraisers, and accountants. Tell them of your desire to buy specific types of property. Give a little background on yourself to build credibility. Stress your ability to act quickly, if you have it, and enclose a business card. The professional receiving your letter may not have an immediate need but may save your card for future reference.

BANKS

Banks constantly have foreclosed properties to sell. If they know of a private investor interested in the type of property they are holding, they will call. If they can sell you the property immediately, they will not lose as much money marketing their foreclosed property. Another advantage to this ploy is the fact that you are dealing with a bank. They may make the loan for the acquisition of the property and facilitate attractive rates and terms.

ATTORNEYS

Attorneys handle a volume of cases involving the sale of real estate. If you can establish yourself as a credible investor with attorneys, you may be in line for some very sweet deals. Your letter to attorneys will make them aware of your presence and interest in real estate. Whether they are dealing with estates, divorces, or other types of cases, you will be on their list of contacts.

ACCOUNTANTS

Accountants may sound like a strange connection for buying property, but they hold some interesting cards in the real estate game. Their clients may be selling their real estate portfolios to invest in other interests. Perhaps the depreciation clock has ex-

pired and their client needs to rotate his investment crops. Whatever the reason, you want to be known by these tax advisors. If you are rehabbing your properties for resale, you should mention this in your letter to the accountants. Their clients may be interested in buying your completed projects.

CORPORATIONS

Large corporations are worth sending a letter to. They frequently transfer their employees and assist in the sale of employees' property. Let these major corporations know you are a ready, willing, and able buyer. When they need to sell fast or are having trouble selling a rundown property, they will call you. Many of these corporations can afford to sell cheap and take a tax loss; this is gold in your pot. Don't overlook these corporate players, they are not emotionally involved and will frequently sell fast to avoid headaches and lost time from production.

REAL ESTATE BROKERAGES

If you are a qualified buyer, you may be able to cut a deal with a real estate brokerage. Offer to guarantee the purchase of any "fixer-upper" they can't sell. Show them how your guarantee makes their firm more desirable to the home-seller. Brokerages like to list property for sale, and they are always battling other brokers for listings. If a brokerage can guarantee the sale of a property, it is much more likely to be awarded the listing.

Qualify your guarantee by requiring an on-site inspection and by establishing a purchase price you are comfortable with. Agree that the brokerage will try to sell the property for three to six months at market value. If this effort fails, you have the opportunity to buy the property at a much lower price. The owners don't realize the profit they had hoped for, but they get a sale when no other offers are being made.

Some real estate firms use this same approach, offering to buy the property themselves if it does not sell. They do this to obtain listings and to make lucrative purchases. Smaller firms can't afford to make these guarantees. If you connect with these firms, you could obtain properties well below market value. The brokerage wins by getting more listings, you win by getting discounted properties, and the owner wins by getting a sale when there are no other takers.

CRUISING

The last two methods to be discussed are very effective. Ride around neighborhoods you think have possibilities. Look for rundown properties with tall grass and deteriorating exteriors. Key characteristics to zero in on are bad roofs, barren yards with poor grass or bad drainage, and damaged siding or peeling paint. The owners of these properties may be facing extensive repairs they can't afford. When you spot such an ignored building, jot down the address. Then go to the tax office and get the owner's name and address. Write the owner a letter and express your interest in purchasing the property.

You know the property is in need of repairs. Due to the condition, it is a good chance the owner has little interest in the property. If he receives a letter from a prospective buyer, he may jump at the chance to sell. Again, you are getting to the owner before the brokers and the public can. You have strong negotiating power, because you are the only interested buyer.

OUT-OF-STATE OWNERS

Make the most of your tax office visit by looking for out-of-state owners. Find local properties owned by people several hundred miles away. These people may have retired, relocated, or been transferred. Obviously, they thought they could maintain their property as rental property. The chances are very good they are no longer happy with being long-distance landlords. Property management firms eat into the rental income, and personally overseeing a rental from out of state is very difficult. These absentee landlords can be outstanding targets for direct mail.

Send them a letter stating your interest in their property. Their response may result in a quick and highly profitable acquisition for you. These out-of-state owners are an excellent place to direct your efforts. They may be thinking of selling but at the same time dreading the rituals of selling by proxy. If your letter arrives in the right hands at an opportune moment, you can dance all the way to the bank with your profits.

STUDY

Developing an ability to evaluate the best properties to pursue is essential to the rehab business. For the best results, invest the time to learn as much as you can about real estate. Most communities offer evening classes to prepare people for the real estate licensing exam. These classes provide a wealth of information. By attending these classes, you will learn real estate law and appraisal techniques. These two subjects alone are worth the price of admission. Most of the classes only last a few weeks, and the benefits will be with you throughout your entrepreneurial endeavors.

Extensive self-study is another way to strengthen your new skills. Read everything you can find on remodeling and creative financing. Study books dealing with appraisal practices; a strong appraisal is the cornerstone of a wise investment. Don't get caught up in the fast talking, no-money-down, real estate riches scheme. Some of these approaches are effective, but most of them are difficult to perfect and extremely risky. They require extended leverage and don't offer a safety net. Many of the once popular no-money-down plans were disabled with the tax law changes of 1986.

You can get rich with real estate, but you will have to earn your money. There are no overnight shortcuts to financial freedom. The best approach is a steady, well-planned investment blueprint. Moving too fast will result in disaster. Real estate moguls are made, not born. Caution and common sense will take you well along the road, and the information here will get you home with money in your pocket.

All these techniques work. I have used them personally and know other successful investors who use these same methods. If you follow my guidelines, you will be choosing from prime properties at discounted prices. The effort expended in finding hidden properties will be well rewarded. Break away from the pack, and blaze your own trail to real estate riches.

SAMPLE DIRECT MAIL LETTER

Roger A. Homeseeker
312 Bellows Road
Canton, Virginia 04039
(804) 555-1234

September 24, 1992

Mr. and Mrs. John A. Propertyowner
1225 Loon Drive
Augusta, VA 04044

Dear Mr. and Mrs. Propertyowner:

I recently drove through the Bay Hollow subdivision and fell in love with the area. Your house on Loon Drive is exactly what I am looking for. I am interested in buying a home in the neighborhood where I can put my hobby to work. I enjoy working around the house, and the location and style of your home are perfect for my needs.

If you are interested in selling your property, I would like to meet with you. I am willing to pay a fair price for the home and will be able to arrange financing quickly. Please write or call me at your earliest convenience. Thank you for your consideration of this request.

Sincerely,

Roger A. Homeseeker

PROPERTIES TO AVOID 4

One of the highest risks an investor runs is being overpowered by low sale prices. The lure of a low asking price is often irresistible. In my brokerage activity, I have seen this happen to all types of investors. Inexperienced buyers are the ones most likely to become infatuated with a property on the basis of price alone. They believe the deal of a lifetime is within reach. Unfortunately, these deals are usually sour and may very well haunt you for a lifetime.

Seasoned investors know they will not get something for nothing, but they are still attracted by low-ball prices. There is something about a low price that makes mature adults leave logic behind. In the real estate business, you have to base your decisions on well-researched facts. It is very rare to find an absolute steal of a deal.

Every investor hopes to find hidden treasure in the jungle of available real estate. There are some true treasures in the underbrush, but you may have to dig for them. Scanning the classified ads for low prices is not normally going to produce a charmed deal. You will have to exert more effort and cultivate your skills to unearth the best properties.

There are some properties that will bring you to your financial knees. These buildings can be hard to identify as losers. Until you gain extensive experience, you are vulnerable to the lure of bad buildings. What looks like your ticket out of the daily grind can be a one-way trip to bankruptcy. Before you lay your money down, learn what properties to avoid.

Many of the warning signs of properties to avoid are generic. They apply to single-family homes and large apartment complexes. Occasionally, a property will break the rules and yield surprising results. These variable factors are noted when mentioned throughout the chapter. Unless specified, the danger signals apply to all real estate investments.

LOCATION

The first quality to evaluate is location. Real estate values depend heavily on location. I have emphasized this before. Location is said to be the most important element in the value of real estate. There is no argument within the industry on the importance of location. Sale prices are typically established utilizing common methods and with some form of justification. If you find a property well below the average market value, there is probably a good reason for the low price.

A good house in a bad location is never a good deal. On the other hand, a bad house in a good location can yield enviable returns. Large multi-family dwellings twenty miles from town will probably not be a solid investment. Motels situated on back roads have less value than lodging facilities along arterial routes. Common sense will answer most of your questions about appropriate locations.

Assuming you are dealing in residential properties, ask yourself if people will want to live in the area. Don't make a decision based on your personal desire to live in such a location. Be objective and ascertain whether the neighborhood will support your rehab efforts.

CHECK THE CYCLE

Look into the past and forward to the future. What is the present life cycle of the community? Is the vicinity stable, deteriorating, or growing? If it is going downhill, refrain from starting a rehab project in the area. Remember the example in Chapter 2 of my first rehab venture. I bought into a declining area and had no hope of increasing the property value against the influence of an undesirable neighborhood. Stable and growing localities are what you should be seeking.

Neighborhoods and business districts go through cycles. First they grow, then they stabilize. Once stable, they may grow or decline. When properties decline, they usually rebound at some point in the future. The period of time between bottoming out and progressing again is difficult to judge. City reforms, grant programs, and development plans can all encourage a growth cycle. Determine the phase of the location you are considering through research.

Real estate brokers are a valuable information source to assist you in ascertaining growth phases of a neighborhood. If you don't know what area to concentrate your efforts in, your first step can be to meet several brokers. You must first know what type of property you wish to acquire (single family, small multi-family, six-unit apartments, etc.) and how you wish to create your profit (quick-flip, owner occupancy, short-term rental, or long-term rental). Give the broker your criteria, and ask her for information on areas that would meet your needs.

After determining which neighborhoods to concentrate on, have the broker compile comparable sales data for surrounding areas over the last year. This is easy for most real estate brokers, because the information is available to them in their multiple listing comp books. Make sure the broker lists the address, asking price, selling price, days on the market, and any unusual features of the property. It is important that you be able to flag buildings that sold rapidly due to extra square footage, recently raised rents, or supplementary storage. In this way, you can accurately define comparable properties.

Be sure to go through the same process with several brokers. Don't provide your broker with information assembled by a previous agent. If you allow each broker to give you his or her unbiased opinion, you can accurately assess the areas and comparable property information they provide. This will give you a clear picture of which areas suit your needs. You will also be able to track the growth or decline of a neighborhood.

All stages have advantages and disadvantages. A prospering area will be more expensive to buy into. Once you buy, will values continue to escalate or will they decline? This is often a gut feeling, substantiated by historical data. If you buy while an area is on the rise, you will be able to profit during the stationary period. These properties should be approached with a quick-flip in mind. Otherwise, you risk holding the property through the stable phase and into a decline. Most investors only buy during a growth cycle, as long as they can get in early.

STABLE AREAS

Stable neighborhoods are on the edge and can go either way. Again, assess past performance and use good judgment. Prices for stable areas will not be cheap. These cycles are usually safe and produce modest returns on your investment. Rock-bottom areas offer the most opportunity for quick cash. You can buy cheap, and if your speculation is accurate, you will see handsome profits quickly. If you misjudge the area and it levels out in its declined condition, you have a problem.

ASSESS YOUR NEEDS

With so many possibilities, how will you know where to invest? Investing is always a gamble; there are no guarantees. Much of your decision will rest on the intended purpose of the property. The desire to sell for a quick profit will not be met with stable areas. Declining areas are definitely a losing proposition. Rapidly growing areas can offer a fast profit. If you are confident the area will continue to grow, it is worth serious consideration.

A neighborhood on the rebound can provide a fast and sizable rate of return. If you plan to rehab the property for a quick sale with high profit, concentrate on these areas. Fast growing sections are also a viable contender for your overnight wealth.

Avoid the stable areas, as it will take longer than you are willing to wait for your investment to mature.

Rehabbing properties for a rental portfolio offers more latitude. Stable areas can be very good for this strategy. If you are willing to hold the property, these areas present the least risk. Determine your goals and invest your time before investing your money. Do extensive research and make a decision based on facts.

ZONING

Zoning is a big factor in property values. A house sitting on land zoned for commercial use may be much more valuable than the average house. A large multi-family building without the proper zoning approvals may be nearly worthless. Don't take a property's present use for granted. A property being used for commercial purposes may be in violation of local laws.

Buying these properties can be a disaster. Suppose you pay high dollar based on the income potential of a property. What happens when you discover, after closing, that the present use violates zoning ordinances? You will be very sorry for not investigating the legal uses of the property.

FUTURE DEVELOPMENT

The reason for a below-market price could be location. Don't think the surrounding properties are the only thing affecting the location of a property. Future development plans could be the reason for the low price. Consider this example taken from an actual case history.

There is a stretch of homes along a busy byway in a predominantly rural location. One or two houses have "For Sale" signs appear in the yard. Then many of the neighboring houses are placed on the open market. At first, their prices are competitive but below average for the county. Later, the prices begin to decrease, yet none of the properties has sold. The houses are representative of comparable homes being sold in other areas of the town. Why aren't these houses selling in the same ninety-day period as similar properties?

As time passes, the prices continue to go down.

For an investor looking for rental or rehab property, this looks like a good deal. Their extended time on the market suggests a good opportunity exists with these properties. Visually, the homes show no signs of danger to the investor. The area is situated in the path of a growing population. Surface indicators point to a good investment. Should you jump in and buy these underpriced homes? Not yet. You must first know why the prices are below those of other homes on surrounding streets.

Looking Beyond the Surface

With some research, you will find the reason for the low prices. Without such investigation, you may regret your purchase for years to come. These homes were priced to sell for a reason. In this example, the catalyst was the proposed widening of the road. As the proposed plans progressed, the prices plummeted. In less than a year, these houses would lose much of their front lawn when the road work commenced. Grass would be replaced by pavement to support increased traffic on the road.

Losing a major portion of your front yard will adversely affect the value of your property. If you bought one of these houses without knowledge of future plans, you might have an extremely difficult time recovering your investment. What looks like a deal for you is really a deal for the seller. Very few people want to live in a home with a fast-moving string of cars in the front yard.

Future development plans can have significant impact on property values. They can drive values up or down. Before you buy any property, research all factors with a potential effect on your investment's value. Are there plans in the works to build a new landfill across from your intended purchase? How will the intent to run high-voltage power lines across your property affect its value? These plans will severely reduce the salability of your investment.

WATER PROBLEMS

You now know several of the factors to assess in a property. You have cleared the location, verified the zoning, and researched future use. The next query applies to the lawn area. Does it have proper drainage? When the first heavy rains come, will diminutive grand canyons carve their way through the yard? Are you going to have a mosquito breeding pond next to the new deck you intend to build? Perform a thorough site inspection on the property grounds. Look for evidence of poor grading and water erosion.

Flood Zones

Is the land in a flood plain? If the property is in the country, will the septic system support additional bedrooms and baths? Does the rural property have a well capable of producing potable water? These are only some of the questions to ask; the list goes on.

Properties located in flood zones or flood plains are difficult to finance. They also require expensive insurance premiums to protect against losses. A cheap house in a flood plain is no bargain. It will be next to impossible to sell and is not a good investment for housing purposes. Flood zones exist for a reason — the potential of damaging water. In our town, a street that runs along the river serves as a shining example of water problems. Every year the ice-out engorges the river, and every year the road is affected by water. On occasion, the river flows across the road, eliminating car traffic altogether. Properties located in flood zones are difficult to rent or sell, especially to people who know the area.

Wet Basements

Location values can be affected by other types of deterrents. If your intended purchase has a basement, how will a high water table affect it? Wet basements are not worth much. A wet unfinished basement loses its value as a storage facility. Finished basements with water problems are even worse. Wet basements are a liability, not an asset. If you are shopping for property during the dry season, how will you know about water problems?

There are many telltale signs to help you determine water problems. Is the ground graded away from the property's foundation? Is the grade of the land consistent, or does it have depressions? If the ground is not graded away from the foundation, you could be looking at a wet basement. Depressions in the lawn collect water and attract unwanted insects. Is the lawn well landscaped? If the area doesn't support a strong growth of ground cover, erosion could be a problem.

Are there any dips or grooves running through the property? These natural channels indicate a seasonal waterway. Are the trees full of fungus or dying? If there is evidence of unusual tree conditions, the ground may be holding a lot of water. Is the area growing ferns, cattails, jack-in-the-pulpit, or blue flag iris? These plants thrive in wet, marshy areas. They are beautiful indicators of wet conditions.

Water Discharge

You have been looking down at the ground, now glance at the roof. Does the building have gutters? Without gutters, the water running off the roof may find its way into the basement. When gutters are present, investigate their discharge location. Does each downspout terminate on a splash block? Splash blocks prevent the water from driving a hole into the ground, but they do nothing to keep your basement dry. Water from gutters should be piped to a location away from the foundation.

Ask if the property has a perimeter drain around the exterior of the foundation. These drains help prevent water from infiltrating the foundation. With your exterior inspection complete, investigate the basement itself. Is there a sump pump in the floor? If so, water is or has been a problem. Does the concrete floor appear to be a uniform color and texture?

When water problems arise, perimeter drains are often installed in the concrete floor. If the concrete looks patched, has a different color around the edges, or has a varied texture, there may have been water problems. If a sump pump is present, where does it discharge? When the discharge is too close to the foundation, the water will seep back into the basement. The discharge pipe should be installed to prevent the water from returning to the basement.

Identifying Signs of Damage

Are the basement walls stained? Is mold present on the walls, floor, or ceiling joists? If the area is carpeted, does it smell musty? Lift a corner of the carpet and look for mildew. All of these are red flags of moisture problems. Look at the owner's personal belongings and mechanical systems. Are they sitting on the floor, or are they on elevated pallets? If they are sitting on pallets, there is a good chance the basement gets wet. Rust at the base of heat units, water heaters, washers, and dryers is another sign of water problems. These are the most common indicators of moisture predicaments.

Water damage is difficult to circumvent and expensive to correct. If your intention is to use a property for rental, you will be barraged with complaints about water problems from tenants. If you plan to sell the property, you must realize most real estate brokers are experienced enough to spot water damage. If the improvements you make to correct wet conditions are not properly installed, you could be looking at a lawsuit. Put water problems on your list of items to avoid.

TREE LIABILITIES

Inspect the trees on the property you are considering. If they are dead or dying, you may have to spend large sums of money for their removal. If these trees fall, you can be held responsible for the damage they cause to surrounding properties. Most people never look for this type of condition. Buying a property and discovering the need for $2,500 to eliminate threatening trees can break your budget. Dead trees reduce the appeal of a property to prospective purchasers. Your only escape would be to sell the property during the winter, when the condition is not as obvious.

COMBAT ZONES

When checking out attractive deals, get to know the neighborhood. Properties located in high crime areas are not good investments. They will be difficult to sell and even harder to keep. These areas do not attract a quality of tenant that will be worth the money. If you do chance upon good tenants, violent areas will quickly run them off. You can assess the neighborhood in many ways. Start with the local police. Inquire about the type and frequency of calls received by the police for the neighborhood.

Do a visual inspection of the subject property and the surrounding buildings. Look for vandalism, abandoned cars, graffiti, and security devices. If stores have bars on their windows, you probably don't want to invest in the area. Vandalism is never a contributor to rising real estate values. If the neighborhood's walls, signs, and buildings have been defaced, avoid the neighborhood.

Are there a number of people loitering on the streets? What do the cars in the area look like? Vagrants and rundown vehicles point to a high risk for your investment. Properties can be rehabbed to become attractive, but neighborhoods are difficult to change. Visit the location at several different times. Evenings, weekends, and when schools let out are good times to judge a neighborhood. Common sense will help you make the decision on a location's visual desirability. If all the homes in the area need to be rehabbed, leave them for seasoned professional investors. This is no place to begin your trail of experience.

ARM YOURSELF WITH INFORMATION

You can learn a lot about a property from the local paper's classified ads. Once you know where your target property is, check the "For Rent" advertisements. Is the area saturated with rental units? If it is, your proposed purchase may be a bust. Carry this line of investigation several steps further.

Ask the local housing authority for information on the rental history of the area. Is there government-assisted housing in the area? You may not be able to compete with government programs. Given the right property, you can capitalize on assistance programs. Most tenants on government assistance have a difficult time locating apartments, so they are less likely to move. The advantage to government programs is that they guarantee your rental income. You end up with stable cash flow and steady tenants. Judge your improvement investment against the potential of assisted tenants to determine whether purchasing the property will be beneficial.

Have your real estate broker provide a detailed report on the sale of other properties along the same street. Check the sale prices and the number of days required to sell the properties. It is a good idea to build a data file on property activity. If you know the areas you are interested in, track the sale and rental activity for each area. Keep a log or database of all the properties similar to the ones you are looking for. If you start this file early, it will be a great deal of help when you are assessing your purchase. You will know which areas to concentrate on and which to avoid. Good deals will stick out like a rose in a briar patch.

EASEMENTS

Easements can have negative effects on the value of real estate. An easement is the right to use someone's land, and there are many types of easements. Most dominant easements convey with the property. Some servient easements do not convey to a new owner. Utility companies and municipalities usually hold dominant easements. These are easements given by you, or a previous owner, for the use of your land. In other words, you need electricity to your home, so you give the power company an easement to lay the underground cable through your yard to the house.

For example, you may have an easement allowing you to bring your driveway across a corner of your neighbor's land to get to your property. A survey should show established easements. A title search lists all recorded easements, as well as any other clouds on the title. Don't make a final and unconditional commitment to purchase any property until the title has been searched and any easements meet your approval.

ENCUMBERED PROPERTIES

If your intended property is encumbered with liens or attachments, you have a serious problem. A thorough title search will expose these parasites. It is then up to you to decide on a course of action. The encumbrances should be removed before you take possession of the property. When these problems are brought to the seller's attention, it is his responsibility to deal with them. If he doesn't have the money to clear the title, negotiate for a reduced selling price. Lower the price enough to offset your costs in removing the clouds from the title, but never leave title problems unattended.

CLEAR TITLE

Title searches are a common part of most real estate transactions. They are frequently performed by attorneys to discover any clouds on the title. A cloud on the title is anything that impairs the seller from conveying total ownership rights in the property. These clouds could be liens, easements, attachments, encroachments, or a mortgage. If you plan to pay cash for a property, you should always request a title search. When financing the property, a title search is routinely required by the lender. Insist on a clear title before buying any real estate.

Dark Title Clouds

Imagine buying a property that sits well off the road only to find you cannot legally access it. The past owner may have had an easement-in-gross, which allowed passage over the neighbor's land. Easements-in-gross do not automatically convey to a new owner. You could have just spent big bucks for a piece of landlocked property. While this may be a solvable problem, it can get costly to utilize your new acquisition. Anytime the cost to convert and use a property exceeds the plausible return on your investment, you should avoid the purchase. Expensive title problems can have an adverse effect on your acquisition costs.

If you buy a property with existing or pending title objections, you are buying trouble. Your attorney should do a thorough title search before you close on the property. Title defects can ruin a property's value. You can do preliminary research at the Registry of Deeds. The information there is public record, and you may view all the documents on file.

Existing title clouds are recorded with the property's deed. Thirty minutes of research could save you days of negotiating and hundreds of dollars in pre-purchase fees. Insist on a clear title with all buildings bought. If the title is suspect, move on to another property.

SURVEYS

Another contingency that should be in every offer to purchase is the right to an acceptable mortgage survey. You may be surprised how many buildings are erected illegally. The error may exist for years without a problem. Just because no one has objected in the past, don't think you are above reproach. Often, all it takes is a change in ownership to expose an obstacle. Many times, no one is aware a problem exists until you have the property surveyed.

A mortgage survey will clearly show the boundaries of the property and the position of all improvements on the property. Improvements include more than simply the house and garage. They could be driveways, parking areas, fences, sheds, or swimming pools. Most property has established town or city requirements it must meet. These are called *buffer zones* or *setback zones*. If any part of an improvement is built inside a setback zone, you could have to pay for its removal.

Merely seeing an improvement on what you believe to be the property you are buying is not enough. Most zoning ordinances require improvements to be positioned away from the property line by a determined distance. When people add on to their home or build a storage shed, they seldom have a survey performed. They think they know where the property lines are, or they measure their property dimensions from a town tax map. Whether through negligence or ignorance, buildings that do not comply with established ordinances can become your problem.

Buying a property with setback violations can be a nightmare. Having to excavate and remove an in-ground pool is an expensive proposition. If you own the property and a complaint is filed, you could have to perform the removal of the pool. There may be some legal actions available to you against the previous owner. Even if you win such a suit, the cost will be astronomical. The best advice is to avoid the problem in the first place. Mortgage surveys and title searches allow you peace of mind and the right of quiet enjoyment. Don't skimp on these professional fees. They are much easier to take than the fees incurred through litigation or code compliances.

CODE VIOLATIONS

Code violations can be motivation for a seller to unload property cheap. I have seen changes in government officials bring about periods of fierce scrutiny. Many times a new administration concentrates on cleaning up slack areas of the system, such as code compliance. A rash of spot inspections may ensue, with code enforcement officers handing out violation orders like free candy. The owners of these affected buildings may prefer to dump the properties instead of bringing them up to code compliance. Code deficiencies can cost a bundle to remedy. Your professional inspectors should make you aware of any existing violations. It is also a good idea to check with the code enforcement office before making an offer. They may know of pending compliance requirements the property is subject to or upcoming county inspections.

INVESTING ON A SHAKY FOUNDATION

Foundation defects can be expensive to correct. Buying a property with a bad foundation is not wise. Very few properties offer the latitude of a low enough purchase price to compensate for foundation repairs. Unless you have allowed for extensive reconditioning in your buying budget, these buildings can break you. Prior to making a final commitment to purchase, have the property inspected by a professional.

Before spending time and money on a professional inspection, rule out the obvious. A comprehensive visual examination can alert you to blatant foundation faults. Is the foundation cracked? Is the roof sagging? Are the interior ceilings cracking or showing nail heads? Are the windows and doors difficult to operate? These are all simple factors to check in evaluating a foundation. If any of these conditions exist, the foundation may not be firm.

ROT AND INSECT DAMAGE

Take a screwdriver with you on your property inspection. Use it to probe exposed beams and joists. Try to stick the screwdriver in the sill plates. If the screwdriver penetrates any of these areas easily, there may be rot or insect damage. Is any of the wood extremely dark or black? This discoloration may prove to be moisture damage.

Are there any lines of dirt running along the foundation or structural members? These miniature tunnels usually indicate termites. Are the floor joists covered with a powdery white substance? Dry rot may be present. Do the floor joists look as if they were shot with a shotgun and birdshot? These numerous small holes could mean powder-post beetles are at work destroying your prospective investment.

Go into the attic and look for small mounds of

sawdust. If you find any, the rafters, trusses, or ceiling joists may be infested with wood-boring insects. This situation can cost thousands of dollars to rectify. Perform these basic inspections before hiring a professional inspector. If everything looks good to you, call a professional to check for the not-so-obvious problems.

REPEAT REHABS

Investors without construction and remodeling knowledge can fall prey to deceiving properties. If you are looking at a too-good-to-be-true deal, beware of first impressions. At first glance, a property may seem to be in better condition than it actually is. Let's look at a possible scenario.

We will call our fictional investor Bruce. Bruce responds to an advertisement for a super-cheap deal. Anxiously, he rushes to tour the property. If the building is as good as it sounds, Bruce doesn't want someone else to buy it before he can. The seller agrees to show the property on short notice, and Bruce is beaming with excitement. This is the first property Bruce has found at such an attractive price.

The goal is to buy the property, fix it up, and sell it fast. When Bruce gets to the property, he is impressed with the exterior condition. The outside does not need much work. A coat of paint, a few shrubs, and the exterior will be all set. The neighborhood is nice, and all Bruce's research shows this area to be a future hot-spot. From outward appearance, this seems to be the property for him. If the inside is anything like the outside, Bruce plans to make an offer immediately.

Too Good to Be True

The seller arrives and shows Bruce around the grounds. She points out the parking, the boundaries, and the new energy-efficient windows. Bruce is impressed, and asks to see the inside. The seller takes him into the basement. It is dry and shows no sign of structural or water problems. A quick look at the furnace and water heater makes him comfortable. They aren't new, but Bruce plans to resell the place anyway.

As he moves through the property, Bruce can't believe how good everything looks. The ceilings have a new textured finish and show no stains. The carpet needs to be replaced, but that's no big deal. Most of the walls are in fair condition. They will need some work, but what's a little patching and painting? While Bruce is looking through the place, the doorbell rings. The seller excuses herself and goes to answer the door.

Bruce peeks in the bathroom and kitchen. They are dated, but appear to be in average condition for a potential rehab project. As his enthusiasm builds, Bruce realizes somebody else is walking around upstairs. He goes to investigate and finds another party inspecting the dwelling. Feelings of discomfort invade. This is his deal—he found it, he deserves it.

Haste Makes Waste

At this point, Bruce is concentrating more on the other buyer than on the property. Feeling threatened, he rushes through the rest of the property and returns to the kitchen. Sitting at the table, he starts running numbers through the calculator. The seller comes in and asks if he has any questions. His response is one of passion. He indicates his desire to make an offer on the building.

The seller sits down and asks Bruce for his proposal. In haste, he offers 5% less than the asking price. The seller refuses Bruce's offer and counters with an offer of 2.5% less than the original price. The other prospective purchaser is still moving around upstairs. What is taking him so long? He wouldn't be spending this much time in the place if he weren't serious about buying it.

Bruce is convinced the deal is fantastic, and he accepts the counter-offer. After completing the necessary paperwork, Bruce gives the seller his check for the earnest money deposit. The purchase offer has only two contingencies. Bruce is entitled to have his deposit returned if financing is not available in the stated amount, and he must receive a clear title with general warranty deed. The deal is cut, and Bruce rushes home to celebrate.

Using his previously arranged credit line, Bruce closes on the property in two weeks. The title was clear, Bruce received a general warranty deed, and the property is his. Unfortunately, real estate does not come with a money-back guarantee. There is no return policy to cover your mistakes. If you make a bad purchase, you have to suffer the consequences.

The investor in our story has made a bad purchase and many mistakes.

The Truth Comes Out

After completing the transaction, Bruce called in several contractors to price the rehab work. When the contractors inspected the home, they found many obscure and costly obstacles. They determined that someone had started a rehab on the property and changed her mind. The reason for the change in heart was extensive, cost-prohibitive work.

Bruce's great deal turned into his worst nightmare. He was the embarrassed owner of a building better suited for demolition than renovation. Bruce's haste and excitement put him in financial distress. By not following the proper inspection methods, Bruce had been sold a no-win deal. The more the contractors looked, the more problems they discovered.

The roof and the upstairs plumbing leaked. The ceiling joists and subfloor were rotting under the upstairs bathroom. When the previous owner found these situations, she had the ceiling patched and textured. This cosmetic band-aid hid the existing damage and presented a pleasing appearance. A thorough inspection of the heating system revealed a cracked heat exchanger, among other defects. The cost to repair the boiler was almost as much as a new boiler.

The attic was infested with wood-boring insects. To remedy the infestation would require a tented fumigation. The fumigation would cost several thousand dollars, and the rafters would need repair. Carpenters estimated the rafter repairs to be $1,123. Then there was the septic field trouble.

The septic tank was metal and rusted through. It would have to be replaced and the leach field was no longer in operating condition. The cost to replace this system would be in excess of $5,000. The cost of mandatory repairs continued to mount. The exterior walls were insulated with newspaper and cardboard. When the seller installed replacement windows, she noticed the lack of satisfactory insulation and decided to give up on the building.

A Rehab Reject

When the previous owner began her remodeling efforts, she found these and other flaws. She decided the repairs would not be justified for her in-vestment plan. Then she patched and hid what she could. This allowed her to offer a visually appealing property for sale. Bruce's quick once-over inspection produced the desired results for the seller. The place looked like a good deal, with only minor cosmetic improvements needed. The deceiving appearance was what the street-smart seller was counting on to get her out of the property.

Everywhere the contractors looked, they found more serious deficiencies. Bruce felt doomed and helpless. He couldn't afford to make the needed repairs; they weren't in his budget figures. In its present condition, the house would be next to impossible to sell. Its condition was not good enough for the average owner-occupant. Savvy investors would subject the property to a detailed inspection.

Renting the home was a possibility, but many of the faults would have to be fixed before occupancy. Impulsive Bruce ended up in a world of trouble. This story is imaginary, but the potential problems are real. You decide whether Bruce went on to patch up the property enough to recoup his investment or got stuck with a lemon. If you are not careful in your evaluations, you could wind up like our impetuous friend Bruce.

There are specialists in the real estate business who thrive on impulsive and inexperienced investors. They buy horrible buildings and do only enough to make them look better. Then they sell them to the unsuspecting buyer for a healthy profit. It is this buyer who is left in the lurch. The first guy bought cheap and sold high. He sold it to the new buyer, who cannot afford the unforeseen repairs. The inexperienced investor is forced to sell, but paid too much to unload the property. This situation can result in foreclosure or bankruptcy.

FIRE JOBS

If you stay in the rehab business, you will be tempted to tackle fire jobs. These are properties damaged by fire and water. Sale prices on these buildings tend to be very low and very intriguing. In reality, fire jobs are complex projects to undertake. Unless you have extensive experience, don't even consider these opportunities.

Renovating a fire-damaged building can challenge the best contractor. It is difficult to assess the extent of damage. Working conditions are not desirable, and many subcontractors refuse the job because of this. Plumbing that looks fine can have melted joints that become a sprinkler system after new drywall has been installed. Wiring can be destroyed beyond repair, but there may be limited visual evidence of the damage. Structural members may have lost their integrity.

The price of these properties is captivating, but you should leave them for professional fire restorers. Contractors capable of completing fire jobs without losing money are rare. Fire pros are specialists and have paid a large price in experience to be successful. Avoiding this type of rehab will reduce your risk and prolong your career as a rehab contractor.

ABANDONED BUILDINGS

Vacant buildings can be very dangerous to buy. If the property has not been in use, it could have a multitude of imperfections. The plumbing could have frozen and never been repaired. Mechanical systems may have seized up and could require enormous repairs or complete replacement. Inspecting these properties can often be difficult. If the electricity has been turned off, you won't be able to complete a suitable inspection. It will be hard to see, and you will not be able to test any of the systems.

Before making an irrevocable commitment, insist on a full, satisfactory inspection of the property, with all systems operational. Buying property based on a sight inspection is unforgivable. Discerning investors know a fine-tooth-comb examination is an integral part of any buying decision. Without the inspection, you are buying an unknown product.

VERIFYING INCOME
ON A VACANT PROPERTY

Vacant houses should be checked out carefully, and empty apartment buildings must be put under a microscope. Any commercial or income property requires exhaustive investigation when being purchased vacant. Beyond structural and mechanical conditions, income properties must be scrutinized for their ability to produce a positive cash flow.

When income property has been vacant, there is little information to base current projections on. How long has it been since the property produced an income? What condition was it in when those rents were received? How much will the property be capable of producing in the current market? Finding the answers to these questions can be very difficult.

A large multi-family property could have all the needed qualities for a profitable rehab, except suppose it won't sell or rent after completion? When evaluating income-producing properties, look beyond the physical condition. Follow the guidelines in the location section of this chapter. Combine these techniques with the advice found throughout this book.

You must be sure your finished rehab project will have a place in the market. Remember, it will take time to complete renovations. You must speculate on what market conditions will dictate upon completion of the renovation work. This is best accomplished by using historical data. Spend enough time on research to protect your investment and rehab efforts.

THOUGHTS FOR REFLECTION

What properties should you avoid? Is there any property you should *never* consider buying? These are two small questions with potentially large repercussions. Some real estate is not worth your time or investment dollar. This does not mean the realty has no value. It only means the value is not worth the effort or risk required to extract it.

There are very few properties that should never be considered. The land value of a property is always worth consideration. Given the proper zoning and a low sales price, some properties are worth buying just to demolish. If the overall package, including demolition, costs less than comparable vacant land, you may have found one of those hidden treasures we spoke of.

It is possible, in some cases, to construct a new building for less than the sale price of existing properties in the area. If the septic and well systems are in good condition, you save by not having to install them. Even when the land will not support septic systems or wells, it has value. In this case, the value is not for housing, but there is still something to be achieved. When you can buy for the right price, any property is worth a few hours of thought. A creative investor will find a way to turn a loser into a winner.

Sifting through available properties may be intimidating early in your career. Don't worry, all investors have felt similar fears and reservations. The ones who didn't are probably not in the game anymore. You should be apprehensive and being a little afraid won't hurt. Buying rehab projects can be risky business.

You will do much better approaching this business with respect than you will with a cavalier attitude. Don't be afraid to make a decision—just recognize the need to make sound decisions. When you learn what properties to avoid, you are well in front of the competition. This takes time, experience, and mistakes. If you are not making any mistakes, you are not reaching your potential.

Mistakes are a part of learning and experience. Expect to make some mistakes — even full-time professionals stumble from time to time. Learn from your mistakes. The first time is experience, the second time is a mistake. If you control your errors to an extent that doesn't stop you, you are doing well. As time passes, you will have fewer learning experiences and more money. The learning process never ends; every day brings changes and challenges. That's what makes being an entrepreneur interesting.

DETERMINING BEFORE AND AFTER VALUES

5

Appraisal skills are as important to learn as rehab procedures. If you don't know how to measure the value of a property, you will have a difficult time making money in the real estate business. This is not to say you must be a certified appraiser. Your knowledge should allow you to do a quick routine assessment of the buildings under consideration for purchase. These skills will make your job easier and will save you time and money.

By learning the basics of real estate appraisal principles, you will be able to reject certain properties quickly. Without this competence, you will waste much of your time estimating improvement costs only to find the project is not viable. Professional appraisers charge anywhere from $150 and up to tell you not to buy a building. If you can come to this conclusion on your own, you have saved money.

It is a prudent decision to have a professional value a property once it has met your quick-test criteria. It is not too difficult for the average person to learn fundamental appraisal procedures, but you should leave the final evaluation to a professional. The appraised value of a property is the deciding factor for a bank, and it should be your ultimate gauge as well.

It would not be realistic to pay for a professional appraisal of every property you are considering. There is enough information in this chapter to get you well on your way to placing a reasonable value on purchases and intended improvements yourself. Expanding on this foundation of knowledge comes with experience. Reading books dedicated to appraisal techniques will quicken your pace in becoming competent at the task.

The fundamentals of real estate appraising will be valuable throughout your investing career. They will help you when you buy, when you improve, and when you sell. They will give you an edge over the competition and make you more efficient. Many of these principles apply to all real estate. Some of the specialized areas pertain predominantly to income and commercial properties. In this chapter, I will emphasize the residential and multi-family approaches. These two categories are the most popular with rehab investors. I will briefly discuss commercial techniques and other specialized areas. You will have no trouble grasping the methods for a basic residential appraisal.

APPRAISAL FUNDAMENTALS

Real estate may have a multitude of values simultaneously. The most common value sought is the fair-market value. In addition to fair-market value, realty can also have the following types of values:

☐ tax value

☐ mortgage loan value

☐ replacement value

☐ rental value

☐ appraised value

☐ inheritance tax value

☐ cash value

☐ insurance value

❏ depreciated value

❏ capitalized value

❏ exchange value

❏ salvage value

The list could continue for several more categories, but these are the best known and most frequently used values. Generally, for a rehab investor, tax value, market value, rental value, and loan value are the areas most scrutinized.

Some of the key factors in determining a property value are listed below. They are:

❏ highest and best use

❏ conformity

❏ competition

❏ anticipation

❏ supply and demand

❏ contribution

❏ change

❏ growth and decline

All these elements are evaluated when determining the value of real estate. One of the most important elements is the determination of the highest and best use of a property. This factor is so influential that Chapter 12 is entirely dedicated to highest and best use.

Types of Appraisals

The two methods of appraisal used most are the direct market comparison approach and the income approach. For residential properties, the market comparison approach is the most common. This is true of single-family dwellings and small multi-family properties. Larger multi-family residential buildings are typically appraised using the income approach. For large rehab projects, the cost approach is frequently used to arrive at an appraised value.

MARKET-COMPARISON METHOD. Using the market-comparison approach, you must find at least three properties with similar qualities to your property that have been sold. These sales should have been consummated in the last six months or less. Us-ing a market-comparison sheet like the example on the next page, you list the qualities of each property.

After all the meaningful information is recorded, you must evaluate it and assign a value to each section. When performing this technique, you will incorporate the principle of substitution. A little later in the chapter, I will give you a clear example of this approach to appraising a property.

Once you have determined the market value of a property, you can calculate the loan value. First, contact several of the area lenders you will be approaching for financing when you buy. Ask them what their loan-to-value ratios are for various properties. Be sure to get separate information for single-family homes, multi-family up to four units, owner-occupied property, and commercial buildings. Depending on owner occupancy, single family and units up to four can have a loan-to-value ratio of up to 95%, with 90% being the average. Buildings with over four units usually have a loan-to-value of about 80%. Find out if the loan-to-value is based on the contract price or the appraised value. Most lenders will work off whichever figure is lower. This means if the purchase price of a single family property is $100,000 and the appraised value is $120,000, the bank will loan 90% of $100,000. In this case, $90,000 is your loan value.

THE INCOME APPROACH. With multi-family properties of five or more units, the income approach carries the most weight in assigning a market value. This method is centered around the annual net income of a property. A vital fact to remember is that this approach deals with net income, not gross income. The rule of thumb for this technique is dividing the net income by the desired rate of return. The number obtained from this mathematical equation is the property value. When we get to the section of the chapter with examples, you will see exactly how this works.

COST COMPARISON METHOD. The majority of rehab projects have to be appraised using the cost approach to figure a completed value. You must estimate the value of your improvements in terms of their cost. This application allows more room for speculation and error, but it is the only feasible way to give value to projected improvements.

There is a detailed explanation of this policy in the example section of the chapter.

MARKET COMPARISON SHEET			
Subject Property	**Comp 1**	**Comp 2**	**Comp 3**
Price	$113,000	$119,000	$117,500
Age	7 YRS.	6.5 YRS.	6 YRS.
Location	QUIET RES.	QUIET RES.	HIGH TRAFFIC ?
Lot Size	70' x 150'	75' x 148'	65' x 150'
Landscaping	GOOD	GOOD	NEEDS WORK
Construction	FRAME	FRAME	FRAME
Style	CAPE COD	CAPE COD	SALTBOX
Number of Rooms	9	9	10
Number of Bathrooms	2	2	2
Square Footage	3	3	3 (4?)
Basement	UNFINISHED	UNFINISHED	UNFINISHED
Garage	YES	YES	YES
Storage	GOOD	EXCELLENT	GOOD
Exterior Condition	EXCELLENT	GOOD	GOOD
Interior Condition	GOOD	GOOD	GOOD
Amenities		DECK	DECK
Association Fees	N/A	YES	N/A
Improvements	NEW SIDING		
Financing			
Date Sold	9-11-92	9-25-92	11-1-92
Adjustments	+ 12,500	+ 13,000	+ 11,000
ESTIMATED VALUE	$125,500	$132,000	$128,500

Determining Values

For an astute rehabber, a combination of these methods is usually the order of the day. In the appraisal process, you must follow designated paths. The first step is to establish the type of value you want to determine; it will usually be the market value. The next requirement is to catalog all the information you need to form an opinion of value. Then, list the sources likely to provide this data. Next, gather the necessary information and make a concise record of your findings. Be sure the information is accurate and applicable.

With these duties complete, put together everything you can on the property you are appraising. Don't forget to include your proposed changes to the property; they will have a significant impact on your final value. At this point, you must decide which appraisal style you will use. In most cases, you will combine at least two of the aforementioned principles of appraisal. With this determination made, analyze your collected data.

Make the necessary substitutions and adjustments to reconcile your findings. (How to do this is illustrated in the example section of this chapter.) When you reach the final reconciliation, you will have a solid estimate for the value of your building. If the numbers are encouraging, move ahead with your investigation and potential purchase.

Classifying the Land

To classify a home's lot, you must separate it into zones. Appraisers use three zones—public, service, and private. The public zone is the area visible from the street, usually the front of the property. Service zones include sections designed for driveways, sidewalks, and storage buildings. The private area consists of a family's outdoor living space. It encompasses the lawn, deck, playground, swimming pool, and other outside recreational districts.

Interior Zones

The interior of the residence must also be classified. Traffic areas consist of hallways, stairways, and foyers. These portions of a home see the most transient activity. These pathways play an important role in the design of a home. If they are broken up and cause congestion, the property loses value. Inhabitants should be able to gain direct access to a bathroom from these high-use areas. Moving from one level of the home to another must be accomplished through a hall instead of through another room. Without the proper layout, a home will be deemed functionally obsolescent.

When rating interior zoning, pay attention to the logical arrangement of rooms and traffic patterns. A residence should include three primary zones—for sleeping, living, and working. Kitchens and laundry areas are considered work zones. Bedrooms make up the sleeping zone, and the remainder of the house is the living zone. With today's lifestyles, you might include a fitness zone and a relaxation zone.

Room Relationships

A kitchen should have convenient access to the dining area and the parking zone. If the home has a separate dining room, it should be adjacent to the kitchen. The family room should be situated as far from bedrooms as possible. It is normally the noisiest room in the house. Your best appraisal will come if the family room's location allows undisturbed use of the rest of the home. A formal living room separated from the casual living space is expected and conforming.

Number of Rooms

Ideally, bedrooms should be on the cool side of the building and away from the noise of busy streets. Given a choice, include a minimum of three bedrooms in your rehab home. Two-bedroom homes limit your potential market share of tenants or buyers. Four-bedroom homes are in demand, but the cost of providing a fourth bedroom can be prohibitive. A three-bedroom home is the most universally accepted home on the market. Look at the surrounding homes and make your decision based on the comparable homes in the neighborhood.

How many bathrooms should a home have? An industry standard calls for one bathroom for every two adults. An additional bathroom should be provided for every three children in the family. Every level of the house should have at least a half bath. By modern standards, a three-bedroom home should include a minimum of one and one-half bathrooms. Two and one-half bathrooms are the most desirable in multi-level homes and properties with more than three bedrooms.

A full bath can be installed in a 5-foot by 7-foot space, but try to make the bathrooms as large as is reasonable. Current trends point to larger bathrooms with more amenities. Look for ways to upgrade a half bath by adding a bathing unit. A half bath can appraise for $1,300 to $1,700, while a full bath's value is between $3,300 and $3,700. Regardless of whether you add a shower or tub, converting the space to a full bath will increase your appraised value by around $2,000.

Type of Construction

Foundations affect the appraised value of any property. Foundations can be monolithic slabs, floating slabs, pier foundations, crawlspaces, and full basements. Each of these foundations has a different appraised value. Slab foundations are the least expensive foundations to construct, because they provide a foundation and a structural floor. Pier foundations are inexpensive, but create problems in cold climates. Full basements are financially feasible in cold climates, and crawlspaces are popular in warmer environments.

Framing methods include platform frame construction, balloon construction, and post and beam construction. There are cost advantages to these various types of framing, but they have little to do with the appraised value of a building. General construction styles have an effect on a property's value, but they are allowed for in the substitution methods of a comparable appraisal.

The types of items to compare cover everything from insulation to roof designs. A house with a gable roof is standard construction, but one with a mansard roof costs more to build. This does not guarantee a higher market value for the house with the more expensive roof. Taking advantage of these types of appraisal techniques separates professional rehabbers from amateurs.

PRACTICING APPRAISAL TECHNIQUES

To start using the principles of appraisal methods, you will need forms. The first form to study is a Location Information Form. An example of this form is at the end of the chapter. The purpose of the form is to establish the qualities of a neighborhood

or business section. The data found on the form will help you determine the value of a given location. Many of the deciding factors are easy to rate, but some require more research.

Information such as family incomes and occupations is not as important as the stage of the location's life cycle and the demand for the area. Neighborhoods move up and down in economic and physical cycles. As we discussed in Chapter 4, neighborhoods may be growing, stable, or declining. Determining this data is critical in making your appraisal. The demand for property in the area is another prominent factor in a location's value. By using a form each time you assess a building, you won't overlook a key area and your appraisals will be consistent.

The next form you will want to use is the Land Evaluation Form (example at the end of the chapter). The knowledge gained in completing this form is essential to the overall value of a property. You can gather much of the needed information from city or county offices. The remainder will be a product of a site visit and firsthand observations. After these two forms are complete, you are ready to move on to the Property Data Form.

The Property Data Form is a comprehensive listing of all the integral characteristics of the building. It provides space for vital information on all the areas having the greatest effect on a property's value. Finding the information for this form is a little more difficult. The level of difficulty can be reduced by using the form as a checklist. When touring the subject property, make notes on the form and fill in all the blanks. This practice will provide you with valuable details and a start in your appraisal process.

A SAMPLE OF MARKET VALUE

At this point, you are ready to work through your first appraisal example. In this example, we are going to appraise a single-family home. Initially, we will determine the existing value by using the direct market comparison approach. The planned improvements are not a factor in this first appraisal. Our goal is only to establish the market value of the home in its present condition. Our subject property is a four bedroom, two and one-half bath ranch on

123 Wallace Street.

To begin, you must itemize the type of information you need and the sources where it can be found. By using the forms previously discussed, you will have a list of the data needed for a complete appraisal. Look over the forms and determine where you will find the required facts and figures. Once you have a plan, begin gathering the particulars.

Obtain and list the information pertaining to the location, the land, and the individual structure. Your completed data should resemble the Property Data Form example on the next page for 123 Wallace Street.

When this is done, you will need documentation to compare to your findings. This step is what makes the process a direct market comparison. Correlating the facts on comparable sales is easy for a professional appraiser. He or she has access to computer-supplied data and comparable sale books. Unless you have obtained this same information from a real estate broker, you are disadvantaged by a lack of facts on recent sales. This disadvantage is real, but it is not incapacitating.

Using Public Records

You can find the bulk of the needed information in the tax assessor's office and at the Registry of Deeds. Your form tells you what information is required, and the records in these public offices provide the information. Tax assessors have detailed information in their files on all the houses within the town or city. Their statistics answer the majority of the questions on the Property Data Form and the Land Evaluation Form. You can obtain the tax value of a property from the assessor's records. The facts not supplied by the tax office can be found in the Registry of Deeds. All this information is public record and easily accessible.

Physical characteristics are found in the tax records. These include, but are not limited to, the number of bedrooms and bathrooms. Other features are the type of construction, age, style, and size. Tax records are excellent sources of detailed declarations. Current sale prices can be discovered in the Registry of Deeds, and utility information can be obtained from the public works department. This information is available without cost and is invaluable in your buying and selling decisions.

Comparing Property Qualities

When making a direct market comparison appraisal, you will make adjustments for dissimilar features. The basic features of your comparable properties should be nearly identical with the property being appraised. The closer the properties match, the easier and more accurate your assessment of value will be. The areas with the most importance are as follows:

❑ age

❑ style

❑ number of bedrooms

❑ land area

❑ general condition

❑ similar locations

❑ size

❑ construction type

❑ number of bathrooms

❑ zoning

❑ total number of rooms

❑ functionality

When selecting comparable properties, seek properties with the most recent sales. Try to avoid using comparables sold more than six months ago. Real estate markets are volatile and can change in a matter of months. A property selling for $135,000 a year ago may only be worth $110,000 today. This principle also applies to price increases. Dig deep to find current sales for your correlation. For a fair comparison, you will need a minimum of three comparables.

The easiest way to evaluate similarities is with another form. This form is called a Sales Comparison Sheet, and there is an example at the end of the chapter. On the Sales Comparison Sheet, all the major categories are listed horizontally. Vertically, you will find spaces for each comparable sale to be distinguished. This form allows you to assimilate all your collected data on a common form. With this method, comparing the similar sales is easy. All you have to do is fill in the blanks and compare the differences

PROPERTY DATA FORM

Address: _123 WALLACE STREET, JIMSON, VA_

Style: _COLONIAL_   Price: _$237,000.00_

Road Frontage: _200'_   Water Frontage: _N/A_

Land Area: _20,000 sq. ft._   Zoning: _RESIDENTIAL_

Number of Rooms: _8_   Number of Bedrooms: _4_

Number of Baths: _2½_   Exterior Dimensions: _28' x 44'_

Deed Book & Page: _BOOK 173, PG 47_   Annual Taxes: _$2,200.00_

Map/Lot/Block: _MAP R-12, LOT 22, BLOCK 4, ROBJOY ESTATES_

Siding: _CEDAR_   Color: _BEIGE W/ BROWN TRIM_

Electric Service: _200 AMP_   Heat Type: _HEAT PUMP_

Type of Hot Water: _ELECTRIC_   Water Service: _PUBLIC_

Attic: _YES_   Sewer: _PUBLIC_

Basement: _FULL, UNFINISHED_   Assumable Loan? _No_

FLOOR PLAN

	1st Floor	2nd Floor	3rd Floor	Basement
Living Room	✓			
Dining Room	✓			
Family Room	✓			
Kitchen	✓			
Bedrooms		4		
Bathrooms	½	2		

and similarities. This sounds a little easier than it actually is.

LOCATION. For the location factor, all comparable sales should be found in the same neighborhood whenever possible. If the comparables are not in the same location, adjustments must be made. Age is usually parallel with residential comparables. Most homes in any given area will have been built during the same period. If the age is different by more than five years, an adjustment must be made accordingly.

LOT SIZE. Lot sizes in city situations rarely affect the appraised value of a property. Exceptions would apply if the lot was irregular or unusable, or didn't offer privacy or parking. In standard appraisals of urban property, lot size does not normally play a significant role in value.

CONSTRUCTION. Construction types must be the same, or adjustments will be required. Style, as long as it conforms to the area, is not critical. You wouldn't want to compare an expansive two-story home with a modest ranch home, but this is rarely a problem. The number of rooms contained in each house, excluding bathrooms and buried basement rooms, should be consistent. If there is more than a one-room difference, you will need to make adjustments in the value.

SQUARE FOOTAGE. Total square footage is a deciding factor. Two houses can each have nine rooms, but one of the houses may be much larger than the other. This has obvious effects on the cost of construction and resale value. Basements, even when finished, are not normally computed as standard living space. This is important in your appraisal and must be a consideration in your rehab plans. Finished basements are popular, but they can prove a stumbling block when attempting to recover your improvement costs.

ROOM COUNT. Bedrooms are one of the largest influences in a home's value. You cannot use a two-bedroom home as a comparable for a four-bedroom home. If the difference is only one bedroom, adjustments can be made. While this is possible, it is much more desirable to maintain equality in the number of bedrooms in each comparable. Bedrooms are vital to assessing value and must be given the credit they deserve. This fact gives you a good direction to point your rehab efforts in.

Adding bedrooms will add value quickly, so look for this potential in every property. For appraisal purposes, a room without a closet cannot be considered a bedroom. Moreover, a room smaller than 8' x 10' will lose value as a bedroom, even if a closet is present. If you intend to convert or add a bedroom, keep these requirements in mind.

Bathrooms are ranked number two in determining the value of a home. They are second only to bedrooms. Follow the same path with bathroom comparison as you would with bedrooms. General condition is always a determining factor. You can make simple adjustments for deteriorating conditions, so don't allow these problems to prevent the use of a comparable.

PROFITABLE EXTRAS. Garages, fireplaces, air conditioning, and other desirable differences can be accounted for with adjustments. These are minor contrasts, and they can be assigned a special value for adjusting the appraised value. The last consideration may surprise you, but you must acknowledge it.

As a rehabber, you are interested in only spending money with the best chance of increasing your profit. Pay particular attention to this advice. In the category of "other space," you will include many potential appurtenances and improvements. Storage facilities and garages could be placed in this group. Any other structures that are not a part of the primary residence will be included in the group. Florida rooms, fitness rooms, and the like are legitimate living space and should receive a standard rating in the "other" category.

This next topic is the most important physical aspect for a rehab artist to consider. In appraisal reports, attics and basements are not equally profitable. A finished attic can be treated as standard habitable space, but a buried basement falls short of this mark. In the "number of rooms" category, converted attic space may be counted. Finished basement rooms are ignored in this column. Keep this in mind at all times during your rehab projections.

Given an option, spend your money in the attic, not in the basement. The cost of creating living space is similar between attics and basements. The difference comes when you try to recover your costs or turn a profit. Attics will beat basements in any professional appraisal report. This single fact can save you from a common misconception among remodelers, so don't forget it!

The date of the closed sale must be considered as well. If the dates vary greatly, or if market conditions have changed dramatically, the sale date may demand adjustments in the estimated value. Under average conditions, a comparable sold within the last six months does not require an adjustment.

Calculating Adjustment Amounts

The most complicated facet of the direct market approach is determining how much to allow for various adjustments. Professional appraisers have experience and computer databases to assist them. You have nothing but books and your wits from which to draw a conclusion of value. Does this mean you cannot make an accurate assessment of real estate values? Absolutely not, you can produce results with your resources that will parallel professional appraisals.

In the early stage of your appraisal journey, using more than three comparables will boost your accuracy and confidence. Given enough comparable sales, you can create tight numbers on the adjustments needed. To illustrate my point, consider this example. You develop a list of nine comparable sales. Seven of these homes have brick exteriors. One of the remaining comparables has vinyl siding and the other has wood siding. The type of siding is the only significant difference between the nine comparable sales. The seven brick homes all sold in a price range between $123,000 and $125,000.

The two houses with different siding sold for less than the brick homes. The house with vinyl siding sold for $118,000 and the one with wood siding closed at $119,500. When comparing so many otherwise identical properties, you can conclude a reasonable adjustment value. In this example, brick houses are worth five to six thousand dollars more than homes with wood or vinyl siding. This figure is only an example; it is not meant as a true comparison of brick versus vinyl siding. The key to success is having enough similar comparables to draw these accurate conclusions.

Every time you run a comparable sales chart, record your findings and file them for future use. The more you practice these skills, the better your accuracy rates become. Continued extensive comparisons will allow you to build a market value ad-

justment for every common factor in a home. Fireplaces may work out to be worth $3,500 on average, and decks may show a value of ten dollars per square foot. This type of historical data is extremely valuable in all of your rehab efforts. It will guide you to the most profitable improvements and protect you from paying too much for a property.

USING BIDS TO DETERMINE COSTS

A possible alternative to this time-consuming process is to consult with a general contractor. Make some sample plans and specifications. In one example, require a brick exterior but request a price for vinyl siding as an optional choice. Carry this out through the most common variances in the homes you are contemplating purchasing. Put your mock plans out to bids from five contractors, and you should get a good feel for what various extras are worth. These price differences are based on improvements or new construction, but they may be applied to older properties.

If a cedar shake roof is 35% more than an asphalt roof in your bid request, you can use a similar rating when applying your appraisal techniques to existing homes. This is one of the quickest ways to develop an accurate database of adjustment figures. Most general contractors are happy to comply with your request for prices. Free bids will provide you with valuable information for making market comparison adjustments.

ACTUAL APPRAISED VALUES

If you want fast, reliable standards to base your calculations on, and you don't mind investing about $100, contact a professional appraiser in your area. Look for someone who specializes in the type of property you are interested in buying, and arrange to meet with her for an hour. Tell the appraiser to assume all your questions are based on standard construction methods, then ask for value differences on the items listed on your Property Data Form. In less than sixty minutes, you can compile a wealth of priceless information. You will know exactly what to figure for square footage costs, how much each bathroom is worth, and the value of a slab versus a crawlspace.

USING THE COST APPROACH

Cost approach appraisals are key tools for rehab investors. Knowing the completed value of your proposed improvements is a pivotal point in the decision to proceed with a given property. If you are going to spend your time and money only to break even, the project is a loser. Cost approach appraisals require slightly different tactics. They deal with the actual cost of a defined improvement.

Cost approach appraisals may be called *summation appraisals*. In this type of appraisal, land value is not a consideration. The land value is rarely used in the assessment, but location has a bearing on the outcome of a summation appraisal. These appraisals have two negative aspects. Construction and remodeling costs vary greatly between contractors. The costs fluctuate depending on where materials are purchased and the profit margin sought by contractors. For these reasons, you may have to make adjustments in your final evaluation.

The other drawback evolves from the highest-and-best-use principle. Some improvements are worth less than they cost to produce. Building or rehabbing a small house on land zoned for industrial use would be a bad decision. For the property to see its full potential, the house would have to be moved or destroyed. Another example would be building a shopping center along an isolated country road. As a final example, remodeling a home in a $100,000 neighborhood until you have invested $250,000 would be ridiculous. Finding a buyer for a house priced twice as much as surrounding properties is unlikely. The expense for these projects is far in excess of their value.

Reproduction and Replacement Costs

When seeking value with a cost approach appraisal, you can look for two types of costs. They are *reproduction costs* and *replacement costs*. The reproduction cost is the amount required to create an exact duplicate of the building or improvement. The replacement cost is decided by the expense to recreate a very similar building or improvement, with equal utility. Replacement cost is the most popular method in summation appraisals. In both cases, current construction costs are used to determine a reasonable value. Finding a summation value may include any of four methods.

THE SQUARE FOOTAGE TECHNIQUE. The square foot method of summation appraisal is a fast way to arrive at a figure. This method is reasonably accurate with new construction of homes and similar properties. If you are contemplating adding on to a property or considering demolishing the structure to make way for a new building, this technique will serve you well. It is not as reliable with rehab projects or remodeling.

Using the square foot method requires finding a common value of comparable new structures. In the case of a house, this can be very simple. In tightly zoned areas, house prices will parallel with marked consistency. A ranch-style home with 1,200 square feet, three bedrooms, and one and one-half bathrooms may be a standard production home. When placed on a lot in the same subdivision, all these homes will have competitive values.

By making adjustments for options, you can easily assign a square foot value to the homes. If all these homes start with a base selling price of $60,000, excluding land value, the square foot factor is $50 per square foot. To arrive at this figure, subtract the land value from the sale price to determine the structure only price. Then divide the number of square feet into the structure price. Cost manuals are another resource frequently used to establish a per-square-foot value. These manuals, available in most bookstores, give precise examples of various types of construction and improvements.

COST ESTIMATING BOOKS. In such a manual, you may find an evaluation for the cost of constructing a detached garage. The manual will provide some breakdowns of cost and an overall cost per square foot to complete the construction. In the final breakdown, the manual might assign a value of $20 per square foot for the construction of a typical garage. Option and adjustment figures may be included to allow adjustments for upgrade features. These features could include electric door openers, additional windows, storage-rated ceiling joists, or insulation.

These manuals are excellent for finding a quick guesstimate of value. There are a few problems with depending on a manual for your cost figures. Manuals of this type are not updated as often as costs change. Most manuals are only modified once a year. Construction costs can change quickly and drastically. If the manual is not current, your estimated costs will go astray. Another concern with using figures found in manuals is the geographical price variations. Construction costs in Maine are vastly different than the same type of costs in California. The best manuals allow for this and provide index factors to compensate for regional differences.

The square foot method is used regularly in determining values for new homes. Under such conditions, the results are fairly accurate. Trying to use this approach with rehab projects is not as successful. Rehab costs are determined by existing conditions and can vary enormously. It is rarely practical to assign a square foot value to remodeling work. Review the example of this appraisal process at the end of the chapter. It will make this fast, on-the-spot procedure easy to understand. While the accuracy of this method is questionable for rehab work, the procedure is helpful. It allows you to make quick assessments capable of producing consistent results.

THE UNIT-IN-PLACE TECHNIQUE. Another frequently used method for cost appraising is the unit-in-place method. This approach is much more time consuming than the square foot method, but it is also more accurate. This procedure requires each element of the construction to be given an individual value. These components of construction may be assigned values found in cost manuals. These manuals will indicate a value for every major item found in construction or remodeling.

The values may be based on a cost-per-square-foot method, a cost-per-linear-foot method, or a cost-per-item method. These values are appointed to each phase of construction or remodeling. Plumbing, heating, and electrical costs are normally given in per-square-foot increments. Plumbing may be assigned a value of $3.20 per square foot. Electrical costs may be given an estimated value of $2.95 per square foot. Framing costs are typically given a per-square-foot value, while foundation expenses are computed on a per-linear-foot basis. (See the example for this type of appraisal at the end of the chapter.) This method offers more precision than the square foot method, but it still leaves something to be desired in accuracy.

QUANTITY SURVEY APPRAISALS. The final approach used with summation appraisals is the quantity survey method. This is the most accurate method and is the best tack to take with rehab jobs. Using the square-foot method is fine for a fast qualification assessment of a property. It can tell you almost immediately if the property has profit potential. The unit-in-place method is also an acceptable quick-test routine for evaluating the pre-purchase value of a property. Both of these methods are fast and accurate enough for making a preliminary decision. If the investment passes either of these tests, use the quantity survey method for your final evaluation.

Before making an offer to purchase, you need concise cost figures on which to base your offer. The quantity survey method will give you extremely accurate figures and protect you from financial losses. This detailed method of cost approach appraising requires a complete itemization of every expense to be incurred in your rehab project. This is a complicated method and may be intimidating to investors without rehab experience. Don't let your apprehension drive you away from the best way of protecting your investment.

The manuals used in the earlier methods have a place here. They will help the inexperienced investor know what types of costs to look for. By assessing your intended improvements and using the manuals as a prompt for ideas, you can develop an estimate sheet. A comprehensive Estimate Form is given at the end of the chapter. This estimate form has a broad category for every facet of rehab expenses likely to be encountered. Use this as a guide and break the categories into sub-categories as required for your job.

After you have designed your personal estimate form, filling in the blanks gives you a total cost for your projected plans. The amounts used may come from a general contractor or subcontractors and material suppliers. Granted, this approach means a lot of work, but it may save thousands of dollars and your credit rating. Buying a property for rehab without accurate cost projections is a financially deadly game. Inspect the example at the end of the chapter for a detailed guide to building a summation appraisal with the quantity survey method. If you are serious about rehabbing your way to riches, it is imperative that you learn to estimate your costs accurately before buying a property.

COMBINING APPRAISAL METHODS

In evaluating properties for their desirability as rehab projects, you should use two appraisal methods. For residential property, use the direct market comparison approach and the cost approach. Do a market comparison on the property in its as-is condition. Perform a cost approach appraisal on the improvements you plan to implement. Then do a market comparison study on the property, based on its future condition after your rehab improvements. This checks-and-balances system will protect your assets and determine the viability of your intended project.

MULTI-FAMILY INCOME METHODS

When dealing with multi-family properties containing six or more apartments, use the income approach of appraisal. This type of appraisal requires information about market rents, present gross income, present expenses, and future income and expenses. The first thing you must establish is the market rent for the area. This is done most accurately with information from closed comparable sales. Without access to comparable sale books and multiple listing service books, how will you determine market rents?

You can peruse the local paper for amounts being asked for rent in the area or contact the local housing authority. The housing authority has historical rental income figures available for your inspection. The ads in the paper give you a good idea of market rents, but remember they are only requested rents. They are not necessarily the actual rents being collected. Once you know the common rental income for apartments similar to the ones under consideration, you can begin the process.

Take the present rental income for the subject property and put it at the top of your paper. Verify all income and expense figures for a property being purchased. Brokers and owners may make an honest, or not so honest, mistake when providing these deciding figures. Allow a figure for annual maintenance and an amount for lost income from vacancies. A vacancy rate can be supplied by the housing

authority of your loan officer.

Calculating Net Income

In most areas, 10% of the gross income is allotted to maintenance, and 5% of the income is removed to allow for vacancies. Subtract these amounts from the gross income. Next, subtract all the known expenses from the gross income. These items could include real estate taxes, utilities, heating fuel, snow removal, lawn care, and a host of other expenditures. After all these deductions from the gross income, you are left with the net income. This is also called the net operating income or net-before-debt figure. This is the money you anticipate having available to pay for the property and your profit each year.

Using a summation appraisal, determine what your improvements will cost. Estimate how much the improvements will allow you to raise the present rents. Keep standard market rents in mind during this phase. If all three-bedroom apartments in the area rent for $550 per month, you won't collect $800 for your units, regardless of improvements. Installing whirlpools and sunrooms will not allow rents to jump far above those of comparable units. Be realistic with your projections and keep them conservative. Getting higher than expected rents is great; collecting substantially lower income than projected will ruin your day.

QUICK METHODS TO TEST THE FEASIBILITY OF A PROPERTY

For a quick-test assessment, add your improvement costs to the anticipated acquisition cost of the building. Divide your projected net operating income by twelve, which gives you the projected monthly net income. If this figure will pay the monthly loan installment on the purchase price, plus the improvement costs, you have a definite winner. Most investors are happy if a property pays for itself after the down payment is applied. Finding one capable of paying its way using the full purchase and improvement costs is outstanding.

Using this basic income approach is probably all you need to concentrate on with income property. You will know how much negative cash flow is acceptable, and this approach gives you an accurate estimate of your net income. If you want another way to determine your investment's value, use the capitalization rate (cap rate) method.

PROJECTING RATE OF RETURN

The cap rate method determines the rate of return on your investment. If you know the appraised value of the property and the net income, finding the cap rate is easy. You simply divide the net income by the appraised value. The result is the rate of return yielded by the investment. As an example, assume your total property acquisition and improvement costs are $300,000. The net income for this example is $30,000 per year. Dividing the $300,000 by the $30,000 gives us a cap rate of 10%. This method is useful if you have a goal for a specific rate of return.

Gross income multipliers can be used with income property, but you need an index number for your multiplier. This can be obtained from past sales. To determine a gross income multiplier (GIM), you divide the closed sale price of a building by the gross income. *Use the gross income, not the net income!* By doing this with several sold comparable properties in the area, you can develop a GIM. For example, a building sold for $260,000, with a gross annual income of $26,000, has a multiplier value of 10. This method allows more room for error and should primarily be used as a fast way to perform a preliminary evaluation.

These are the only methods required for the average investor dealing in multi-family properties. Work the numbers tightly and don't overestimate your projected income. Do some homework for historical data in your area. Maintenance and vacancy rates vary from neighborhood to neighborhood and region to region.

As an alternative to learning these skills, you can rely on professional appraisers. If your time is valuable, it may be more cost effective to engage an experienced appraiser. I have always preferred doing my own appraisals. It is the best way to ensure meeting your financial goals, but there is nothing wrong with hiring a professional. When buying your first rehab deal, it is wise to invest in a certified appraisal. The cost will not break your budget, and it will give you a clear written report on the property's value. In addition, it will show you how the pros do it.

I learned my first appraisal techniques in this way. Since then, I have done extensive reading and attended classes to enhance my skills of property assessment. If you plan to be in the business for a long time, these same steps will benefit you over the years. No matter how you do it, know your project's before and after values before making a commitment to purchase. Going into a deal without adequate cost projections will cause you grief at some point.

Even if you are lucky on the first few, there will be one waiting to pull you down. It costs very little to establish these values, and you risk so much if you don't. As a seasoned contractor, investor, and broker, I can't emphasize enough the importance of knowing what you are getting into before you sign on the dotted line. The policy of determining before and after values is crucial to successful real estate investing. This single tactic removes a huge portion of the risk associated with real estate speculation.

MARKET COMPARISON SHEET			
Subject Property	**Comp 1**	**Comp 2**	**Comp 3**
Price			
Age			
Location			
Lot Size			
Landscaping			
Construction			
Style			
Number of Rooms			
Number of Bathrooms			
Square Footage			
Basement			
Garage			
Storage			
Exterior Condition			
Interior Condition			
Amenities			
Association Fees			
Improvements			
Financing			
Date Sold			
Adjustments			
ESTIMATED VALUE			

LOCATION INFORMATION FORM

Property address _____

Legal description _____

_____

Lot dimensions _____

Zoning _____

Road frontage _____

Shape _____

View _____

Land area in square feet _____

Topography _____

Hazards _____

Landscaping _____

Deed restrictions _____

Drainage _____

Easements _____

Improvements _____

_____

UTILITIES

Public water yes/no   Public sewer yes/no

Electricity yes/no   Gas service yes/no

Cable TV yes/no   Telephone yes/no

COMMENTS _____

_____

_____

_____

LAND EVALUATION FORM

Property address _____

Legal description _____

_____

Lot dimensions _____

Zoning _____

Road frontage _____

Shape _____

View _____

Land area in square feet _____

Topography _____

Hazards _____

Landscaping _____

Deed restrictions _____

Drainage _____

Easements _____

Improvements _____

Water frontage _____

Wooded or open land _____

Accessibility _____

Land's best points _____

Land's worst points _____

COMMENTS _____

_____

_____

_____

_____

SALES COMPARISON SHEET			
Subject	Comp 1	Comp 2	Comp 3
Square Footage			
Lot Size			
Utilities			
Number of Rooms			
Number of Bathrooms			
Number of Bedrooms			
Kitchen			
Family Room			
Living Room			
Den			
Laundry Room			
Basement			
Attic			
Storage			
Construction			
Interior Condition			
Exterior Condition			
Parking			
Schools			
Location			
Price			
COMMENTS			

SQUARE FOOTAGE APPRAISAL EXAMPLE

CRITERIA
Living space—$60.00 per square foot
Buried basement living space—$20.00 per square foot
Site improvements—$10,000.00
Exterior steps—$1,000.00
Appliances—$1,000.00
Land value—$20,000.00
Subject house is a 1,040 sq. ft. ranch-style home
1,040 X $60.00 = $62,400.00
No basement = 0
Site improvements = $10,000.00
Exterior steps = $ 1,000.00
Appliances = $ 1,000.00
Land value = $20,000.00
Total estimated value is $94,400.00

LINEAR FOOTAGE APPRAISAL EXAMPLE

CRITERIA
FULL-FOUNDATION COST—LABOR & MATERIAL $33.00 per linear foot
2" x 6" FRAMING COST—LABOR & MATERIAL $45.00 per linear foot
ONE-STORY SIDING COST—LABOR & MATERIAL $27.00 per linear foot

EXAMPLE
You plan to build a full foundation for a home with the dimensions of 24' x 46'. You add all the linear footage of the foundation to arrive at a number of 140 linear feet. This figure is multiplied by $33 to give you an estimated foundation cost of $4,620. The same principle applies to framing, siding, and other similar costs.

QUANTITY SURVEY COST APPROACH EXAMPLE

Survey and Soils Test	$ 600.00
Site Work	10,000.00
Water and Sewer	4,500.00
Demolition	.00
Foundation	4,200.00
Framing	5,800.00
Windows and Exterior Doors	1,700.00
Roofing	875.00
Siding	3,800.00
Heating	4,700.00
Plumbing	4,250.00
Electrical	3,975.00
Insulation	1,630.00
Drywall	3,890.00
Paint	2,775.00
Interior Doors and Trim	1,876.00
Cabinets and Vanities	2,300.00
Floor Coverings	3,650.00
Accents and Accessories	475.00
Trash Removal and Cleanup	720.00
Landscaping	900.00
Loan Fees	1,200.00
Other	.00
TOTAL COST	63,816.00

ESTIMATE FORM

Survey and Soils Test	_____
Site Work	_____
Water and Sewer	_____
Demolition	_____
Foundation	_____
Framing	_____
Windows and Exterior Doors	_____
Roofing	_____
Siding	_____
Heating	_____
Plumbing	_____
Electrical	_____
Insulation	_____
Drywall	_____
Paint	_____
Interior Doors and Trim	_____
Cabinets and Vanities	_____
Floor Coverings	_____
Accents and Accessories	_____
Trash Removal and Cleanup	_____
Landscaping	_____
Loan Fees	_____
Other	_____
TOTAL COST	_____

CUTTING YOUR BEST DEAL ON REHAB PROPERTY

6

Successful real estate investors all have a common trait. They are consistently effective in winning negotiations. The negotiation victories vary in nature, but winning them is the investors' key to success. Developing bargaining skills is done through experience and study. You may be surprised to find you use these same skills frequently in your daily life. It might be asking your supervisor for a raise or convincing your spouse to concur with your dinner selection. Anytime you try to sway an individual to agree with you, you are using negotiating skills.

Honing your ability to persuade another person will serve you well in real estate transactions. Take a look at your habits and personality, what do you see? When you buy a car, do you pay the sticker price? Do you perform every request made of you, or do you rebut some demands? When you bought insurance, did you buy from the first company you spoke with, or did you shop for the best price? Using these questions as examples, explore your hidden talents. Perhaps your job requires the ability to dicker.

You may find you don't have the self-confidence to enter into mediation. Before buying your first rehab property, inspect your strength when it comes to haggling. You don't need to be overpowering or domineering to win negotiations. You simply need the ability to discuss a subject in a way that yields a beneficial outcome, preferably in your favor.

If you find yourself uncomfortable with your capability to bargain, start reading. There are numerous books on basic arbitration methods. Reading these books and absorbing the basic principles will give you a foundation to build your personal skills on. You must develop your own style for negotiating. Using a dry sales pitch will not produce satisfactory results. The person on the other side will quickly recognize your intentions and raise a shield to protect against your sales assault. Once the shield goes up, the task of winning becomes much more difficult. If the other party is expecting a hook, he won't take the bait.

Taking basic sales skills and adding your personal touch increases your effectiveness in winning the battle for control. You may not recognize your actions as sales skills, but much of our life is built around negotiating. Parents are experts at negotiating. They are constantly bargaining with their children to obtain the desired goal. Parents of teenagers learn from experience the art of gentle persuasion. Many jobs involve the use of manipulation skills. Getting what you want is usually a matter of successful negotiating. Whether you operate a cash register in a fast-food establishment or run a multi-million dollar corporation, you use these sales skills.

This chapter will shape your existing skills and teach new methods for getting the most from your investment dollar. After a long and diverse career in real estate, I have learned what works. I have been involved with offers and counter-offers from both sides of the table. The principles of making a deal are the same for the buyer and the seller. The difficulty is in the execution of the principles. Average sellers are not prepared for a well-planned assault of camouflaged bargaining chips. If you plan your approach and substantiate it, you will emerge the victor.

DON'T SHOW ALL YOUR CARDS

The element of surprise is an important component to winning any real estate deal. If a seller believes you are buying the property to make a profit, he may become difficult to deal with. Even if you are paying a price normally acceptable to the seller, he can become obstinate. The human instincts of greed and envy frequently take over when a seller discovers you are an investor. The seller assumes that if you are buying the property as an investor he isn't selling it for a high enough price. Often the seller begrudges the idea of you making money on his property. There are several simple ways to overcome this common problem.

If you are working through a broker, be careful what you say. Unless you pay an agent to be your representative, real estate brokers work for the seller. The broker may be mediating the deal for you, but she is compelled to disclose everything she knows about the deal to the seller. If you brag to the broker about being a well-to-do investor, this information will be given to the seller. Telling the broker your plans for the property can shut your door to opportunity. Giving your creative ideas to the broker raises two hazards. If your plans are viable, the broker may try to purchase the property herself. This may not seem ethical, but don't believe it can't happen. The second risk is having the seller become privy to your plans.

EXPOSING YOUR IDEAS CAN COST YOU THE DEAL

Exposing your valuable ideas to the broker or seller can cost you the deal. Maybe the seller hasn't considered any options beyond selling the property as is. If you plant the idea for using it as rental property, he may decide not to sell. The broker may be blinded by making a commission until you show your intentions for converting the property into a multi-family dwelling. This idea could mean much

more money to the broker than a quick commission. If this happens, your chances of obtaining the property are greatly reduced. The best advice is to keep your ears open and your mouth shut.

THE OWNER-OCCUPANT ADVANTAGE

Buying a single-family or small multi-family property permits you to present yourself as an owner-occupant. Giving the impression of buying the property for your residence removes the risk of jealousy. Neither the broker nor the seller will think twice about your interest, if they believe you plan to live in the property. This modest advice will defuse your first major complication, the greed factor. You want the seller to believe he is getting the best of the transaction. When he assumes you are buying a home based on desire and emotions, he will concentrate on meeting a pre-set price goal. If you don't use this approach, the seller's original bottom-line figure may become substantially larger.

Usually, rehabbers are looking for neglected properties in need of repair and renovation. You can concentrate on this point to whittle away at the sale price. This tool is most effective when the seller considers you an average home buyer. The assumed identity of a typical buyer will help you here. Don't let on about your plans to renovate the house for a profit. If you are handy, don't let them know it. Pointing out the defects and stressing the cost of professional repairs will give you leverage in lowering the price.

The homes you are seeking will not appeal to the buying public. Most buyers want a comfortable home to purchase and inhabit without the cost and inconvenience of repairs. This public preference will discourage a seller after months of rejection. The longer a property has been on the market, the better your chances are for a sweet deal. Playing on the home's deficiencies is a proven way to justify a price drop. Working this angle requires planning and a tactful approach.

DEALING WITH BIASED SELLERS

Unfortunately, sellers often believe their homes are worth considerably more than they are. If they have emotional ties to the dwelling, the sale price will be high. They are not looking at the home as a business venture. To the sellers, it is their home; to you, it is a real estate money machine. The conflict in these views will push negotiations apart if your statements are not presented properly.

You must be cautious with your comments so as not to insult the seller. Telling a seller her house is dilapidated and in need of major renovations can have the same effect as saying her daughter is ugly. The channels of communication and negotiation may quickly close. Be cautious not to appear insulting or derogatory. A few pages from now, we will discuss using inspections as a way of focusing on the property's shortcomings without insulting the owner. At this point you are initiating the mediation process. You must see the property and get acquainted with the owner. This is where you begin to formulate a plan of attack.

When you tour a property for the first time, pay attention to the seller's comments. Strolling through the house with all your attention riveted to the building's condition is a mistake. Too many buyers listen to the broker and concentrate on the property's physical condition. It is very important to pick up on signals the seller is sending out during your inspection. In a way, the seller will become your business partner for a limited period of time. It is crucial to know what makes this partner tick, what buttons to push to get positive responses. Brokers routinely ask the seller to be absent during the showing. They know the seller can weaken their ability to sell you the house.

REQUEST THAT THE SELLER BE PRESENT

Professional brokers are skilled salespeople. They are accomplished in the methods required to side-step your questions. Without the seller's presence, the broker can probe for information without giving you the answers you need. Brokers also tend only to address problems you raise, whereas sellers will often volunteer unsolicited information.

What will happen if you ask a broker what the heating bills have been for the past two winters? Occasionally, the broker will provide copies of the fuel bills, but more likely she will tell you she has to get the information from the seller. This buys time and gives the broker a reason to meet with you a day or two later. She will use this meeting as an opportunity to close on the sale. Many purchasers forget to follow up on their request for fuel bills. If you continue to insist on the heating cost history, the broker will probably try to get by with a general statement from the seller. She may say the seller has not kept records on the fuel costs, or the cost is average for this age home. These noncommittal answers are not what you want.

Look for the Seller's Reactions

If you look the seller in the eye and ask the same question, he will say something instinctively. He is not a trained sales professional and will let valuable information slip out. You can learn a lot from watching facial expressions when asking a deciding question. If he hesitates or looks uncomfortable, pursue your line of questioning. When he doesn't want to talk about a subject, you have more reason than ever to want a truthful answer. Brokers may try to break in and answer the question for the seller. If this happens, politely address the question to the seller again. If the broker still tries to answer it, get blunt. Tell the broker you assume the seller knows more about the property than the broker does, and ask the question again.

Don't Let Brokers Get in Your Way

If you feel the broker is spinning you around and blocking the answer to your question, ask to speak with the seller privately. Point out that this is the seller's home, and you want it to be your home. You have a fondness for the property in common. There is no reason the seller can't or shouldn't speak with you openly about the home. If your request is refused, leave the property. There is something they don't want you to know. When this type of problem arises early in the consideration of a property, it is best to move on to greener pastures. If you can arrange for the seller to be present at the showing, you have a better likelihood for making a deal later.

TAKING NOTES

A voice-activated micro-cassette tape recorder can make an enormous difference in your negotiating strategy. Carrying one of these cassettes through the showing will give you a record of the information obtained in the showing. Be certain to dictate notes about the property, so the seller and broker will not be disturbed by the tape recorder. You can then openly or inconspicuously record the broker and seller. A clear tape recording is definitely more accurate than your memory.

Making the seller available for questions can be a difficult proposition. The real estate broker will want the meeting avoided, and the seller may have an adverse reaction to being interrogated. If you meet resistance to having the seller present, and if the property is a real gem, forgo the requirement on the first showing. For investments with only moderate appeal, insist on the seller's attendance at the initial showing. When the broker denies your request, relinquish your interest in the property. This move will almost certainly guarantee you an audience with the seller.

GAINING CONTROL

When the time comes to consider an offer, insist on talking with the seller. Brokers will try to discourage you from meeting the seller. Tell the broker you will only feel comfortable submitting an offer when you know whom you are dealing with. Explain that you believe in dealing with people on a one-to-one basis, not as nameless strangers.

If you convince the broker and the seller you will not consider the building without meeting the seller, the appointment will come together quickly. The fear of the seller tainting the deal is overshadowed by the possible loss of a sale. When you get the face-to-face showing with the seller, you are gaining control. Throughout the negotiations, this control will be a factor. Forcing the seller to do the showing your way is a sure sign of your power. This power will be cultivated as the negotiation process proceeds and should give you the winning hand in this game.

BUILDING THE SELLER'S CONFIDENCE

Meeting with the seller allows you to establish a relationship. You can casually make statements such as, "Financing is not an issue," or "I just want to be

sure I will be comfortable with the house." These comments build the seller's confidence in your ability and desire to buy. The only time to lay back from these power-plays is when the property is a must-have deal. If it is unconditionally special, waive the early maneuvering of control, and wait for an opening later in the bargaining.

Once you gain control and have the seller's attention, it is time to exercise your newfound skills. While seeing the house for the first time, I told you to pay attention to the seller and listen rather than talk. This elementary advice is a cornerstone of strong negotiating skills. The best salespeople listen more than they talk. It is especially important to implement this technique in the beginning. It is easy to gather valuable bargaining information from the seller's initial comments, but you must be attentive. If you take accurate notes during your time with the seller, you can use the information to formulate your game plan. Without a plan, you leave yourself susceptible to sales tactics, false information, and weak negotiations.

ON-THE-SPOT DECISIONS

Never make an on-the-spot offer to purchase the property. You need to step away from the building and the sales pressure to evaluate your findings. Never allow yourself to look overly anxious about a property. Avoid affirmative statements such as, "When I make my offer," or "When we get to closing." Always use the word "if" as a sign of your tentative position. Gather the information you need to make a decision, and tell the broker you will get back to him. The broker may mention several other showings scheduled for the property, or that there is another party who may be submitting an offer later in the day. Regardless of what the broker says, repeat that you will get back to him, and leave it at that.

DEVELOPING YOUR STRATEGY

It is important to develop your strategy in a comfort zone, without coercion. When you are back in the office or at home, you can replay the tape and contemplate your next move. Having this detailed accounting of the showing is invaluable in your decision making. Review your notes or recording carefully—this is where your planning will start. Make your plans accurately, and you will get the real estate at the right price or determine the deal isn't worth doing. For the time being, don't let the threat of another buyer pressure your decision. Remember, another interested party may present an offer, but it is not necessarily a signed deal.

ESTABLISH YOUR BOTTOM LINE

You must establish your purchasing limits before you enter the bargaining arena. All too often, investors are manipulated or persuaded into offering more for a property than they intended. Remember our friend Bruce in Chapter 5? He was influenced by the presence of another party. This guy could have been the seller's husband, but Bruce let his desire for the property rule out this possibility. Anytime you let your emotions influence your opinion, you weaken your ability to negotiate for the best deal. It is easy to justify paying more than you had planned when you are consumed with excitement and blinded by imaginary profits.

Determine the Property's Value

What considerations go into your planning? The answer to this question depends on the type of property you are planning to buy. The considerations are also predicated on the reason for your purchase. Some of the components are consistent; they are applicable to every purchase. Market appraisal predetermines the value of a property. You learned the techniques to assess property value in Chapter 5; now is the time to use them. Remember the difference between genuine value and appealing price. First you establish your price limit, then you must relate each individual property's price to its value.

Properties have market value and they have emotional value. As a purchaser, you must avoid emotional bonds, but you also need to be able to identify a seller's personal attachment to a property. Some sellers love their homes; others can't wait to move. A primary question to answer is why the seller is selling. The presence of seller incentive, or lack thereof, determines which course of negotiation you take. Is there a pending divorce or foreclosure, or

significant tax liens? Is the seller being transferred to a new location by his company? How long has the seller owned the property? Is this a voluntary sale or a forced sale? The reason for the sale may be the single most important question to answer.

Question the Reason for the Sale

When the seller has to sell, you have the advantage. Inquire about the reason for the sale with the seller and the broker. Ask the broker first, before meeting with the seller. Then ask the seller why the property is being sold. If the two answers don't match, raise your first red flag—something is amiss.

When the seller is being forced to sell, you can play hardball in your purchase offer. As an owner of a rundown home that must be sold, the seller may be at your mercy. Never take an answer to your question for granted. Research your query further to determine if you are being told the truth. Sellers of real estate are not always the most reliable sources of information on the property.

Verify the Reason for the Sale

At some point during your inquiry, ask for the name of the seller's attorney. Call the attorney and inquire about details of the property, such as deed book and page information. At the same time ask if the property is in the seller's name only. When asked such an innocent question, many people will expound on the circumstances surrounding the sale. Verifying tax distress sales is easy through the assessor's office. You would be amazed how often a bogus divorce or spurious death is used to conceal the true reasons for a sale. Protect your money and credit with an extensive investigation.

The Advantage of a Motivated Seller

Finding truly motivated sellers will make your negotiations move much more smoothly. They must sell, but you don't have to buy. If you are a qualified buyer, the broker and seller will treat you like royalty. Determine the maximum price you are willing to pay for the property. To accomplish this, you will need to perform several tasks. These challenges include a before-and-after appraisal. This technique is described in detail in Chapter 5. Essentially, it requires a professional appraisal of the property in its present condition, and a report on its projected value when your plans are complete.

Using the Inspection to Your Advantage

Intensive inspections must be provided for in your purchase offer. A sample Inspection Addendum to the purchase contract is shown at the end of the chapter.

Your offer should be contingent upon inspection results meeting your satisfaction. A multitude of areas need to be inspected. Request a water test and septic inspection for any real estate without public utilities. The water should be tested for any impurities and radon. The septic system inspection will protect you from unexpected costly modifications or replacement. Enlist the services of a licensed professional inspector. Pest inspections expose insect and termite infestations. Checking the roof before buying can eliminate the need for a new roof when you get the first rain.

A professional structural inspection will turn up any serious defects in the body of the home. A visit by the code enforcement officer can save you a lot of money after the closing with multi-family properties. In-depth mechanical inspections alert you to outdated or inefficient plumbing, heating, air conditioning, and electrical systems. A little legwork at the Registry of Deeds will disclose liens and easements that affect the value of the property. Require an inspection of every item you can think of. The results from these inspections provide ammunition for your demands of a lower price.

If you are confident in your own abilities, you can do the inspections personally to save money. Saving money is good, but professional inspection reports add credibility to your reduced offer. If you have documented evidence from professionals regarding deteriorating conditions, you have more leverage in lowering the sale price. It also turns the inspector into the bad guy. Someone unrelated to the deal becomes the bearer of the bad news, and you do not risk insulting the seller with your personal opinions.

How should you coordinate the needed inspections? Inspections are typically done after the contingency contract is signed. You can request inspections prior to making an offer, and this is the best time to require them. Inspection results presented after an offer reduce your negotiating power. You

risk losing the cost of these inspections when they are done before having a signed contract, but they give you power.

Ideally, you should learn to perform preliminary inspections yourself. This eliminates the need for out-of-pocket expenses before striking a deal. You can use your assessment to disqualify a property and save yourself time and money. If the property presents problems that will allow you to dicker on the price, enlist professionals to corroborate your findings. Be careful when you bring serious deficiencies to the seller's attention. It is imperative to use the property's bad points to lower the price, but done callously, you will alienate the seller. Using a printed inspection form will make your accusations less personal and more effective. There is an example of an Inspection Report Form at the end of this chapter. Prepare a similar form for your own use and incorporate it into your arbitration arsenal.

FLASH YOUR CASH

Establishing a pre-approved credit line gives you another lever to use in lowering a sale price. The ability to produce a bank check for the full purchase price without applying for a loan is a powerful incentive. Few investors enjoy this capability, but if you have it, use it. After you acquire the property, you can arrange long-term financing to free up your credit line.

Having the ability to perform quickly on an agreement to purchase also strengthens your bargaining power. If you are able to settle on property in a very short period of time, a desperate seller will jump at your low offer. When people are facing foreclosure or divorce arbitration, time is of the essence. These sellers are anxious to complete their transaction in the shortest possible time. Estate sales can provide this same benefit. Impatient family members are often burdened by financial obligations while trying to put an end to an unpleasant duty. These people are likely choices for a reduced offer. Get to know the seller and his motivation for selling. This information can be the difference between a windfall and wasted time.

Another dependable negotiation tool is financing. Terms, conditions, interest rates, and creative financing are instrumental in cutting your best deal.

These facets are addressed in Chapter 7. In general, financing has a significant impact on the value of a structure. This is particularly true when buying income properties. There are a few secrets in structuring the financing of a deal. These secrets are not common and virtually go unnoticed by many purchasers. Creative methods can transform an otherwise losing proposition into an amiable deal.

CREATIVE SETTLEMENT METHODS

The first of these often overlooked tools is the delayed settlement. A delayed settlement can become a strong bargaining chip when the seller needs time to locate a new home. It is also helpful when a seller needs to receive the sale proceeds at a specific time. This could be the next tax year or the seller's fifty-fifth birthday. By delaying the closing of the sale, the seller may gain meaningful tax benefits.

As an investor, you can use this to your advantage. The average home buyer will want possession when his loan is approved and closed. This can usually be done in less than ninety days. For the seller with tax consequences, your ability to defer the closing for several months may be worth a sizable discount on the sale price. Another creative negotiating tool is the reverse mortgage. This is an alluring alternative when the present owners are elderly and in need of money.

Reverse Mortgages

Put yourself in the position of these elderly homeowners. They have lived in the house for forty-two years and reared two fine children under its roof. Their grandchildren have enjoyed the tire swing in the old oak tree out back, and the home is filled with loving memories. Now they are living on a fixed income and are being forced to part with their beloved home. This is a painful decision, but they have no alternative. You can do yourself and the elderly couple a huge kindness under these circumstances.

Because of their close emotional attachment to the home, their asking price may be steep. Even though they know they should sell, they will be reluctant to accept any purchase offer. It is too arduous for them to meet the demands of parting with a slice of their family history and moving into an apartment. This reluctance often makes negotiating a standard deal difficult. There is an option that allows both the seller and the purchaser to win. Your trump card is the *reverse annuity mortgage*.

With this mortgage, the couple is not forced to move, but you are assured of an outstanding profit potential. Assume their home is paid for and is worth $125,000. The asking price for the house is established at $132,500. Obviously, this is no bargain as it stands, but with the use of a reverse mortgage the deal can turn to gold. In the reverse mortgage, you offer to pay the couple to continue living in their home. How does this make sense? Well, this is how it works.

You negotiate with the couple for a sales price of $80,000. When they bought the house forty-two years ago, they probably paid less for it than you did for your new car. Their only reason for selling is to gain enough money to live. You offer to pay them a fixed monthly amount and allow them to live in the property for a determined period of time. Let's say you pay them $300 per month and allow them to live in the house for ten years or until one of them passes away, whichever comes first. The $300 payments are subtracted from the purchase price. When added to their supplemental income, the $300 is enough to allow the couple to live comfortably. The monthly income combined with the incentive of not having to move may justify your price reduction.

During the time that the couple lives in the property, they continue to maintain it. Historically, the property will appreciate in value each year. You have an iron-clad contract to purchase the home for $80,000, and every monthly installment applies to the purchase price. The contract contains provision for the settlement of the property in the event of their death. In ten years or less, you will own the home for only $80,000. Today's market value is $125,000. If you assume a conservative annual appreciation rate of 5% per year, the home's value in ten years will be over $200,000. Your profit before improvements will be $120,000. After making $300 per month payments for ten years, you will have reduced the acquisition cost at the time of closing to $44,000.

Your gain is the financial reward of a solid business deal. The couple's benefit is living a financially secure retirement in their own home. You both win, and when you take possession of the property, your improvements cause the profits to soar. If you are wondering where you will get the money to make the monthly installment, you did well to consider this point.

Most banks will loan up to 80% of the appraised value for an investment property. With a solid contract, the lender should be willing to loan against your contract. They have the comfort of knowing you will only owe $80,000 on a $125,000 house. If the bank loans 80% of the appraised value against your purchase contract, you will receive a mortgage for $100,000, based on today's value. If you have to make $300 monthly payments for ten years, your total cash outlay will amount to $36,000. All this time, the property value should be escalating and increasing the value of an 80% loan-to-value mortgage. The odds are good you can borrow the monthly installment mortgage from a liberal lender and make a no-money-down purchase with an astronomical rate of return.

Obtaining a loan from a major lending institution in this way may be difficult. As our economy has softened, banks have become more conservative. Before you make any commitments, be sure you can cover the monthly payment to maintain control of the property.

Life Estates

Life estates are similar to the previous example. In a life estate, the seller is guaranteed the privilege of remaining in the home until his death, rather than for a specified period of time. In either case, you can take ownership prior to the expiration of the life estate. If you need the tax advantages of the property, you can become the owner of record and allow the seller to continue inhabiting the dwelling. This type of creative purchasing broadens your negotiating options. These are long-term acquisition plans, but with proper planning and foresight you will still want profitable deals in ten years.

Retaining the Seller as a Tenant

When shopping for multi-family property, you might score with an offer to keep the seller as a tenant. The basic reasons for a seller to accept this offer are the same as the couple in the reverse mortgage example. In this case, offer the seller a lower price in exchange for a long tenancy at reduced rates. The overall savings on the purchase price will more than offset the reduced rental income. The seller will not have to move and will benefit from years of below-market rent.

If you take this tack, include a rental escalation clause in your agreement. Get the seller to agree to an annual rental increase of a set amount. This clause will help your future cash flow and will increase the value of the property when you sell. Seller/tenants make excellent resident managers. They know the building and the other tenants. The seller's continued presence can make your job as landlord much easier.

Creating a Partnership

Another tactic is to offer the seller a partnership interest in the equity of the property. Buy the building well below market rate and offer the seller a piece of the action. You assume all the improvement or management responsibilities, and the seller speculates for a handsome profit. This method can provide you with the opportunity for a no-cash acquisition. If the seller is retaining a percentage of ownership, he will have a vested interest. Use this vested interest in lieu of your down payment. Some sellers will respond favorably to deferred earnings and the chance for a higher financial gain down the road.

Buying at the Right Time of Year

Seasonal shopping provides the investor with additional buying leverage. Certain seasons are traditionally slow for real estate sales. For single-family homes, the best months to buy are January, August, November, and December. Average home shoppers are not as active during these times. August is known for its heat, as well as the preparation and expense of getting the kids back to school. November and December are associated with holidays and bad weather. January is a time for recovering from holiday spending and preparing for tax payments. These times are excellent for the foraging investor.

Being active when most of the market is dead will turn up outstanding buys. This seasonal strategy extends into multi-family properties. December and January are excellent times to find your best deal. Landlords are tired of frozen pipes and outrageous heating bills. They are looking ahead to the new year's property tax increase and summer seems years away. Your willingness to purchase their ball and chain will put you in the driver's seat. There is irony in this approach. You place the building under contract in January, and the seller is elated to be getting out from under the heating bills. In most transactions, the closing will not occur for forty-five or sixty days. By this time, the heating season is basically over, and you enjoy a long summer of good rents and no heating expenses.

COMBINING NEGOTIATION TECHNIQUES

Now that you have had an overview of cutting your best deal, let's review the prime points to ponder.

1. Evaluate your natural negotiating skills. On paper, list your strengths and weaknesses. Read books stressing sales and bargaining skills. Don't stop studying until you clearly understand the basic principles of negotiating. As you walk the trail to financial freedom, remember what you do in various situations and note the results. Scrutinize your successes and discover which tactics work. Learn from your failures, and always look for ways to improve your methods. This approach will enable you to develop a consistent winning strategy.

2. Utilize the element of surprise. Don't disclose your intentions for the property or your identity as an investor. The only time to break this rule is when you are building a solid relationship with a professional, ethical broker. This exception was discussed in Chapter 3.

3. Deal with the seller as a fellow homeowner. Disarm any potential complications by approaching the seller on common ground.

4. Know the risks involved when pointing out problems with a property. This is a requirement of successful rehab negotiations, but you must use the right procedures.

5. Meet directly with the seller whenever possible. This tactic allows you to assess spontaneous answers to your questions.

6. Don't allow a broker to bully you. You are the

buyer, and without a buyer the broker will not receive a commission. The broker may work for the seller, but she won't get a paycheck unless you buy the property.

7. Make an accurate record of the seller's statements. If you don't remember the outcome of your questions, they were a waste of your time. Remember, meeting with the seller lays the groundwork for your bargaining battle plan. The more comprehensive your notes, impressions, and information, the more likely you are to secure success.

8. Pay close attention to the seller's comments and actions during your tour of the property. This technique allows you to assess the seller and look beyond the smoke and mirror games of the broker. Acquainting yourself with the seller will allow you to ask the right questions and uncover potential areas to exploit.

9. Probe the seller for pertinent information. Investigative questioning will expose the truth in the sale. You will know you are dealing with facts, not fallacies. In this way, you will discover target areas to aim for when the heavy deliberations begin.

10. Never make on-the-spot offers. It is important to step away from the situation and reflect on what you have seen and how you wish to proceed.

11. Set limits on your offer. Knowing your top-dollar offer before engaging in the contest will keep you out of trouble. It is easy in the heat of arbitration to get into a bidding war. Avoid this disastrous problem by establishing your highest bid beforehand.

12. Substantiate the value of the property. This includes your before and after market values, as well as the worth of the property to the seller.

13. Determine the reason for the sale. Knowing the seller's motivation is imperative to planning an effective negotiating ploy and presenting the most appealing offer possible.

14. Find motivated sellers. Financial distress creates motivated sellers, and you are much more likely

to strike a winning deal with the lure of money on your side.

15. Plan for extensive inspections. Comprehensive inspections open the door for justified price drops. Professional inspections carry more weight and can push a seller into a corner. Using the Inspection Report Form at the end of the chapter will take the edge off your presentation of the defects. The seller will recognize the form as a standard inspection checklist. This will soften the blow of your concentrated attack on the building's shortcomings. When faced with damaging evidence, many sellers panic that they will not be able to sell the property to anyone. Showing the sellers why the home is worth less will convince them to take your offer while they can.

16. Use financing terms as a bargaining chip. Financing plays a major role in real estate investing. It is worth your while to understand all the options available to you. Read Chapter 7 for complete details on financing.

17. Establish a pre-approved credit line. Having available cash gives you an uncommon edge in asking for a price reduction. Explore the possibilities with your banker and establish the credit line as soon as you can.

18. Use a delayed settlement. This simple tactic can be a deciding factor in winning your war of words.

19. Don't forget other creative methods. Reverse mortgages, life estates, life tenancies, and seller ownership participation add a new dimension to your bartering tactics. Under the right circumstances, they are mighty tools.

20. Shop in the off-season. This is a proven technique when seeking a good buy. Perform market research to establish the slow times in your area and when they arrive, get busy. Learn to emphasize seasonal advantages to sellers. After all, how many other people are likely to buy the house right before Christmas, or put an income property under contract prior to the winter fuel season? Point out the advantages you can offer a seller during otherwise unappealing seasonal periods.

Winning in real estate negotiations becomes easier with experience. In the early going, experiment with combining several techniques. Don't forget to try the one approach not yet discussed. Sometimes the best way to get what you want is simply to ask for it. Don't be afraid to test the direct approach. I have seen this method produce unusually good deals in the past, and it could be what works best for you. Finding good deals is a numbers game. The more offers you make, the better your chances of having one accepted.

Be prepared, persistent, and methodical, and you will find yourself in control of your slice of the real estate market. For many investors, negotiating for a property is what makes real estate an adventure. Once you gain some experience, refining your horse-trading skills is an exercise you look forward to. When you have perfected your abilities, the financial rewards will exceed your expectations. This is when you realize your efforts were not unavailing. Owning and controlling real estate is not only a monetary success, it can give you self-confidence and a great deal of satisfaction.

Negotiating is one of the most important elements of being a successful investor. Take enough time to understand the fundamentals before trying to buy your first investment property. The methods employed are different than those used to acquire a personal residence. Emotions cannot be allowed to enter into a business decision. This is often the hardest thing for novice investors to learn. Don't be so anxious that you fail in your first project. The real estate and rehab business is timeless. You can afford to take the time to do it right, but you cannot afford to be wrong. Learn to master negotiating skills, and you will know how to control your life. These skills will serve you well in everything you do.

INSPECTION ADDENDUM

This addendum shall become an integral part of the purchase and sale agreement dated
_____, between _____,
Purchasers and _____, Sellers of the real property commonly
known as _____. Within _____ days of acceptance of the
above mentioned contract the Purchaser shall order an inspection of the property located at
_____, from a qualified representative of the Purchaser's choice
at the Purchaser's own expense. This inspection shall include the items indicated and checked below:

_____ Roof

_____ Heating system

_____ Cooling system

_____ Foundation

_____ Plumbing

_____ Electrical

_____ Appliances

_____ Chimney

_____ Septic

_____ Well

_____ Code violations

_____ Drainage systems

_____ Structural integrity

Other:_____

In the event the Purchasers are not satisfied with the inspection results, they may void this contract if written notice is given to the Sellers by _____. Seller agrees to allow reasonable access to the property for the purpose of this inspection. Additional terms and conditions are as follows:

_____

_____

_____

Purchaser	Date	Seller	Date
Purchaser	Date	Seller	Date

INSPECTION REPORT FORM

Item	Poor	Fair	Good	Excellent
Foyer				
Hall				
Kitchen				
Living Room				
Dining Room				
Master Bedroom				
Family Room				
Bedroom 2				
Bedroom 3				
Bedroom 4				
Bedroom 5				
Master Bathroom				
Bathroom 2				
Bathroom 3				
Half Bath				
Closet Space				
Floor Coverings				
Interior Paint				
Plumbing System				
Heating System				
Electrical System				
Basement				
Attic				
Insulation				
Garage				
Deck				
Siding				
Exterior Paint				
Lawn				
Roof				

COMMENTS

FINANCING 7

Financing is a critical aspect of buying real estate. When you entertain the thought of renovating real estate, you must address the financing issue. You have to master financing principles to enjoy a prosperous investing venture. Buying and renovating buildings can involve several types of financing. Acquisition financing is one of the first forms of funding available for getting into the business. Construction or improvement loans are often necessary to perform the required work on the properties. If you decide to keep your purchase, a permanent loan will be part of your long-range plans.

These three basic types of financing can take many forms. They can be obtained from banks, savings and loans, credit unions, and loan companies. Loans can be originated with a mortgage broker, or private investors may be solicited for real estate funding. The seller of the property may be willing to contribute to the financing of the building. Insurance companies are prominent lenders for real estate, and there are other less common sources available to the creative buyer.

The types and terms of loans available are as diverse as the properties they finance. Traditional lenders offer a multitude of loan plans. These programs include balloon mortgages, fixed-rate programs, adjustable-rate mortgages, and a wide spectrum of variations on each type. Independent and non-traditional lenders have even more to offer. They utilize every option in developing a creative financing plan to meet any investor's needs. Before you can confidently seek financing, you must understand the various types of loans available. Different properties require different kinds of loans to make

them economically attractive.

By the end of this chapter, you are going to know more about financing than many bankers. You will learn to choose the best loan for each style of real estate. I am going to show you some creative financing techniques that make conservative bankers break out in chills. When you learn to control financing, you will be able to control unlimited amounts of real estate. To appreciate the benefit of the techniques discussed, you must understand the loans available. Let's start with a brief look at the most common forms of real estate loans.

FIXED-RATE LOANS

One of the oldest and best known types of financing is the fixed-rate loan. These loans are based on an annual percentage rate of interest that does not change throughout the life of the loan. If you originate a thirty-year loan at 10% interest, the rate will remain at 10% until the loan is paid in full. For years, these were the standard of real estate loans. The advantage to these loans is the ability to know what your interest rate will be from day one to the last payment. The disadvantage is a higher monthly payment and frequently many more discount points.

Discount Points

Each discount point is equal to 1% of the loan amount. On a $100,000 loan, a single discount point is worth $1,000. In today's banking world, points are a common part of every real estate closing. The points can be as few as one or as many as six, or more. There is no set limit on the number of points a lender may charge. Points may be called prepaid interest, origination fees, service fees, or (incorrectly) closing costs. Regardless of what they are called, each point relates to 1% of the loan amount.

In the volatile world of money matters, lenders don't want to commit to long-term fixed interest rates. When they do, they load the loan with points up-front. This provides a quick yield on their money and reduces their exposure for future losses on fixed-rate loans, if the rates escalate. The disadvantage to you is more money out-of-pocket when you purchase a property. Before you pay excessive points for a fixed-rate loan, speculate on how long you plan to own the property being purchased.

If you are buying to create a retirement rental portfolio, fixed-rate loans may be your best choice. If you are planning to sell in seven years or less, there are better options available. Most investors work on a plan requiring the sale of their properties every three, five, or seven years. In these cases, fixed-rate loans with excessive points are a waste of money.

ADJUSTABLE-RATE LOANS

Adjustable-rate loans have taken a bad rap in the past. People are afraid of them; they think they will start with a 10% interest rate and be faced with a 16% rate in a year or two. In the earliest types of adjustable-rate loans, this was not an unreasonable fear. The early versions did not have annual caps or lifetime caps. The rate of the loan floated with the economy and could fluctuate greatly in a short period of time. Many of these early loans also used negative amortization to allow extremely low starting rates. You could borrow $75,000 today, make payments for two years, and wind up owing more than you originally borrowed. This type of loan spelled disaster for many home buyers.

Unscrupulous real estate brokers sold people houses with these loans, knowing their ability to make the payments in future years was highly unlikely. The increasing monthly payment and remaining balance forced many buyers to lose their homes. During these times, the public turned against adjustable-rate loans. The modern versions are much safer and offer many advantages.

Assume you are buying a home and financing $100,000. You can take a fixed-rate loan at 11% and pay four points, or you can choose an adjustable-rate loan. The adjustable-rate loan starts at 8% interest and requires one discount point. The adjustable loan has a 2% annual cap and a 5% lifetime cap. The adjustable-rate loan has a conversion option you can exercise after the second year. The cost to exercise this option is $500. You plan to keep your house for five years, so which is the better loan for your purposes?

With the fixed-rate loan, your discount points total $4,000. This amount must be paid at the time you settle on the purchase of the property. Your monthly payment will be about $952.32, for the life of the loan. You are paying about $674.54 in interest each month. In five years, your monthly interest cost will amount to about $40,472.53. Combining your monthly interest cost and your discount points, your hard financing costs total about $44,472.53. If you could have invested $3,000 of your discount points in a conservative investment, with an 8% yield, you would have earned about $1,469.53 in five years. When you add this lost interest income to the cost of your fixed-rate mortgage, your total cost is about $45,942.06. How does this compare to the adjustable-rate loan?

Your discount point on the adjustable-rate loan would be $1,000. Your monthly payment the first year would be about $733.77. Assuming the worst, we will say the interest rate increased the maximum amount for the second year. At 10% interest in the second year, your monthly payment would be about $877.57. If we assume the interest reaches the maximum increase in the third year, your rate is 12%. If you elect to freeze the interest rate at 12%, it will cost you $500. Let's say you decide to exercise your lock-in option and freeze the interest rate at 12%.

Your monthly payment for years three, four, and five will be about $1,028.61. At the end of five years, you have spent $1,000 in discount points and $500 in a conversion fee. Your monthly interest expense has amounted to about $39,699.37. Your total hard financing costs equal about $41,199.37. If you invested the $3,000 you didn't have to pay in points in a conservative investment, with an 8% annual yield, you would have earned about $1,469.53. When you deduct this earning from your hard financing costs, your total financing costs, compared equally to the fixed-rate loan, cost you about $39,729.84.

The adjustable-rate loan cost you approximately $6,212.22 less than the fixed-rate loan. The savings were made, even though the interest rose to its maximum amount each year. In these loans the rate does not always increase. The interest rate can go down by as much as 2% each year. While it is uncommon for the rate to drop, it is not unusual for the rate to rise moderately. If this had been the case, the savings would have been much larger.

This example should make the benefits of an adjustable-rate loan clear. If the loan has annual increase caps and allows for inexpensive conversion, it is a bargain in a five-year plan. There are many types of adjustable-rate loans available. Not all of them offer conversion features, but most of them limit interest rate increases on an annual basis and a lifetime basis.

A big advantage to the adjustable-rate loans is their low out-of-pocket expense. The money saved on discount points can be put to much better use if you don't plan to keep the property for an extended time. The money can be applied to improvements or used as a down payment for another property. Another advantage is the lower monthly payments in the first two years. This allows more latitude for repaying improvement loans. It also helps in generating a positive cash flow if the property is used for rental purposes. By the time the rate increases, rental charges have increased to offset the additional loan payment. Adjustable-rate loans deserve a serious look; they can be the best type of financing for almost any property. Fixed-rate and adjustable-rate loans are the two most common conventional loans. That is not to say they are the only type of loans out there. There are many more financing plans available.

GOVERNMENT LOANS

There are FHA, VA, and FmHA loans. These loans are associated with the government. FHA loans are insured by the Federal Housing Administration (FHA). The down payments required for these loans are usually less than for conventional loans. They are typically fixed-rate loans, with more lenient qualification guidelines than a conventional loan. With an FHA loan, you may finance a portion of the closing costs involved in purchasing a property. FHA loans may be obtained by owner-occupants or investors, for properties with up to four units. They are available through most large lending institutions.

The Veterans Administration (VA) designed the VA loan. It is a loan program developed to assist qualified military veterans. These loans do not require a down payment, and the seller must pay all discount points required in the closing of the loan. The Veterans Administration guarantees a portion of the loan. When the loan is repaid, the veteran's benefits are restored and may be used again. VA loans require the purchaser to be an owner-occupant.

Farmers Home Administration (FmHA) loans are targeted to limited income individuals. They are available for loans on property in small towns and rural areas, with populations below 20,000. FmHA loans are not generally suitable for rehab purposes.

BLENDS AND BLANKETS

Some of the lesser known types of loans include blanket mortgages and blend mortgages. A blanket mortgage is a single mortgage covering multiple properties for security. These mortgages can be used in creative financing to limit the amount of down payment required to purchase a property. Blend mortgages merge a new mortgage with an existing loan.

Normally, the interest rates from both loans are blended to arrive at the established interest rate for the new loan. Blend mortgages offer an option in creative financing. The buyer may be able to assume the seller's existing low interest loan. By using the blend method, the new loan, for the difference between the assumed loan and the amount needed to purchase the property, may be more economically appealing. This merging of the two loans can produce a lower overall interest rate than a completely new loan.

INSTALLMENT LOAN CONTRACTS

Installment loan contracts (also known as land contracts) are a form of owner financing. This type of financing is easy to obtain, but it is very risky. If the seller owns the property free and clear, he can offer this type of loan to a prospective purchaser. If the seller owes money to a lender for the property being sold, be careful. In older note agreements with lenders, sellers could offer installment loan contracts to new purchasers without violating their note agreement. In new loans, this practice is prohibited by a "Due on Sale Clause."

These clauses give the note holder the ability to demand payment in full if an installment loan contract is entered into by the seller. If this occurs, the seller is forced to pay the loan in full, upon demand, or forfeit the property to the note holder. If, as a purchaser, you have given a down payment or made payments, you could lose all your money and the property.

In the average installment contract, the seller retains legal ownership of the property until it is completely paid for. As a purchaser, your investment is at risk until you have a clear title to the property.

If creditors are legally allowed to attach the seller's property for non-payment of debts, they will be attaching what you thought was your property. Until you are the owner of record, the property may be seized by others, as an asset of the seller. Be very careful if you consider an installment sale contract.

OTHER TYPES OF MORTGAGES

Shared-Appreciation Mortgages

Shared-appreciation mortgages (SAMs) are another means for creative financing. These mortgages are described in detail when we explore creative financing methods. SAMs allow two or more people to participate in the ownership and appreciation of a property.

Wraparounds

Wraparound mortgages are yet another method of imaginative financing. They allow a property owner to refinance an existing loan to extract equity from a property. Blend mortgages are used to combine an existing loan with a new institutional loan to get the financing needed. We will discuss both of these further in the execution of creative financing techniques, later in the chapter.

Junior Mortgages

Junior mortgages are mortgages subordinate to existing mortgages. These are commonly known as second and third mortgages. They can play a big part in structuring an attractive financing package. I will delve into these loans later in the chapter. When we start examining the use of creative financing, all these borrowing tools will be discussed.

Construction Loans

Construction loans (also called term loans) are used for short-term financing. They can be used for acquisition and construction or improvements. Frequently, with rehab projects, you will obtain a construction loan to acquire the property. This loan will also advance money on a progression basis to pay for construction or improvements. Construction loans allow you to borrow the money for the initial purchase of your property. After acquiring the property, you must make the improvements or build the construction before drawing money from the construction loan.

There are predetermined guidelines regarding draw schedules. A representative for the lender performs a site inspection of the completed work. After the inspection, the lender advances a percentage of the loan for all completed and approved work. Most construction loans are established with a term of nine to twelve months. At the end of this term, the loan must be renegotiated and renewed, or paid in full. Most lenders expect the loan to be paid when the expiration date arrives. This can be done with one of the forms of permanent financing described above.

There are other types of loans available, but the ones listed are the loans frequently used for acquisition and permanent financing. Now that you are aware of the different styles of loans, let's learn how to use them. This section of the chapter deals with implementing creative financing. For aggressive investors, inventive financing is a crucial part of the investment plan. Here are some proven ways to get the most mileage from your money.

STRUCTURING FINANCING

Structuring the financing for a single-family home is different than it would be for a four-unit dwelling.

Both of these will be drastically different from financing a six- or ten-unit apartment building. The steps required to finance a rundown property lead you on a different trail than financing a normal property. The following section offers examples for each of these properties.

Single-Family Home

In our first example, we are going to finance a single-family home. The home is in livable condition but is a prime rehab property. It is the worst house in a good neighborhood. The work needed is largely cosmetic, and the seller is being forced to sell below market value due to a divorce settlement. The average home in this neighborhood is valued at $135,000. The appraised value of the subject property is presently $85,000; you are buying it for $75,000. The desperate seller is willing to pay your closing costs. In this situation, you are going to start with a term loan.

After preparing a comprehensive loan package, you go to see several loan officers. You apply for a term loan in the amount of $108,000. This is 80% of the anticipated value of the home, once your rehab improvements are made. When the loan is approved, some lenders will advance the full amount of money needed to acquire the property. You may have to give a small cash down payment, or allow the lender to place a mortgage on your home or another investment property, to secure the subject property. This will depend largely on the lender, your credit-worthiness, and your track record. Established investors should be able to acquire the subject property without a cash down payment.

Once you own the property, the renovations can be started. If you have done your cost projections accurately, the total rehab expenses will be less than $20,000. Each time a significant amount of work is complete, the lender will advance money from your term loan to reimburse the cost of the improvements. Acting as your own general contractor should save you 20% or more on the cost of the improvements. If you do any of the work yourself, your savings will grow rapidly.

When the work is done, have the house appraised by a certified real estate appraiser. When the bank appraised the proposed improvements and the existing structure, they estimated a completed value of $135,000. Your finished appraisal should reflect a finished value between $128,250 and $141,750. All certified appraisals should be within a 5% range each way. For this example, we will assume the property's finished appraisal determined a value of $130,000. What does this mean to you?

You paid $75,000 for the property and invested another $20,000 in improvements. Your total investment is $95,000. The house is appraised at $130,000. You have made a profit of $35,000 for your efforts. This is a handsome profit for a part-time venture, using nothing but your head and your credit line.

Now that the job is finished, you will need to obtain permanent financing or sell the property. If you decide to sell the property, you may be able to maintain the term loan until the property is sold. If you need to obtain long-term financing, there is good news. Most banks will allow non-owner-occupied property to be financed with a 20% down payment. If you plan to live in the property, you may only need a 5% down payment. At the most, as an owner-occupant, your down payment will not exceed 10%.

The property is valued at $130,000. With a 20% down payment, the amount you may finance is $104,000. You only have $95,000 invested in the property. If you borrow 80% of the home's value, you will walk away from the loan closing with money in your pocket. There will be closing costs and points to pay, but the financed amount will pay off your term loan and your closing costs and points. There should still be a few thousand dollars left over to put towards your next purchase.

Under these circumstances, you were able to buy the property with little to no money down. You worked with the lender's money during the renovations and made a healthy profit. Once you get the hang of it, rehabbing your way to riches is fun.

Financing a Four-Unit Deal

Our next venture is the purchase of a four-unit apartment building. The same basic principles used on the single-family home apply to this purchase. There are a few differences in strategy. With an income-producing property, you must make allowances for the rental income. How much will be lost in rents during the rehab process? Will rents be able to be raised after the improvements are made? Are the improvements going to reduce the operating expenses? These are all questions the lender will want answered.

You can avoid large rental income losses by renovating one apartment at a time. When the apartment is completed, put a tenant in it and renovate another unit. This process will allow you to rework the building with only one vacancy at any time. If you are going to occupy the property, you may not have any vacancies during the remodeling. Leave your apartment for last, and rotate the tenants into the apartments as they are completed. When you finish the last unit, you are already home. Exterior work will not adversely affect your tenants. If interior work can be done one room at a time, you may be able to maintain full occupancy during the remodeling.

If your improvements include new windows, insulation, or modern heating and cooling systems, your operating expenses should drop. When you show the lender how your improvements will reduce your annual operating expenses, they will be more inclined to approve the rehab loan. Even if you are planning to sell the property, these improvements will make the property more valuable to the new buyer.

To answer the question about raising rents, you will have to do some market research. Check with property management firms and read the papers to establish market rate rents in the area. Use similar properties in the comparison to establish your projected ceiling on rental income. Evaluate your improvements and draw a conclusion as to the probability of raising the rents. If you are upgrading the bathrooms and kitchens, you should be able to demand higher rent. Adding storage, replacing floor coverings, and modernizing the apartment offer justification for a rent increase. If the market research shows support for increased rent, the lender will be more likely to approve your loan request. The rest of the scenario is the same as for the single-family example. Four-unit buildings can be well worth the extra work; they are one of the most sought-after income properties.

Commercial Apartment Buildings

Our final example addresses the financing of commercial apartment buildings with six to twelve units. When you step into the financing ring for these buildings, the gloves come off. There are no set rules in this arena. Commercial loans are rarely sold on a secondary market, so this allows the lender to make their own rules. If you can convince the lender your plan is solid, you can get the loan. There is little concern over qualifying ratios or private mortgage insurance companies. It is simply a case of the best proposal wins.

Apartment buildings with over six units require a completely different approach than buildings with four units or fewer. Much of the decision on the loan is based on the qualities of the building. In smaller buildings, the loan approval decision is usually based on the purchaser's credit history and his or her ability to repay the loan. In these larger buildings, most of the decision is based on the building. Credit status is still important, but the building itself must possess good numbers.

The loan officer will want to see operating statements for the last year or two. He will want to verify the numbers from the owner's tax returns. What he is looking for is the "Net Before Debt Number." This is the amount of money available to make a loan payment with; it is the rental income less expenses. The expenses could include real estate taxes, water and sewer service, fuel and utility expenses, maintenance, and management. Most lenders deduct 10% from the gross income for the management of the property. Depending upon historical data, they will deduct another 5% for vacancies. Once all known expenses are deducted from the gross income, you are left with the "Net Operating Income" or "Net Before Debt Number."

Appraisers use rental income figures with a gross rent multiplier to determine the value of the property. The higher your income is, the more the building is worth. Income is the primary basis for establishing value on these commercial-grade properties. This is of the utmost importance to you as an investor and a rehabber.

Unlike smaller buildings, which use market comparison approach appraisals, you will be dealing with income approach appraisals. All your rehab attention should be aimed at areas to raise rents. Using a market-rent study is imperative in deciding the viability of your rehab project. You have to do substantial research before applying for a loan. When you sit down with the loan officer, it is best to have all your facts and figures. This builds confidence and proves professionalism on your part.

In this final section, we will explore some unique and creative financing tactics. The example with the single-family home showed some aspects of creative financing. In that example, you were able to buy the property without using your own money, and you made an attractive profit. This section will expose other methods for structuring "buyer-friendly" financing.

BUYER-FRIENDLY FINANCING

When you are trying to buy a property, who has the most interest in your ability to purchase the real estate? The seller has the highest motivation in seeing you obtain financing. With this in mind, use the seller's need to sell as leverage. There are many ways a seller can participate in your financing. Some types of loans restrict certain forms of seller financing. This is a minor inconvenience, so use your head. There are plenty of ways to prosper from an aggressive seller.

The most common type of seller participation is in the form of second mortgages. The seller agrees to hold a note for part of the sale price. Under the right conditions, these second mortgages can make it possible for you to purchase the property without a down payment. If the lender is willing to lend 80% of the appraised value and the seller holds a 20% second mortgage, you may not need a down payment. This is a popular and effective way to buy real estate with limited cash.

The seller may be willing to owner-finance the entire purchase price to you. If there are no "Due on Sale Clauses" and the seller conveys title to you, this is an excellent way to obtain property. Beware of installment sales contracts and "Due on Sale Clauses." Have your attorney advise you on any real estate purchase agreement. Ask the seller to pay your closing costs and points; this can save you thousands of dollars. Refer to the advice given in Chapter 6. The information there covers life estates, reverse mortgages, options, leasehold estates, and other tools you can use in seller financing.

Partners

Consider creating a partnership. If you find a super deal but need money, turn to investors and offer them a partnership interest in your find. Try to secure an option on the property before making other investors aware of its existence. Without contractual control of the property, your investor buddies may buy it out from under you. You can turn a profit from the beginning with this type of deal.

Let's say you have the building under option for a sale price of $150,000. Its rehabbed value will be around $275,000. You find three investors and offer them a 25% interest in the property. As limited partners, their ante is $50,000 to get a piece of the action. Their investment covers the total acquisition cost. This leaves you as a 25% partner, with no money invested. By finding the property and putting together the deal, you have one-fourth of the deal, with no out-of-pocket cash. When the property is sold, you will get 25% of all the profits. How can it get any better?

If you decide to use this technique, you might want to make some preliminary preparations. Your partners may resent putting up all the money for the purchase of your found property. Now, finding the property and structuring the deal are certainly worth something. After all, the partners would not have a deal if you had not handed it to them. No matter how justified your actions are, they will resent being the only money players.

There is an easy way to protect yourself from this animosity. Establish a corporation and engage a close friend or relative as a vice president. His or her last name should not be the same as yours. When you find the right property, put it under contract in the corporate name and include a clause allowing the contract to be assigned to another buyer. The clause might read, "Realty Wealth Builder, Inc., and/or their assigns." This clause allows the corporation to have contractual control of the property and to sell their contract to another party. Have the corporate vice president sign the purchase offer.

Your corporation puts the property under contract for a sale price of $150,000. You then enter into a contract with your corporation to purchase the property for $200,000. You sign the contract personally as the purchaser, with an assigns clause, and your corporate vice president signs as the seller. When you structure the deal with your partners, they will feel better about putting up their fifty grand.

This procedure reduces your risk of irate limited partners. It is not illegal or unethical. You are using your knowledge and legwork for your interest in the partnership. With the described approach, your partners don't feel abused, and everyone gets what he wants. The partners would get the same return without the corporation, but they wouldn't be happy thinking you got the best end of the deal.

Reducing Out-of-Pocket Expenses

Using blanket mortgages can reduce your out-of-pocket expenses. If you have equity in other properties, you can use that equity as down payment for new properties. The lender will attach a first or second mortgage on your other properties, for security. Then they will loan the money, allowing the purchase of the new property.

Wraparound and blend mortgages can also make the most of your equity in other properties. With the wraparound, you can refinance an existing property to pay for a new property. Wraparounds can be used on a new property as well. If there is enough spread between the purchase price and the value, you can employ a wraparound mortgage to bridge the gap between owner financing or an assumable loan. Blend mortgages are used in similar ways. You combine the existing loan or owner financing with an institutional loan to meet the financing need. These are favorable when the existing or owner-financed portion is financed at a low interest rate.

Balloons

Balloon payments are risky, but they can keep your monthly payment low. If you use a balloon payment, set a term at least one year later than you anticipate owning the property. If you plan to keep a property for five years, make the balloon payment due in seven years, or upon the sale of the property. Balloon payments require a lump sum payment at a predetermined date. These are excellent tools to use when they are used prudently.

Interest-only loans and loans with accruing but unpaid interest are also attractive for cash flow purposes. These are similar to balloon payments and must be handled with great respect. Don't put yourself in a position to lose your property if you cannot

perform on a large payment. Make sure the property will appreciate enough to refinance to pay the payment on the balloon note, or that it can be sold before the payment is due to pay off the balloon payment.

Alternate Loan Sources

Mortgage brokers, private investors, and loan companies are all capable of making loans with creative terms and conditions. These sources can be dealt with on a business level. If you have a satisfactory business plan, they can arrange your financing. Be careful with these lenders—they may not be as dependable as the local bank.

If you are having trouble arranging a loan for improvements, consider this option. Ask your contractors to participate in the rehab venture. Request that they provide their labor and materials for a percentage of the profit when the property is sold. Some contractors will be happy to oblige. They can use the rehab work to keep their crews busy during slow times or broken schedules. This tactic conserves your cash and still gives you the opportunity to enter the rehab business.

Found Money

In urban areas, you may be able to obtain special financing for your renovations. Many cities offer low interest loans and grants for housing improvements. These interest rates can be as low as 4%, and the grants may never need to be repaid. This type of rehab financing maximizes your profit. Contact your local housing authority to determine what programs are available in your area.

Sweat Equity

If you are handy and like to be physically involved in your projects, the sweat equity factor is fantastic. Any work you do yourself propels your profit into a higher tax bracket. Acting as the general contractor should save you about 20% on your improvement costs. Doing the work yourself creates staggering profit figures, unless your time is more valuable in other venues. Maybe it will be more profitable for you to subcontract the work and locate additional properties for renovation. Before becoming a hands-on remodeler, evaluate where your time is best spent.

Sell the Lender

Financing can make or break your real estate deal. If you prepare a solid business plan, lenders will be impressed and willing to work with you. But before you ask a lender to gamble on your proposal, remove any opportunity for doubt. Spend enough time researching market conditions and real estate values to provide the lenders with a request that will prove irresistible. If you apply yourself, you can find financing for almost any project. Once you develop a successful track record, the lenders will come to you. If you convince the lender your project is profitable, they will be more than anxious to grant your loan.

NETWORKING WITH BROKERS AND INVESTORS 8

The more active you become in the rehab business, the more help you will need. Your time is a precious commodity and must be used efficiently. As a white-collar rehabber, your time is best spent finding properties and coordinating the rehab process. When you attempt to budget your time, you are faced with decisions.

Determining how to spend your time can be extremely difficult. All aspects of your venture are important. What should you concentrate on and what can you delegate to others? Consider this partial list of responsibilities:

❏ structuring financing

❏ locating properties

❏ supervising rehab work

❏ creating feasibility studies

❏ selling

❏ selecting contractors

❏ acquiring property

❏ accounting

❏ preparing cost projections

❏ marketing

❏ buying material

❏ selecting products

All these tasks are required of the active rehabber. Each job has its own importance. When you attempt to prioritize them, you may become dismayed. In many ways, they are equally important. If you neglect any one of these chores, you will not maximize your rehab profits. Obviously, an individual cannot perform all these functions with the utmost competence. Because of this, you should contemplate enlisting help in your enterprise.

If you plan to make a lot of money with your rehab business, you will not be satisfied with the results possible from only your personal efforts. To become a high-roller, you need to build a network of competent assistants. These do not have to be payroll employees. In fact, you would do better without a salaried staff. Independent contractors are the most effective choice for most white-collar rehabbers.

EMPLOYEES

When you expand your operation, payroll employees can put a big dent in your profits. If you are paying the employee $8.00 per hour, the employee may be costing you $12.00 to $15.00 per hour. This extra hourly cost is due to many factors. They include:

❏ payroll taxes

❏ insurance benefits

❏ paid sick leave

❏ unemployment tax

❏ social security

❏ paid vacations

❏ worker's comp insurance

❏ unproductive time

These examples are only the most common additional costs incurred with employees. Depending on your specific circumstances, there could be many other hidden charges associated with employees. Independent contractors charge a higher hourly fee but may be less expensive.

INDEPENDENT CONTRACTORS

If the independent contractors are properly insured and in compliance with local regulations, they may be your best bet. Even when the independents appear to cost more, they may cost less. You pay only for services received. You are not faced with paying employees for the entire day when they only produce five hours' work. Until you refine your business and gain experience, independent contractors are an excellent choice.

If you agree to pay an independent contractor a flat fee, you know what your cost will be. If the cost is a little higher than the anticipated cost of an employee, consider this. The fee is set and will not exceed the agreed-upon amount. You know and can budget your cost. With an employee, you can only speculate on your cost to complete the same job. Do you want to pay a carpenter to sit around drinking coffee and telling stories to his buddies? When the carpenter is contracted for an established fee, he socializes at *his* expense, not yours.

Hopefully, you understand the value of dealing with known costs. As an investor, it is critical for you to have the ability to project accurate expenses. Without this ability, you will not last long in the competitive real estate business. Property appraisals only support so much; you cannot always add on to the price to make up for your underestimated projections.

BROKERS AND INVESTORS

Real estate brokers and investors can play a vital role in your success as a rehabber. Experienced rehabbers have the ability to do everything necessary in the rehab business. Having the knowledge does not mean they have the time. Typically, each investor, or rehabber, has his own strong suit. If you are a carpenter, you may not want to subcontract the field work to another carpenter. If you are a tradesman, you might consider contracting brokers and financial experts.

In either case, you are not likely to be the best person for every aspect of the rehab process. Recognizing and accepting this fact is the first step to reaching the big league. Trying to do everything yourself will undoubtedly hold you back. What gets done may be done correctly, but how much can you do? This chapter is dedicated to showing you how to make the most of your personal talents and abilities.

MAKING THE MOST OF YOUR ABILITIES

Is It Feasible?

One of the first steps of the rehab business is performing feasibility studies. These studies tell you if your ideas are viable. Can you subcontract this phase of the business to an independent? You could, but most investors want to produce their own information for the feasibility of a project. You could hire an outside agency to provide information, but the cost is prohibitive, and you are never sure of the accuracy of the report.

Smart investors personally determine their risk factors. The only exception would be for major developments. If you are planning a shopping center deal or similar project, you may very well need the services of professionals. For average rehab deals, you can spearhead this part of the venture.

Finding It

Locating suitable properties can be done by independent brokers. Your time is better spent with more exacting duties. Unless you are well-versed in the real estate market, good brokers are well worth the effort required to cultivate them. You will learn more about assessing and choosing brokers later in the chapter.

Financing It

Financing plays a fundamental role in the rehab

business. Without good financing, you will be limited in your ability to make the most of your existing financial resources. Experienced brokers can help with financing. They should be tied into many aggressive lenders. Other investors are another source of financing options. Astute investors have many money sources. In addition, they can help you maximize your financial leverage. Investor participation is also discussed later in the chapter.

Putting It Together

Property acquisition can be expedited and enhanced by a qualified broker. Real estate brokers who specialize in investment properties know the ropes. They have the experience and contacts to make your deal come together quickly and easily. Their commission is a small price to pay for the advantages you receive, and in most cases, they are paid by the seller.

Projections

Before committing to a building, you will need cost and sale projections. Cost projections can be gathered from general contractors. You should maintain an active interest in this part of the business. Never blindly accept the numbers provided by general contractors. You must shop prices carefully. Identical services can have dramatic variances in price.

Sale projections should come from information provided by active brokers and your feasibility study. When you are buying with the intent to sell soon, knowing the market is critical. Brokers can provide indispensable information in this area. It is a mistake to accept a broker's recommendation openly. He has many reasons for encouraging you to proceed with a project. He may be paid a commission on the sale to you and a commission on the sale after the rehab is complete. This is acceptable, if the project will sell promptly and profitably.

Keep in mind that the broker gets paid either way. If you buy a loser, he makes money selling it to you. When your completed project does not sell in a timely fashion, you are on the hook. The broker made money when you bought it; if he sells it again, great, if he doesn't, you lose.

Marketing Plans

Developing a marketing plan is instrumental to your overall success. Again, good brokers can be an important asset in this aspect of the business. They are trained professionals in the art of marketing. Should you leave this phase entirely in a broker's hands? No, never become so distant from your business that you trust others to make your money for you. Real estate and rehab projects are not effortless. To realize satisfactory results, you must stay involved. This is no business for an absentee owner.

Product Selections

Product selection can have an enormous impact on your profits. Contractors can help with product selection, but don't accept everything you are told. Something as simple as the type of plumbing fixtures used can make a noticeable difference in your income. You must take an active interest in product selection.

If you do your own cost projections, you must know what products will be used in the renovation process. Until the cost of materials is determined, you cannot accurately project your improvement expenses. It is a good idea to work with local contractors when making product selections and budgets. The people working in the trades know what products are popular in the area.

Electric heat may be cheap to install, but will anyone be willing to buy the property with electric heat? Maybe you like a tiled shower, but is the public willing to pay extra for your preference? These questions can be answered by interviewing contractors and talking with salespeople at building supply centers. In product selection, consult others and depend on yourself.

Material acquisitions may be handled by your independent contractors. Providing a detailed specifications sheet ensures your satisfaction with the materials provided. If you engage a general contractor, you can leave material acquisition to the contractor. There is more on this subject in Chapter 11.

Supervisory Requirements

Supervising the rehab work requires some of your time. If you act as your own general contractor, the time spent on this phase is substantial. When a general contractor is retained, your supervisory time is greatly reduced. Chapter 10 explains the pros and cons of this debate.

Choosing tradesmen to perform the renovation work is a big responsibility. This process can erode your time quickly. You are required to put personal effort into this part of the rehab procedure. Chapters 10 and 11 instruct you on your options in this perspective.

Sales

When it comes to sales, who should be in charge? You should always be in control, but you may not be the best person to procure sales. Selling is an art and can be handled in countless ways. Should you attempt to sell your own property? This is a complex question; it will be addressed a little later in the chapter.

Keeping the Books

Are you comfortable with accounting for your business? Accounting for all aspects of your business can be a monumental task. Contracting the services of a professional may save you thousands of dollars. Certified public accountants are adept at taking advantage of every angle to conserve your tax dollar. During the rehab process, you must maintain impeccable records. The tax consequences of this business have tremendous effects on your profits. Chapter 15 exposes and examines tax considerations.

Delegating Duties

When reflecting on all these choices, what responsibilities are the easiest to contract to an independent? In addition to ease, which tasks are best handled by an independent? The answers to these questions depend on your personal qualifications. For the average investor, a competent real estate broker is the first independent contractor to consider.

Real estate brokers are professionals and have expert knowledge in many fields affecting your rehab venture. They work with financing, marketing, sales, market studies, and property procurement. Of the twelve items listed for independent contractor consideration, brokers can provide assistance with five of them. One proficient broker can eliminate nearly half of your responsibilities.

REAL ESTATE BROKERS. If you are able to develop a strong relationship with a qualified broker, you are on your way to high profits. The right broker can do much of your job for you. There are two problems with this plan. The first is finding the right broker. The second is finding a broker with the skills to perform all five of the job descriptions effectively.

Real estate brokers are only human. They cannot be expected to be the best in every aspect of real estate. Brokers usually have certain areas of specialization. A broker may be dynamite at selling your completed properties and a disappointment in locating potential projects. The broker with strong financing skills may fall short in his ability to project market conditions and demands. It is rare to find an individual fully versed in all facets of your business needs.

BROKER NETWORKS. The solution to this problem is networking. Building a stable of real estate professionals takes time, but the results are worth the work. Many brokers are accomplished in more than one phase of their business. A selling broker should be well educated in financing. Brokers with a gift for finding potential properties are in touch with the market. Putting together a team of brokers can produce outstanding results.

Finding brokers worthy of your trust is not easy. It requires trial and error. The best brokers are always busy and may be difficult to contact. When you walk into a real estate office, it is typically an inexperienced sales agent who greets you. Your needs require an experienced, streetwise broker. Inexperienced agents can do little to propel your business forward. Occasionally, they may be suitable for the chore of finding potential properties.

TAKE A LOOK AT THE ROOKIES. These new salespeople are anxious to work with you. They don't have an established clientele and will welcome your business. Their inexperience may work to your advantage. If they are hungry, they may scour the market to find properties for you. This makes the rookies worth a look.

WHO'S UNDER THE MICROSCOPE? Full-fledged, investor-oriented brokers will want to qualify you as much as you want to qualify them. These brokers have an established source of buyers and sellers. Before they spend time with you, they will want to verify your credentials. Successful brokers can pick and choose their clients and customers. Some of them may have an attitude problem. When brokers consistently structure big deals, they can begin to envision their position as superior. This trait is not desirable; avoid these brokers. Expect to be heavily questioned by good brokers. The best brokers require you to jump through hoops before devoting their time to you.

Direct your broker selection based on the job required and the facts available on the brokers. Let's look at each element the real estate broker can contribute to, and what type of agents may be acceptable. If you are just starting out, your first need is to evaluate market conditions. This research will help you determine if your proposed rehab plans are viable.

BROKER SELECTION PROCEDURES

If you know what questions to ask, an inexperienced broker can fill this need. You may refer to the Preliminary Market Research Form at the end of the chapter. This form provides the questions you need answers to. Circulating copies of the form among brokers is an excellent way to obtain information.

Divide the forms among several brokers in different agencies. Offering several salespeople the chance to work with you will expedite your broker evaluations. By receiving multiple answers to your questionnaire, you will be able to draw more accurate conclusions on the market status. New agents will jump at the chance to impress you with their market knowledge. This is an advantage to your planning and purchasing strategy.

Deciding which brokers to solicit is easy. Read the advertisements in your local paper. When you find the same broker advertising several properties, give her a call. Brokers with the most exclusive listings should know the most about present market conditions. When you call, ask her to send you information on the properties she has for sale. A seasoned broker will probe you for information before sending the requested information.

She will tactfully inquire about your buying power and desires. When this happens, note the broker's name for consideration as your selling broker. If the broker seems excited and agrees to send information without grilling you, she is not the broker you want selling your properties. Log all the

names and phone numbers of the agents you contact. This log will prove helpful throughout your broker selection process.

There is a Broker Selection Log at the end of the chapter. It will help you keep track of all your broker contacts and results for future reference. When your information begins arriving, note who sent what and how extensive their package is. If you receive detailed information on the type of properties you inquired about, you are on the trail of a good selling broker.

Once you have established the market conditions, you can proceed to the procurement stage. Inexperienced agents can be suitable for property procurement. If they are willing to work, they can put some good deals in front of you. Established brokers may be reluctant to show you every property meeting your criteria. Some successful brokers will only send information on their exclusive listings. This is what you want from your selling broker, but you should not accept this tactic from a procurement broker.

Multiple Listing Service

When you are looking to buy, you should have information on as many properties as possible. Most brokers belong to a multiple listing service (MLS). These services allow all selling brokers access to other broker members' listings. The settled brokers shy away from sending information from the multiple listing book. When a broker sells another broker's listing, the commission must be split. Established brokers attempt to sell only their own listings. They generally have several and want to maximize their income by selling only their own listings.

Financing Assistance

After finding the property you want, financing becomes an issue. An experienced broker can be of great assistance in arranging suitable financing. Busy brokers know where to go for all types of financing. Investment brokers have generous skills in creative financing. Inexperienced brokers will only know how financing is supposed to work. Their learning has come from books and training sessions. The mature broker has firsthand knowledge of how to make financing work. She will not accept set ratios and policies. Financing is an area in which established brokers are invaluable. Their contacts with lenders can save you weeks, or even months, in finding the best financing. Brokers with a high percentage of sales are the best choice when it comes to structuring a loan. They could not close many sales if they did not know how to work with lenders.

Surveying the Market

When you have purchased your property, you should conduct a marketing survey. This will involve talking with brokers on what features are desired by their buyers. This information should be gained from brokers with a high ratio of closed sales. The information is your map to the improvements to be made on your property. Inexperienced brokers are of little help with this research. They will give opinions, but you need solid facts. Only consult with seasoned brokers on the improvements to make.

Selling Brokers

As you near completion of your rehab project, selling the building is high on your priority list. Experienced selling brokers are the best suited for this assignment. Inexperienced brokers are going to cost you time and may cost you a sale. Experienced listing brokers may not possess the skills needed to sell a property. It is not unusual for listing brokers to live off the sales of other brokers. They list the property, advertise it, and wait for another broker to sell it. This is definitely not what you want in your selling broker. You need an aggressive, proven selling broker.

Selling brokers are easy to choose. Request evidence of their sales records for the past year. Set parameters on the types of sales closed. If you are selling single-family homes, look only at this type of sales activity. If income property is your forte, be sure it is also the broker's strong suit. Ask to see comparable sales books or copies of their agency's closing records. Either of these will identify the selling broker and the type of property sold.

Before you choose a broker, put them through a few tests. These tests will eliminate many of the unproductive salespeople and expose the best of the bunch. The first element to test for is the ability to find suitable properties for you to purchase. In addition to the example given earlier, use the following techniques to perfect your broker selection.

Procurement Brokers

Procurement brokers may be new or experienced. Choosing a broker for this purpose does not require much effort. You can simply contact several brokers and advise them of the type of real estate you are seeking. By giving the brokers a detailed summary of what to look for, you can test several at the same time. There is no risk at this level of broker selection.

You should continue your search for prime properties while waiting for the brokers to produce. It will not take long to determine which brokers are best for this job. The ones bringing you satisfactory properties are the winners. You have nothing to lose by enlisting the services of multiple brokers for this task. You should maintain a list of all the brokers solicited. Each time you communicate with a new broker, enter his or her name in the Procurement Broker Selection Log provided at the end of the chapter.

As the brokers begin to show results, log the information. After inspecting the buildings they find, enter comments on each property into the log. The more detailed your notes are, the easier it will be for you to refine your army of brokers. This test is simple; the brokers turning up viable properties are the ones with whom you want to be associated.

SELLING IT YOURSELF

Should you attempt to sell your own properties? This is a question with many answers. If you are good with people and don't mind long hours, you may be able to sell your own property. Brokers are supposed to be professionals in the sale of real estate. Many of them will not exert the effort you will to sell the building. You have the most at stake and the strongest motivation to close a sale.

Listing your property with a broker is not assuring a sale. Never list your property with a broker until you are convinced the broker is a successful salesperson. There are definite drawbacks to trying to sell your own property. Some of them include the following:

❑ advertising expense

❑ working nights and weekends

❏ legal complications

❏ time management

❏ dealing with the public

❏ trying to be objective

❏ lack of industry contacts

❏ inexperience

Advertising

Advertising is expensive, and some properties require extensive advertising to sell. Brokers have a continual roll-over of buyers to work with. They frequently take a buyer calling on one ad and sell the buyer a different property. As a for-sale-by-owner (FSBO) seller, you don't have this advantage. Every time you make a mistake and blow out a prospect, you have lost advertising money. Every respondent to the ad should be thoroughly worked to sell the property.

Nights and Weekends

Many buyers are only able to view properties after work. This means many night and weekend appointments to show the property. If you have a full-time job, are overseeing the rehab work, and are trying to show the property, your time will be severely crunched. Do you have time to do the job needed to procure the sale of the property?

Legal Considerations

Licensed brokers are aware of current laws and regulations involving the sale of real estate. These restrictions are plentiful and strict. As an investor, you may not be aware of what is required of you when selling a property. A minor slip in your selling activity can result in a serious lawsuit. Even using an attorney will not protect you completely. The lawyer will not be there when you are showing the property. If you don't make the proper disclosures or you say the wrong thing, you could be in for a major lawsuit.

Time is Money

Time management is absolutely essential to your rehab deal. Selling your own real estate requires many hours of your attention. As an investor,

there is probably some other, better use of your time. There will be broken appointments, unqualified buyers, and disinterested buyers to destroy your time efficiency. Brokers are paid only when the property is sold and closed. This is a big consideration when you are thinking of acting as your own broker. Determine what your time is worth and take that into consideration when making the brokerage decision.

People Skills

Many people do not have the people skills necessary to be sales people. If you have a quick temper, you have no business in the sales game. Do ignorant people irritate you? If they do, avoid selling your own realty. Some buyers have no concept of what real estate sales are all about. Unless you can carry your weight and the weight of uneducated buyers throughout the sales process, find a good broker.

Can you be objective when a prospective purchaser complains about your workmanship? Will you lose it if a buyer says you were crazy to buy the property? How will you react when a buyer says your price is outrageous? Maintaining a cool disposition is only one of the requirements of a good salesperson. For a broker, it is easy to field these types of comments. Brokers are not personally offended and can continue selling the prospect. Some people do not have the self-control to contain themselves when insulted. If you cannot be objective, you will not be very successful in the sales business.

Contacts

Brokers offer another advantage. They have contacts throughout the real estate industry. When they need a strong appraisal, they know who to call. If a portfolio loan is required to make the deal, they know what lender to contact. When time is of the essence, they can pull a few strings to expedite the loan processing. These professional connections can save a deal from destruction. As a rehabber, you may not have developed these contacts. Don't underestimate their importance when making your decision on who should sell your property.

Experience

Perhaps the largest single factor to consider is experience. Seasoned brokers have sold hundreds of properties. How many have you sold? Experience is not something you can gain quickly. It takes time and sales activity to develop and refine sales skills. Unless you have a property so desirable it will sell itself, engaging a broker can be a very wise decision. You should have a good idea of whether you can sell your own property. If time is not critical, give it a try. If you don't like the job, or are not good at it, contact an experienced selling broker.

INVESTORS

It may seem strange to seek assistance from other investors, but they can provide unequalled help. Experienced investors can provide advice, money, and an outlet for your completed properties. If you have a knack for finding and converting properties to their highest and best use, investors will be happy to buy them. When you need creative financing, private investors may be your best source for money. While you are learning the business, working with other investors can speed up your learning process.

Learning the Business

The first use of other investors is to learn the business. If you are new at the game, watch how the pros work. While specific trade secrets may never be revealed, you can learn from talking with other investors. You will not only learn what to do, you will also discover what *not* to do. Rehab investors can be found in a variety of places. You may find them at the local lumberyard. They could be at the corner tavern or in the barber shop.

Many of these investors belong to clubs in the community. They use these clubs to network with their rehab associates. Clubs are frequented by brokers, investors, attorneys, accountants, loan officers, and almost everyone else involved in the rehab business. While you may not think of a CPA being in the rehab business, don't assume she isn't. White-collar rehabbing attracts people from all walks of life. If they are not involved as investors, they are involved through their profession.

Test Your Theory

Once you have established a rapport with other professionals, use them as a sounding board. Be careful not to give them ideas that might undermine

your success. These attentive investors are a perfect audience to try your ideas on. If they feel the project is viable, it should add to your own confidence. Frequently, the professionals will give you advice on how to proceed with your deal. Sift through the advice and extract what you believe to be credible.

Inside Financing

If the investors are convinced you are on to a winner, they may offer to help with the deal. This help could come in many forms. Suppose you are telling a doctor of your rehab plans and she expresses an interest in participating. You may be able to use her funds to finance the project. It will cost you a percentage of the deal, but having a solid financial partner can solve a lot of problems. The doctor can help with financing in many methods. She might pledge a letter of credit to secure the property. Her line of credit may be used to acquire the building or to pay for the improvements. This leaves your credit open for other deals. By giving a percentage of the first deal to the doctor, you can tackle a second project with your own credit.

The attorney you met on the racquetball court may be looking for a nice multi-family building to invest in. If your casual conversation exposes your rehab work on just such a property, you may have an easy sale. It is not uncommon for investors to network with each other for the acquisition and sale of properties. Some investors are looking for run-down properties to renovate. Others are looking for newly renovated buildings to produce rental income. When the two investors meet, their meeting can be a long-term, profitable marriage.

Quiet Leads

If you are looking for buildings to rehab, the professionals you are talking with can help. Loan officers are a great source of leads. They have knowledge of neglected and abused buildings through their job. They may know of anxious sellers, wishing for an offer to purchase their property. When buildings are on the verge of foreclosure, bankers know it. If you are a known rehabber, some of these special opportunities will come your way. These exceptional deals are common among rehabbers inside the network circle.

As a rehabber, some investors are a good source

of properties for you to buy. Heavyweight investors can buy property the average rehabber will struggle to purchase. These wealthy investors can afford to buy at auctions. To buy property at auctions, you must have quick access to cash. There is not time to apply for a loan and have it processed. You must have an established credit line to win at the auction. These top-rank investors are capable of buying good rehab projects very cheap.

Most of these investors buy at the auction and sell on the open real estate market. They make their money on the spread between wholesale and retail pricing. If you tie in with one of these guys, you can be on to a steady source of viable rehab projects. Buying directly from the heavyweight eliminates brokerage commissions. He buys the house at auction and sells it to you for a profit. You rehab the house and sell it to the homeowner for a comfortable profit. Everyone wins, and your job is made easier through your inside procurement process.

As your relationships grow, you may wish to create real estate partnerships. Partnerships allow you to do a larger volume of business with less of your own money. There are countless ways to structure realty partnerships. Talk with your attorney and tax advisor to see what will work best for you.

General Investor Advice

Many investors enjoy talking about their accomplishments. While this talk must be sifted through for facts, you can learn much about the business from casual chats. Regardless of your experience, there is always something new to learn from other investors. Make a point of talking with known investors. Merely knowing the right names to drop can give you an advantage.

Listen more than you talk. You are supposed to learn, not teach. Develop a list of investors you can call upon for various reasons. As you become known in the business, opportunities will find you. Networking with people in and around the rehab business will pay big dividends.

PRELIMINARY MARKET RESEARCH FORM

```
TO: Bill Broker
FROM: Harold Homebuyer
MAILING ADDRESS: 4 Rosewood Drive, Brunswick, ME 04011
```

I am interested in buying a single-family home in your area. I would like you to provide some market information on the sales in the area. The aspects I am interested in are as follows:

Location: Eagle Lake Estates, Greenville, ME

Please provide information on all properties currently for sale and recently sold similar to the home described below:

```
    Wood-frame, saltbox-style home
    3 bedrooms
    2 bathrooms
    Eat-in kitchen
    Full basement
    Forced hot water heat
    1 acre wooded lot with public road frontage
    Attached two-car garage
    Carpet and vinyl floors
```

Please forward this information to me as soon as possible. I am prepared to purchase a home now and appreciate your prompt attention.

BROKER SELECTION LOG					
Name	Phone	Poor	Fair	Good	Great

PROCUREMENT BROKER SELECTION LOG					
Name	Phone	Poor	Fair	Good	Great

WALK AWAY FROM THE CLOSING WITH MONEY IN YOUR POCKET

9

Buying real estate without a down payment is a perennial topic in the realty industry. There have been several books written solely on the topic of purchasing property without a down payment. Seminars are given across the country on the subject of highly leveraged acquisitions. Any relevant magazine is filled with advertisements selling cassette tapes, books, and information on buying without a down payment.

For these services and products to thrive, there must be a high demand for information on the subject of leveraged purchases. There are even promotional television shows centered around the topic. Are these books, tapes, seminars, and other promotions profitable? If they were not profitable, their originators would not continue to spend thousands of dollars in advertising. These products and services are capable of netting a creative entrepreneur big money.

Where is the money made? Most of it is made by the promoters of the products and services. They make a very comfortable living off the income from hopeful investors. Does this mean the plans are a scam? No, many of the plans are workable, but most are not easy to master. Is it possible to buy real estate without a down payment? Yes, anything is possible, but putting all the elements together to buy without any money down is rare. Part of this is semantics; there is a difference in buying without a down payment and buying without giving up your cash.

Can real estate be purchased without providing a cash down payment? Absolutely—you can buy many types of properties with creative financing and without cash. It is possible to have other people make the down payment for you. In addition, it is not uncommon for a shrewd investor to leave the closing with more money than he came in with. Sorting through viable financing options and fairytale deals takes a little time and thought.

Anytime you buy a property without a down payment, you are placing your credit at risk. Highly leveraged purchases can put you in deep financial trouble. This is the first element of the financing deal you should address. You must weigh the risks against the benefits. There is much temptation once you know the mechanics of putting together a no-money deal.

THE ENVIABLE EIGHTIES

There are a tremendous number of bankrupt investors who were paper millionaires during the 1980s. Before the tax reform laws of 1986, investors were very aggressive in the residential real estate market. There were more opportunities than they could take advantage of. From 1980 to 1986, the "No-Money-Down" philosophy ruled the real estate roost.

During these years, investors were willing to gamble. They would pay more than the current market value of a property if it could be acquired without using their cash. This procedure was preached as being the best way to provide for retirement. Many novice investors entered the lucrative waters of rental real estate to ride this wave to riches. The market trend was set. Prices began to increase at inflated rates. Sellers knew they could ask several thousand dollars more for a property if they participated in creative financing.

Tax advantages were tremendous and buying was easy. Lenders were lenient with adjustable-rate mortgages; they saw a chance to recover from the slump of the late '70s and very early '80s. The current conditions were conducive to a fast and furious real estate market. The increased activity and inflated prices affected all real estate. Prices soared across the board. These rapid appreciation rates encouraged investors to count on a steady increase in property values. This false sense of security prompted investors to pay too much for properties to obtain them without down payments.

Partnerships and syndications started to sprout everywhere. Land development kicked into high gear and speculative building was at a fevered pace. Everyone wanted to cash in on the wealth of real estate opportunities. During these times, many of the suggestions being offered were valid. Today, these same tactics do not hold true. Tax reform and a leveling economy have changed the complexion of no-money-down deals. They are not what they used to be. Instead, these once popular transactions can mean financial destruction.

CHANGING OF THE TIMES

This is not to say there is no place for a leveraged real estate purchase. Opportunities still abound for the skillful investor. If you didn't learn from past mistakes, you should learn from reading before putting your money and credit on the line. Many of the present-day promotional programs are still using old methods from the boom times. If you fall into this mindset, you will most likely have a short-lived real estate career. Techniques that worked then will not work now.

Buying properties with limited or no cash is still very possible. What you must understand is when you should exercise these creative financing skills. Under today's tax laws, you have fewer advantages.

With the leveling economy, rapid appreciation may be nothing more than a fantasy. Before you try to become a real estate millionaire, you must understand the risks and proper procedures for reaching your goal. Becoming a paper millionaire is relatively easy. Being able to maintain your holdings and avoid financial difficulty is more difficult.

Present procedures for acquiring wealth without cash require different approaches than outdated stratagems. For the remainder of the chapter, you will learn how and when to use modern creative financing methods to establish your real estate empire. Whether you use these programs to build a rental portfolio or to expand your rehab potential, you will benefit from the full use of your available resources.

Inflated Prices

The largest fault with the old no-money-down plans was paying too much for the property. There was a window of opportunity, during the heyday, when this practice was tolerable. Property values were escalating rapidly through temporary appreciation. If you knew how to buy and when to sell, you had a good chance of seeing a profit. In the present real estate market, property values are not surging. In many places, values are stable or declining.

A Fine Example

If you pay more than fair market value for a building today, you are putting yourself in jeopardy. If values do not increase dramatically, you could lose your investment. By today's standards, a more conservative approach is warranted. The following example shows exactly how a deal that worked in the '80s would cause you grief today.

Imagine you find the perfect property to rehab. You plan to renovate the property and hold it as rental property for two years. At that time, you plan to sell for a premium profit. The property you are buying was worth $135,000 about six months ago. The seller is willing to sell the home for $135,000 if he receives the full amount at the time of closing. Assuming a conservative average annual appreciation of 5%, the property should be worth $138,375. Being a creative investor, you offer the seller $147,000 for his property, if he will meet your terms.

You request the seller to hold a promissory note

for $29,400. In addition, you request that the seller pay your closing costs. The note amount is equal to 20% of the purchase price. This is typically the amount required for a down payment from an investor. The seller is taking a risk to hold the note, but if all goes well, he will make an extra $8,625. Greed is a powerful emotion, and many sellers will ultimately give in to this type of offer.

If the seller has substantial equity in the property, he will only be risking $20,775 of his potential profit. If he doesn't take your offer, he may not see another one. The seller is gambling $20,775 to make an extra $8,625. You have agreed to pay the note in full at the end of three years. The note may be secured by the real estate in the form of a second mortgage. This security interest gives the seller an undeserved peace of mind.

After deliberation, the seller sees the potential rate of return on his gamble. It is clear he could never match the return with a normal investment. Your offer is accepted, and the deal is done. With some persuasion, you are able to get the property financed for 80% of the sale price. The other 20% is being held by the seller as a note. You have no down payment invested in the home. You are counting on increasing the home's value and selling it in two years. Your balloon note with the seller isn't due until the third year, or until the property is sold. How could you get hurt?

You rehab the house and find a suitable tenant to rent the property. There is a negative cash flow, but the tax advantages outweigh the monthly loss. By writing the losses off against your other income, you are making a paper profit. The surrounding properties have shown impressive appreciation rates for the last year or so. There is no reason to believe your rental house will not be worth a bundle at the end of the targeted two years.

Old appreciation rates were around 5%, now they are hitting 15%. This is largely due to a concentration of sales similar to the one you participated in. The inflated sale prices are driving appraised values up, and demand is strong. Going into the second year, everything is on track for your rich reward.

You paid $147,000 for the house and invested another $15,000 in it for improvements. The house was worth $138,375 when you bought it. Your improvements were worth the $15,000 you invested.

The completed package had a value of $153,375 when you completed the renovations. Due to your creative financing, your total investment at that time was $162,000.

Now it is two years later and time to sell the property. You had hoped for a 15% annual appreciation, but the rate proved to be 11%. Based on the 11% appreciation rate, the house is now worth $188,973. You took some cash losses in rental income, but they were offset by tax advantages. You list the property with a real estate broker, and it is sold for $188,000. Your cost of sale for closing costs and real estate commission is $14,880. You pay off the second mortgage from the sale proceeds and net a profit of more than $11,000.

You have made over $11,000 in cash and saved thousands of dollars in taxes. The money made was made by using only $15,000 of your own money. In two years, you basically doubled your money. Another benefit of the deal was a stronger net worth during your ownership of the property. For two years, you were able to show the equity in the property as an asset. At the end of the two years, the equity equaled $26,973. Showing this paper asset enabled you to have more buying power for other properties.

Some investors would have leveraged the paper equity to purchase more properties. This type of deal was common in the past. For a while, these deals worked and some people became very wealthy. The investors who didn't sell soon enough became financially distraught. They saw the market turn, then tax reform, and their dreams turned to nightmares.

Attempting to do this same deal today would be foolish. The real estate market and investing strategies have changed. If you have read about these no-lose deals in older books, be aware of the problems you will encounter with the rules of today's real estate game. Look back through the example and note how the recent changes in real estate investing affect the deal.

Shaky Sellers

The first effect is nervous sellers and lenders. If these players were in the earlier game, many of them suffered heavy losses. Sellers will not be as easily swayed to hold paper for their profit. Today's sellers were either personally affected by the fall of the market or have read about the unfortunate sellers who were. This education makes them very skittish when you ask them to hold a second mortgage. History has proven that the second mortgage holder, in a highly leveraged deal, rarely recovers his note amount.

Busted Bankers

During the peak of the fast-paced real estate boom, lenders were scurrying to come up with creative financing plans. Today, loan officers are very wary of creative financing and are playing the role of conservative banker. Many financial institutions have failed because of bad real estate loans. Countless loan officers have been terminated for making marginal deals. Creative financing is still alive, but it is not the wild card it once was.

The Tax Axe

Tax reform had a major impact on real estate investing. While it was once fashionable to buy property for a tax loss, the rules have changed. The tax laws are complicated and restrictive. In the old days, you could shelter your primary income with real estate losses. Now your options are much more limited, and in many cases, a real estate loss is a true loss.

The tax law changes greatly altered real estate investment tactics. What was once a paper loss is now a very real cash loss. You must be much more deliberate in choosing your realty investment. Not having the safety net of tax savings makes every investment more dangerous. Some tax benefits are still available, but they cannot compare with the huge advantages of the past.

Lack of Appreciation

Appreciation rates account for another important change. These rates fluctuate from region to region, but in general, appreciation rates are down. Seeing a 10% annual increase in property values was no surprise in the mid '80s. Present values are not doing so well. Some areas have stabilized and are showing little to no annual appreciation. Other areas are actually seeing values fall. This factor alone kills the deal of the last decade.

Using the same figures in the above example,

run the numbers and see how you would fare with a 5% appreciation rate. Keep in mind, 5% may be considered a generous appreciation rate in the present real estate market. Your total investment in the example is $162,000. The actual value is $153,375. In the example, the investor recovered his negative cash flow in tax benefits. You may not have this luxury today, but for the sake of simplicity, assume the rental scenario is a break-even deal.

With an appreciation rate of 5%, at the end of two years your investment is worth $169,095. The time has come to sell and you list the property with a broker. In the above example, the cost of sale was about 7.75% of the sale price. In this case, 7.75% of the sale price is equal to a rounded figure of $13,000. When this number is subtracted from the sale price, you are left with $156,095. You owe $162,000 on the property, so how did you do? You lost about $6,000.

In reality, you probably lost more than $6,000. By not having the tax advantages, your cost of holding the property could be substantial. In a sluggish economy, low appreciation rates will bury you in a highly leveraged deal. This example should make it clear why the dream deals of the past must be left in the past. Now that you have had your history lesson, we will move on to the modern approach of maximizing your investment dollar.

RESIDENTIAL DEALS

Residential properties are the most difficult to finance without a down payment from your personal assets. Single-family homes and multi-family buildings with fewer than four units are referred to as residential in this text. If an apartment building has more than four units, it is considered a commercial property for loan purposes.

Most residential loans are sold on the secondary market. For these loans to be sold, they must conform to set criteria. The criteria are strict and unbending. Lenders cannot afford to make exceptions to the rules if they wish to sell the loans. Because of these rules, creative financing is limited on residential properties when institutional financing is involved.

As an investor, the down payment required for a residential property is generally at least 20% of the sale price. Down payments of 30% are becoming more prevalent in residential loans. These large down payments are typically required to be made with the purchaser's assets. With this the case, how will you be able to buy residential property without heavy cash?

There are several ways to accomplish your goal. Lenders base their loan amount on a percentage of the property's value. If you are buying a home priced at $100,000, many lenders will loan $80,000 on the property. In this example, you must be able to cover the $20,000 difference. There are ways to do this without depleting your cash.

Equity Leverage

If you own other real estate, the equity from it can be used as a down payment for your new purchase. Existing equity in other properties is frequently used to satisfy down payment requirements. By giving the lender a satisfactory security interest in one of your properties, they will forgo a cash down payment. Normally, the amount of equity you can leverage will be the difference between your existing loan amount and 80% of the property's value.

If you own a house with an appraised value of $100,000 and owe $60,000 on it, you should be able to use $20,000 of your equity as leverage. This is arrived at by finding 80% of the appraised value and subtracting any outstanding loans on the property. In this example, the remaining amount of equity is $20,000.

Pledged Security

You may use other types of investments to secure a property. Let's assume you have a certificate of deposit (CD) in the amount of $20,000. The CD is earning interest and you don't want to cash it in for a down payment. Instead of cashing the certificate, pledge it to the lender. By pledging the CD to a lender, you will meet the down payment requirements of the home to be purchased. The CD is still yours, and you continue to receive the interest earned on the certificate.

If you default on the new property, the bank can take the CD to help cover their loss. As long as things go well, you maintain ownership of your CD. You will not be able to cash the certificate as long

as it is pledged to the lender. In quick-flip rehab projects, this is rarely a problem. Once you sell the rehabbed home, you regain full control of your CD.

This type of pledged security can be almost anything of value. You might pledge a coin collection, stock holdings, or any other negotiable instrument. Creative financing of this sort is respected and welcome. As a rehabber, you have another method available to you. This method does not apply to investors merely buying real estate. It only works when you will be increasing the value of the property.

Sweat Equity

This plan works best when you act as your own general contractor for the rehab operation. As a rule of thumb, general contractors account for 20% of the total cost of improvements. This 20% can be parlayed into your down payment. Here is an example of how you may structure such a deal.

The house you are buying is priced at $70,000. After renovation, the property is expected to be worth $145,000. The anticipated cost to make the improvements is $40,000, if you act as the general contractor. Your total cash investment will be $110,000. You plan to sell the property during, or immediately following, the renovation process.

You present a well-prepared loan package to your banker. The loan request is for an acquisition and construction loan. This type of loan is usually issued in an amount equal to 80% of the property's completed value. In this case, that amount is $116,000. The bank will have your proposed plans appraised to obtain a reasonable completed value.

The lender will then lend 80% of the appraised value, if you are a qualified borrower. These loans allow the use of funds to make the initial acquisition. After acquisition, future disbursements will be made on a progress-payment basis. As work is completed on the property, the bank will advance funds to reimburse your expenses, up to the 80% amount.

This is a good deal for the rehabber. You do not need a cash down payment to acquire the property. Many material suppliers and contractors will work with the understanding that they will be paid by the bank. Once their labor and material are in place, the bank inspects the work and issues payment for the completed work. So far, you have not had to use any significant amount of money. Your only expenses have been loan application fees and closing costs. Some lenders even allow these fees to be paid from the acquisition loan.

When the remodeling is complete, you own a $145,000 house with only $110,000 invested. None of the $110,000 is your money; it is all borrowed. The term of most construction loans is between six and twelve months. Before the construction loan matures, you sell the property for $145,000. You have earned $35,000 and never used your own money to do it.

This may seem impossible, but it isn't. This is a very common approach for professional rehabbers. Your first project may require substantial documentation to gain loan approval. Until you build a track record, lenders may require some form of personal security from you. Once you are a proven rehabber, this deal will allow you to move freely, without much cash.

As good as this deal is, there is a down side to it. If you are unable to sell the property, you could be in trouble. It is best to arrange for permanent financing for the completed property. When the construction loan is due, you will be expected to pay the loan in full. Construction loans can be renewed, but don't bet the house on it. To protect yourself fully, be pre-approved for a take-out loan. This take-out, or permanent, loan allows you to satisfy the construction loan and affords more time to sell the property.

OPM

Another method worth mentioning is partnership financing. Using other people's money is a goal of many investors. The other-people's-money (OPM) method is used daily by seasoned investors. The avenues for manipulating the OPM method are limited only by your imagination. Here are a few of the most common ways to use someone else's money to launch your venture.

Asking the seller of a property to hold a note for a portion of the price is the most common OPM method. This may be a promissory note, a second mortgage, or a loan secured by another property. Forming a partnership is another route you may want to examine. Limited partnerships were very popular in the '80s, but now general partnerships are in fashion.

Tax reform removed many of the tax advantages for limited partners. Losing this advantage turned investors to general partnerships. Partnerships should be formed by attorneys. The risks can be high for each partner, and the stakes in the real estate game are big. If you plan to form a partnership, consult your attorney and tax advisor.

With a partnership, it is possible for you to share an equal interest in the deal without providing any of the required capital. If you are a business professional, you might want to look for tradespeople to act as your partners. In this situation, you would assume responsibility for all administrative duties and business responsibilities. The tradesmen will provide the knowledge and labor to perform the renovations.

Let's say you find an ideal rehab project and place it under contract, subject to financing. You contact your tradespeople and offer them a position in the deal. If you can find a mechanical contractor and a carpentry contractor, you have most of the bases covered. You have the property under contract for $80,000. The contract may be executed by you or your assigns. The two contractors show an interest in the deal and ask what will be required of them.

You explain they will each be responsible for $40,000 in the acquisition loan. In addition, each contractor will provide labor and materials for the work to be done, with payment to be made upon the sale of the finished project. Each contractor will receive his normal fee for the work required. You show each contractor what your responsibilities will be. You will take care of arranging financing, coordinating the project, and accounting for the job cost. Marketing, showing the property, and all other administrative duties will fall into your bailiwick.

If you do a good job of showing your value to the deal, the contractors will go for it. The property you have under contract for $80,000 will be worth $148,000 when renovations are complete. The street price for the improvements is $38,000. The contractors will profit from doing the work for their standard rate. Much of the cost for improvements is labor. These contractors will do well with the profit earned from doing the work.

Getting a third of the overall profit is gravy for the contractors. The house is finished and you sell it for $148,000. By selling it yourself, there is no real estate commission to pay. This was part of your worth to the deal. The gross profit from the sale is $30,000. The gross profit is divided equally between you and the two partners. Each of you receives $10,000.

The contractors each received $10,000 in investor profit and the profit from their labor and materials. You received $10,000 for coordinating the deal and risked nothing in doing it. Doing a deal like this requires some time and several good contacts. Once you are able to put together a few successful partnerships, you will have investors asking you to include them in your deals. This is an ideal way for an individual with damaged credit or little cash to get into the game. The other partners provide the credit and the money; you provide your time and collect a nice check when the project is sold.

Similar deals can be made with all types of investors. Big-money investors may provide the required financing if you do the legwork. For high-income professionals, having a partner in the field is worth a fair percentage of the deal. If you are a tradesperson, you can key in on investors with strong credit and cash. You can provide the labor and legwork while they finance the project. This marriage can produce extremely good results.

Portfolio Loans

Commercial and portfolio loans offer a great opportunity for creative financing. Portfolio loans are loans the lender does not wish to sell on the secondary market. Commercial loans are not subject to the same rules that pertain to residential properties. These two types of loans are what most investors are looking for. When you combine these loans with a commissioned loan officer, you have a winning combination.

In portfolio and commercial loans, if you can sell the lender on your idea, the deal can be done. If the loan officer receives a commission for every loan written, your odds for approval improve rapidly. This is the sector most successful investors concentrate on. Portfolio loans can be obtained for single-family homes and open the door to creative terms. Commercial loans apply to residential dwellings with more than four apartments and to all business property.

When you enter the arena of these loans, the gloves come off and there are no rules. An impressive loan application package carries a lot of weight in these circumstances. For these deals, you must sell the loan officer on your plan. You don't have to conform to set ratios or guidelines; all you have to do is impress the lender.

INCOME PROPERTY

Buying income-producing property for rehab is an excellent path to follow. With the proper navigation, you can walk away from the purchase with money in your pocket. You will not need a down payment, and you can leave the closing with more money than you entered with. Six-unit apartment buildings are one of the best places to ply these tactics. The profits possible from these buildings will keep you up nights. Check out the following example and see if you are suited for this type of deal.

Income property is evaluated on its ability to produce income. The appraisal process for these properties is very different than the appraisal techniques used to place a value on a single-family home. Appraised values are very important to the investor and to creative financing. It is difficult to stretch a residential appraisal more than 5% above comparable properties. This problem does not exist with larger apartment buildings.

Your equity, borrowing power, and net worth are all affected by the appraised value of your holdings. The higher you can push the appraisal, the better your financial statement will look. Single-family homes are frequently throttled by existing values in the neighborhood. If surrounding homes are worth $120,000, it is difficult to justify an appraisal of $175,000 on your property. This setback can be eliminated with apartment buildings containing more than four apartments.

When you step into commercial financing, these apartment buildings are valued based on their ability to produce income. This leaves a lot to speculation and opens the door for some really creative financing. Assume you want to buy a rundown six-unit building for $160,000. The building is structurally sound and all mechanical systems are in good working order. The improvements needed are largely cosmetic. There is room for improving the use of some of the space associated with the property.

The property has two vacancies and has a historic vacancy rate of 7%. The seller's tax returns show annual maintenance costs to be $1,300. The present owner manages the property personally and pays the property's utility expenses. The seller is very motivated to sell before the winter heating season. You see a chance to buy the property cheap and turn it into a strong money machine.

The property has been for sale over the last five months. The seller has not received an acceptable offer and is getting desperate. The present owner owes very little on the property and could easily hold a 20% second mortgage if he wanted to. The stage is set. It is up to you to make the most of this outstanding opportunity. What would you do? If you are not sure, read on.

The Right Moves

You know the seller will accept $160,000 for the property, but you are not sure if he will hold a second mortgage. The heating season is getting close and the expense of heating this old building is staggering. You know the seller wants to sell, but you must determine how to cut your best deal.

You should do a full-blown research study on the property before trying to buy it. If you create tables and charts showing the historical performance of the building, you can stun the seller. First, you will be accepted as a serious buyer—a shopper would not go to the trouble to build a feasibility study. Second, you will have hard numbers to show the seller. Many sellers are not aware what it costs them to maintain an income property. When you lay it out with charts and graphs, the seller will see the reason behind selling quickly.

If you do a good job on your data gathering, you will have the seller's attention. Showing the seller the benefits that will be derived from selling will soften his opinion of the building's value. Next, you offer the seller $160,000 for the building with two conditions. The first condition is a professional inspection of the property's structure and mechanical systems. The second condition requires the seller to hold a 20% second mortgage on the property.

With enough research, you will know about what the seller owes on the property. Provide him with an accounting of what the sale will net him. Stress the advantage of taking some of the profit in install-ments. Set an assumable balloon mortgage, with interest-only payments, for a five-year term. Detail the additional profit the seller will earn from the interest and the tax advantages of not taking all the profit at once.

When these terms are agreed to, go see your friendly commissioned loan officer. Present a professional loan request for an acquisition and improvement loan. Show the lender what your intended improvements will do for the cash flow of the building. Ask the lender to have the property appraised based on its value after your improvements.

Using historical data from the local housing authority will add credibility to your proposal. Run several spreadsheets on the property's performance after it has been rehabbed. Show the banker a worst case/best case scenario and expected performance on the building. Document your projections with proven historical data.

For every improvement you plan to make, note the expected increase in income from the improvement. Show the lender what adding a coin-operated laundry will do for the building. Detail how adding secure personal storage facilities will boost the rental income. When replacing inefficient windows and doors, provide a report on the value of new energy-efficient windows and doors. These heat-loss reports can often be obtained from your local utility company, without any cost to you.

Stress the structural integrity of the property and the solid mechanical systems. Include copies of the professional inspections you had performed on the apartment building. Include as much paperwork as you can without being ridiculous. Loan officers believe the written word and thrive on documentation. Providing a comprehensive loan-request package enhances your ability to obtain a loan.

The bank's appraiser will appraise the building based on its completed value. If you have done your paperwork correctly, the anticipated value will be impressive. After providing clear evidence of the costs you will incur doing the renovations, the loan officer should grant your loan. The seller will hold a 20% second mortgage and the bank will lend a total of 80% of the completed value in progress payments.

If your spreadsheet projections have done their job, this is an easy deal to make. The completed value could easily be set at a figure of $275,000. Remember, with this type of property, the appraised value is largely based on the income produced by the property. This is totally different than a comparable sale appraisal, such as the ones done for single-family residences.

Your improvement expenses are budgeted not to exceed $40,000. You purchased the property with no cash down payment and the seller is holding a 20% second mortgage, with interest-only payments for five years. The property is completed on budget and the total cost of the building is now $200,000. If you sell the property for $275,000, you have made a very respectable profit.

The building will be easier to sell because of the assumable second mortgage. The new buyer may assume the original second mortgage with interest-only payments. This keeps the debt service lower and provides a more attractive cash flow. The payoff to the bank is $168,000 and the second mortgage is for $32,000. This leaves you in a strong selling posture.

With a $275,000 sale price, the new buyer only needs to assume the second mortgage and pay off the $168,000 to clear your credit line. The $75,000 spread can be handled in many different ways. You could offer some owner financing to the new buyer and request security in a different property for the paper you hold. If you want all cash, the assumable second reduces the amount of down payment required from the new buyer.

To cover 20% of the sale price, the new investor will only need $23,000, instead of $55,000. This is made possible by the original second mortgage. You could hold this paper and still walk away with a $52,000 profit. The options become mind boggling if you structure the deal properly. The final result is a huge profit from a deal with none of your money invested in it.

These are the types of deals experienced investors make. When you plan to rehab a building, your alternatives far exceed those of the average real estate investor. Creative financing is still a very viable tool for the rehab investor. Using your head can permit you to avoid using your money. When you achieve success with the OPM method, you have the potential to make an unlimited income.

ACTING AS YOUR OWN GENERAL CONTRACTOR

10

By now, you have learned there are scores of ways to turn a profit in rehabbing rundown properties. Acting as your own general contractor is one of the best ways to increase your profits by as much as 20% of the rehab expense. Who wouldn't want to cash in on this kind of extra money? There is no gimmick here; the extra money you receive will be hard earned. Before you close the book and rush off to "general" your first project, there are some facts you need to know.

This book was not designed for the tradesman looking to hammer the nails and solder the pipes. It is intended to show business people how to make money in the rehab business. Depending upon the business you are in, you may have the makings of a general contractor. Some people are naturals, and others never get the hang of it. This chapter will show you how general contractors make their money and what you must do to put the money in your pocket instead of theirs.

The general contractor must bear the burden of all responsibility for the refurbishing process. His responsibility begins with the planning stages and does not cease until the project is complete. His knowledge must cover everything in between. The knowledge does not have to be deep, but it should go below the surface. Inexperienced general contractors can ruin a job and its budget before you can blink.

Don't be too intimidated. This is not to say you must have ten years of field experience to general a job. I am saying you must recognize the responsibilities and meet them precisely. Many of the requirements demanded from a general contractor are similar to those found in other businesses. Your past employment background may serve as experience for your rehab job. One of the most important elements of a good general contractor is the ability to organize and execute a plan.

Putting a general contractor's responsibilities into chronological order may help you to appreciate them. As we go through the job description, make mental notes on your proficiency to do the job. For the following examples, assume the rehab project is a large-scale single-family renovation. The house is in rough shape and requires the services of several trades to get it on the market as a desirable home.

THE PLANNING STAGE

In the beginning, a general contractor works with the customer to plan the improvements. As a rehabber, if you act as your own contractor, you have to make your own planning decisions. For the most part, this should not be a problem. You can always consult with suppliers and architects if you need help. Your subcontractors can provide plenty of good information on specific aspects of the job.

Once the desired results of the job are known, the contractor must lay out the job on paper. This can be done by an architect, and sometimes by a lumberyard representative, but normally the contractor does the layout. If you know what you want, doing the layout is not much of a problem. Code requirements come into play with your layout, and the code officers should be consulted before final plans are made. Code officers can be very helpful when they are approached with respect.

When the preliminary layout is sketched, it should be shown to the code officers and subcontractors. If there are any problems with the design, this is the time to discover them. You don't want to wait until you are well into the job to find the plumber has no place to run his main vent. Up to this point, most individuals can handle the job of general contractor. When the plans have been approved by all parties, it is time to seek material and labor prices. This part of the job is where some investors decide they don't want to be general contractors.

SHOPPING PRICES

This is where the real work begins and personalities get in the way. Shopping for material prices is not too bad. Suppliers are available during the day and will give you advice on most questions. Subcontractors are a different story. They can be a very independent bunch. Subcontractors are not known for their lavish offices and secretaries. Many subs work from their homes and have an answering machine to take their daytime phone calls. This can be very discouraging to the office-based investor.

Some of the best subcontractors will have to be dealt with late in the evening. For the investor only willing to work normal business hours, general contracting is not a good business to enter. The shopping phase is rife with other irritants. For a hard-driving entrepreneur, the personalities encountered during this phase may be overwhelming. The cogs of the construction business can move very slowly for the unknown general contractor.

Suppliers may not be willing to do a take-off from your sketches. They may insist you provide an itemized material list for them to price. This isn't too bad, if you know how to make an accurate take-off. If you are like the average real estate investor, you have limited knowledge in this area. Looking at a line drawing and developing a detailed list of construction materials can be a monumental task. There are some ways to circumvent this problem.

You can play hardball with the suppliers and hope they will do the take-off for you. You could prevail upon your subcontractors to provide a list of all the materials they will need. In either case, you are at risk. Unless you know enough about the process to spot-check the material lists, you can fall victim to an underestimated budget. Professional general contractors know approximately what will be needed. With a quick scan of the list, they can tell if there are any major discrepancies.

Once you have found a satisfactory way to determine your labor and material needs, you must still negotiate prices. Some of the skills needed for this phase are explained in Chapter 11. Negotiating for the best price is time consuming and can be very frustrating. Incompetence is not uncommon among suppliers. The employees will not have much interest in an unknown contractor and may be unwilling to assist you. If this happens, talk to the manager. The manager wants to increase monthly sales figures and should be willing to work with you.

Follow the advice in Chapter 11 on specification sheets and negotiating techniques. If you don't mind investing your time and suffering through a few headaches, you can accomplish this part of the job. When shopping prices with subcontractors, be prepared for minimal cooperation. In a healthy economy, good subs are busy with regular generals and will not cater to you. Slow times will change these factors. If work is scarce, you get more attention. Even when the subs are interested in doing your work, you may have trouble getting into a construction mindset.

Tradespeople are a breed all their own. They have their own language and their own principles. If you approach them with the proper attitude, they are very congenial. If you approach them with a chip on your shoulder, you are in deep trouble. Be selective in how you represent yourself to the subcontractors. You can count on becoming aggravated by some of them. They will not meet the criteria you expect of a business owner. When this happens, stay calm; don't start throwing your weight and college degrees around. If you do, you will be hard-pressed to find subcontractors.

Contractors can be a tight-knit group. If you get off on the wrong foot, you can alienate every contractor in the trade. Composure and approach mean everything in manipulating subcontractors. If you start spouting off about holding a mechanical engineering degree, you're done for. These people respect *people*, not degrees and financial statements. What will win you awards on Wall Street will cost you plenty with subcontractors.

With practice and finesse, you can obtain the pricing you need. This phase may add to your stress level, but it is something most investors can learn to do. Allow plenty of time to shop prices on your first project. After you have established contact and credibility with subcontractors, subsequent jobs will go much smoother. With your plans made, your specifications detailed, and your prices nailed down, you are ready to get your permits.

PERMITS

Different locations have varying requirements for permits and code enforcement. Code enforcement officers can bring your job to a standstill. Never try to bully the code officer. Even if the code officer is wrong, be very diplomatic. Avoid going to the code officer's supervisor. If you are having a problem with one of the officials, try to work it out with that official. If you go over his head, you may be in for a miserable life as a general contractor.

In most locales, you will need the following permits: plumbing, heating, electrical, and building. As the general contractor, you will probably be responsible for obtaining the building permits. Mechanical permits will be supplied by the individual trades.

To be issued a building permit, you should be prepared to submit plans and specifications for your proposed improvements. Allow a week or more for the code enforcement office to review your submissions. When your plans and specs are approved, you will be issued a permit. Most jurisdictions allow the owner of the property to act as a general contractor. Some locations may require you to be licensed before issuing a permit. This regulation is worth investigating before you spend too much time on your plans to act as general contractor. Once you have your permit, you are ready to start the job.

PUTTING THE JOB IN ORDER

As the general, you are responsible for scheduling material deliveries and subcontractors. While this is a vital aspect of your job, it only requires strong organizational skills. If you have doubts as to which contractors are needed first, ask the contractors.

You may also use the Contractor Schedule form at the end of the chapter as a guide to scheduling.

Getting the right subs in at the right time is necessary for a smooth-running job. If you put the electrician in before the plumber, you may have problems. It is much easier for an electrician to choose an alternate route for wires than it is for a plumber to make magic with his pipes. Adhering to a structured schedule makes the whole job more efficient.

Men without materials can't work. The general contractor is responsible for material acquisition and delivery. Plan your deliveries in advance and order accordingly. If your supplier is top-notch, that is all you have to do for this phase. Unfortunately, most suppliers fall short in the service department. They may promise a delivery date and not keep their promise. The material shipped may be the wrong product. Materials account for many of the general contractor's ulcers.

There are no guarantees in the rehab business, but you can improve your win-loss statistics. Order materials early enough to allow for problems. If the material doesn't arrive on schedule, you won't have work crews standing still. If the material delivered is incorrect or defective, you have time to overcome the obstacle. Check every delivery for accuracy. It is not unusual to be shorted material or to receive the wrong material. If you cannot identify the different types of material, have your subcontractors check the delivery. Don't allow your job to be stopped due to mistakes in material deliveries.

THE PAPERWORK

Successful general contractors maintain good records and detailed paperwork. The paperwork begins before the field work. You will need clear contracts with all your contractors. The contracts should be in writing to be enforceable. There is a Sample Contract at the end of the chapter.

The plans and specifications for the job should be attached to and made a part of the contract. Have each contractor sign the plans and specifications to avoid future arguments.

When the plans and specs are signed by the contractor, he will not be able to say he misunderstood what you wanted. There can be no charges for unspecified labor or material. If a change in your agreement is required, complete a change order form. You will find a sample Change Order at the end of the chapter. All your terms and agreements should be in writing. Following this rule will save you future frustration and money.

To protect your property from liens, have a lien waiver signed with every payment made to contractors and suppliers. (There is an example of a Lien Waiver at the end of the chapter.) Any time you disburse money to a sub or supplier, insist on having a lien waiver signed. If you fail to do this, your property could become encumbered with liens. Mechanic's and materialman's liens are filed to protect suppliers and contractors who have not been paid for their service or material. Any lien on your property will have an adverse effect on your ability to sell it. The lien waiver is your proof of payment and protection from liens.

Maintaining detailed records of your expenses is welcome at tax time. When the property is sold, your tax consequences are based on your profit. Without good expense records, you may have to pay additional taxes. Keep solid records and document every improvement expense. When the property is sold, you will only pay taxes on the profit amount. The acquisition cost of the property, improvement expenses, and cost-of-sale expenses will be deducted from the sale price. You will be taxed on the difference between the total cost of the project and the sale price.

GETTING THE JOB IN GEAR

When materials have been delivered and checked, it is time to bring in the subcontractors. Using your contractor schedule, you must call your subs and put them on notice. Let the subs know how you have them scheduled, and confirm their availability for the selected dates. This part of the job is pretty easy. If you have your schedule worked out, all you have to do is call and set up the subs.

Staying on Track

Initial scheduling is simple; maintaining the schedule is not so effortless. Unless you are the exception, your job will not go as planned. It is very rare to have a job schedule stay on track throughout the job. When something goes wrong to displace

one of the subs, many of the subcontractors will have to be rescheduled. Making these adjustments will try your patience.

Making changes to your schedule on short notice creates an array of challenges. Several subcontractors can be adversely affected by a single delay. Follow this example for a clear understanding of how a simple problem can derail your job.

The plumber and electrician are on schedule and nearly complete with their rough-in work. After checking your schedule, you confirm the insulation contractor and the drywall contractor dates. With the plumber and electrician winding down, you order insulation and drywall. It is delivered on time and the job is going smoothly. The insulation and drywall delivery requires much of the home's floor space to accommodate the bulky materials. The material is stocked in different rooms, and you are proud of the job you're doing.

The next day, the code officers are coming to inspect the plumbing and electrical work. Once the inspections are approved, you can insulate. The plumbing inspector is first to arrive. He inspects the plumbing and issues his approval for the rough-in. The electrical inspector arrives later in the day. It is near quitting time, but at least she showed up. During her inspection, the electrical inspector finds code violations in the wiring. She rejects the work and suspends concealment of the wiring.

The rejected wiring has to be corrected and reinspected. The insulation contractor will not be able to install the insulation tomorrow. If you hurry, you may be able to keep the drywall contractor on schedule, but you have to hustle. You must contact the electrician and get the work corrected immediately to have any chance of maintaining most of your schedule.

By the end of the night, you have reached the necessary subs. The electrician is going out to make the corrections in the morning. The insulator anticipates going to the job after the inspection, and the drywall contractor is still on schedule. Morning arrives and so does the electrician. He makes the necessary corrections, and you have the inspection scheduled for early the next day.

You are on the job, waiting to meet the electrical inspector. She comes in and checks the work. This time it passes inspection, and you have permission to conceal the work. As agreed, you page the insulation contractor to start your job. It is getting late in the morning, and you have not seen or heard from the insulator. Calling his office and pager is not producing results. It is mid-afternoon when the insulation contractor arrives.

Your blood pressure is soaring and your anger is apparent. The insulator explains why he was late. He went to work on another job while waiting to be paged. It was a new house and the driveway was muddy. His truck got stuck in the mud. Well, it is a good excuse, but it doesn't help your situation. Now the insulation won't be installed until tomorrow, and it will need to be inspected by the code officer. This throws your schedule off again.

This time, the drywall contractor must be postponed for a day. When you call to make this change, the drywall contractor says he can't comply with the changed schedule. He has a job scheduled with a mandatory completion date. Starting your job late will make him late on the other job, and he will have to pay a steep penalty for being overdue. While his position is understandable, it is not what you would have liked to hear.

Now you must wait for the drywall contractor to complete his other job before starting yours. You have a contract with the contractor, so you can't bring in another sub. It's not his fault you are not on schedule. The painter and trim carpenter will also be affected by this slowdown.

A few days ago, your job was going full speed ahead. Today, it is stopped in its tracks. All this trouble was caused by one failed inspection. This type of thing happens, and the stress of keeping the job together can become intense. If you are going to run your own show, you must be willing to deal with this type of situation.

Reaching the Finish Line

When you are approaching the completion of the job, expect plans to go astray. It is typical for the most problems to pop up near the end of the job. The last two weeks of the job can be the most complicated for the general contractor.

During this critical time, multiple subcontractors are working in the property. The plumber and electrician are setting fixtures. The drywall contractor and painter are doing their final work and touchups. The flooring contractor is installing carpet and vinyl. Carpenters are scurrying around doing all sorts of jobs. The job is swarming with subs working around each other's work.

In the excitement and rush to complete the job, accidents happen. The plumber may tear your new vinyl floor when installing the dishwasher. Your flooring contractor may damage the painted walls with his work. The painter could spill paint on the new carpet. These accidents do happen and are hard to eliminate. As the general, your supervisory and administrative skills must be sharp to avoid disaster.

PUNCH-OUT

When the job is complete, there will still be items to be touched up and adjusted. The paint work almost always needs a final touchup. The plumber's compression fittings may need to be tightened. Cabinet drawers might need to be adjusted. Doors may require attention to close properly. This type of work is known as *punch-out work*. The general contractor must do a final inspection of the completed job and create a punch-out list.

Going through the job with an eye for detail is how this list is made. The punch-out inspection should be done before final payments are made to the subcontractors. If the subcontractors are paid prior to punch-out, they can be very difficult to get back on the job. You must make a very concise inspection. If you omit an item from your list, getting the problem corrected later may be difficult.

CLEANING UP

The last responsibilities of the general contractor include cleaning the newly improved home. Progressive general contractors hire independent contractors to provide cleaning services. Getting the rehabbed house ready to sell will take more work than a broom and vacuum. Professional cleaners are well equipped for the job and adept at their specialty.

If you plan to clean your own job, be aware of what you are getting into. There are windows and doors to clean. They have to be scraped and scrubbed. The new fixtures have to have stickers removed. The floors need to be vacuumed several times to remove loose particles and dirt. Vinyl flooring needs the black letters of the name brand removed. Cabinets need to be vacuumed. Faucets must be shined, and the exterior must be cleaned up. This is not a project you can complete in a couple of hours.

Most general contractors are happy to pay the price of professional cleaners. I suggest you allow for professional cleaners in your job-cost budget. If you prefer to do the work yourself, you can. If you get into it and change your mind, you have the money budgeted for professionals.

SETTLING UP

When the job is complete, the general contractor will be looking for final payment. General contractors work on a percentage basis. They take their total cost for all labor and material to be supplied and add their fee to the figure. The general contractor's fee is usually a percentage of the total charges made to the contractor. The percentage varies, but 20% is a common markup.

If you act as your own general, you will save this expense. In the rehab of a house, your savings could easily amount to more than $5,000. Saving 20% on your improvement costs is always a pleasing proposition. The work required to save this money may not be as pleasing. You have to decide for yourself whether the money saved is worth your time and effort.

Now that you have an idea of what a general contractor does, evaluate your abilities. Draw comparisons between the general contractor's duties and your past work experience. Take into account your personality. Be honest in the evaluation; you will only be hurting yourself if you overestimate your abilities. If you are unsure of yourself, plan to use the services of a professional contractor.

For your first project, working with a general contractor has many benefits. You will be exposed to the rehab process without being responsible for every aspect of the job. You will learn from watching how the job is done. This experience will enhance your ability to act as your own general contractor. If you hire a general contractor for the first job, you may be able to run your next project alone.

Being the general contractor is not easy. The job demands working long hours and staying in con-

trol. If the general loses control of the job, the results will be very disappointing. Before making your final decision, answer the following questions. They will give you a good indication of your ability to be a general contractor.

Are you an organized person? If you don't possess strong organizational skills, you will not do well as a general contractor. Don't try to convince yourself you can become organized to run your job. If you are not organized by nature, you should hire a general contractor.

Do you enjoy dealing with people from all walks of life? If you don't enjoy working with the public, you will not like being a general contractor.

Are you able to follow instructions? The ability to follow your plans and specifications is critical. If you stray from your game plan, your job will be left to chance. With so much at stake, you must follow your plans.

How much do you know about construction and remodeling? While you don't have to be a skilled tradesman, you must have a basic knowledge of each trade. If you act as the general, you must keep the subs honest. When you have no rehab knowledge and lack the ability to understand the excuses subs are giving, you cannot maintain control. Controlling the subs and suppliers is a critical element in profitable general contracting.

Can you make quick decisions and deal with stress? As a general contractor, you will have to do both. You are the one everyone else will come to with questions and problems. It is your job to solve the problems and answer the questions.

Can you motivate others? Motivation of the work crews and suppliers plays a significant role in your performance as general contractor. If you are unable to project an image of authority, you will not fare well as a general.

Are you easily intimidated by people? The person in charge of the job wears the title of General Contractor for a reason. You will be the general in charge of all operations. As leader of the project, you must be capable of standing your ground. If an irate subcontractor begins to abuse you verbally, you must end the conflict. This can get interesting when the sub is a 300-pound brick mason, with arms the size of your legs. These conflicts are common enough among the trades to take into consideration.

Will you be able to maintain accurate records of all financial activity involved with the rehab? Unless you are willing to throw money away, you need concise records for your tax filing.

Do you have the desire to learn to be a good general contractor? If you are only trying to save money, you won't make a very effective general contractor. Money is strong motivation, but you must have the desire to learn how to do the job right. When you learn how to run the job properly, the cash savings will be there.

Do you have time to run the job? This is a big question, with no room for adjustment. Time on the job and spent running the job cannot be taken lightly. You may need to spend several hours a day working with the project. Some of this time will be spent on the job site. Much of your time will be spent on the telephone. Review your time needs carefully, before getting in over your head.

There is a compromise you might want to contemplate. If you think you can do most of the duties of a general contractor but aren't sure, consider this. Construction managers and consultants are a reasonable substitute for a general contractor. When you can handle many of the job requirements, these professionals can pick up the slack. The cost of these services depends on how much help you need.

When you need technical assistance, construction consultants are the answer to your needs. For an hourly fee, they will answer your questions and provide professional advice. Most consultants limit their services to advice. They seldom get involved in the coordination of your project. If you need help running the field crews, a construction manager is your best choice. Construction managers perform any of the requirements of a general contractor.

Construction managers and consultants add another dimension to the general contractor question. Their services are an efficient way to pay only for the services you need. The fees charged are frequently based on an hourly rate. But some construction managers charge a percentage of the job's cost. For most rehab investors, the hourly-rate basis is the best payment plan.

Take some time to digest what you have read. Due to space constraints, many of the lesser duties of the general contractor have been omitted. The information in this chapter has provided enough facts to make you think. It is by no means all-inclusive of the general contractor's job description. Classify your needs, abilities, and desires before making a final determination on the supervision of your job. If you can run the job personally, your financial reward will be substantial.

CONTRACTOR SCHEDULE		
Phase	**Scheduled Date**	**Completed Date**
Survey and soils test		
Site work		
Water and sewer		
Demolition		
Foundation		
Framing		
Windows and exterior doors		
Roofing		
Siding		
Heating		
Plumbing		
Electrical		
Insulation		
Drywall		
Paint		
Interior doors and trim		
Cabinets and vanities		
Floor coverings		
Accents and accessories		
Trash removal and cleanup		
Landscaping		
Other		

SAMPLE CONTRACT

American Contractors
51 Bondwell Street
Brunswick, Maine 04011
(207) 555-1234

PROPOSAL—CONTRACT

TO:	Mr. & Mrs. Fallow	Date: 6/11/92
ADDRESS:	21 Baker Street	
	Topsham, Maine 04086	
JOB LOCATION:	Mr. & Mrs. Fallow's home in Topsham, Maine	

PROPOSAL EXPIRES IN 30 DAYS, IF NOT ACCEPTED BY ALL PARTIES

American Contractors proposes the following:

American Contractors will supply all labor and material for the work referenced below:
American Contractors will provide all labor, material, and supervision to construct a 24' x 18' ranch-style addition to the Fallows' home. The construction will be to the following specifications:

SPECIFICATIONS

FOUNDATION
Concrete will be 3000 psi slab a minimum of 4" thick, and include a 6 mil poly vapor barrier. All concrete will be reinforced with wire mesh and rebar as needed.

FRAMING
All lumber to be kiln-dried, construction grade. 2" x 6" exterior walls and 2" x 4" interior walls, 16" on center with interlocking double top plates. Prefabricated, engineered roof trusses will be covered with ½" plywood roof sheathing, with H-clips and 20-year asphalt roof shingles. There will be 8" galvanized drip edge on eaves and a "Cor-a-vent" ridge vent with perforated vinyl soffit vent. Wall sheathing will be ½" plywood. The subfloor will be ¾" T&G plywood with ¼" underlayment where vinyl flooring will be installed.

WINDOWS
Windows to be insulated, energy-efficient vinyl-clad, double-hung, with screens.

EXTERIOR DOORS
Exterior doors to be wood.

SHINGLES
Shingles to be 20-year asphalt.

SIDING
Siding and exterior trim to be wood, pine clapboard, stained, with wood trim.

ENTRY STEPS
Entry steps to be pre-cast steps.

FLUE/CHIMNEY
Masonry flue to be installed in addition. Chimney to be concealed by drywall in family room and be capped with brick where it exits the roof.

PLUMBING
One toilet, one vanity and lavatory with faucet, one fiberglass bathtub/shower combination with faucet, and two hose-bibbs. All plumbing fixtures are priced based on being any of the standard colors. If high-fashion colors are desired, there will be an additional charge. Hot water will be provided by a domestic coil in the boiler of the heating system.

HEATING
Heating system will be a forced-hot-water system with baseboard heat, connected to the existing boiler.

ELECTRICAL
Electrical work will include wiring for all mechanical equipment, telephone jacks, smoke detectors, ground-fault circuit interrupters, and cable TV. The panel box will be upgraded to a 100 amp circuit-breaker system. The light fixture allowance will be $400, at builder's cost.

INSULATION
Exterior walls will be R-19 and attic will be R-38.

DRYWALL
Walls and ceilings to be $\frac{1}{2}$" drywall; bathroom will have $\frac{1}{2}$" moisture resistant drywall. All drywall to be prepared for paint.

INTERIOR DOORS AND TRIM
Interior doors will be flat, hollow-core lauan. Interior trim will be colonial beaded trim.

PAINT
All walls and ceiling will be primed and painted with one color paint. The standard color is off-white. Interior doors will be sealed and interior trim will be painted.

FLOOR COVERINGS
The bathroom will receive vinyl flooring. The remainder of the addition will have carpet as a finished floor. The finished floor allowance is $1,800, at builder's cost.

LANDSCAPING
Landscaping will include shrubbery along the front of the foundation, lawn seeding, and straw.

Payment will be as follows:

The amount due for this work is thirty-five thousand six hundred dollars ($35,600.00). This amount will be payable on a progress billing basis.

      If payment is not made according to the terms above, American Contractors (A/C) will have the following rights and remedies. A/C may charge a monthly service charge of one and one-half percent (1¹/₂%), eighteen percent (18%) per year, from the first day default is made. A/C may lien the property where the work has been done. A/C may use all legal methods in the collection of monies owed to A/C. A/C may seek compensation at the rate of $30.00 per hour for their employees attempting to collect unpaid monies. A/C may seek payment for legal fees and other costs of collection to the full extent that the law allows.

If A/C is requested to send men or material to a job by their customer or their customer's representative, the following policy shall apply. If a job is not ready for the service or material requested, and the delay is not due to A/C's actions, A/C may charge the customer for time spent. This charge will be at a rate of $30.00 per hour, per man, including travel time.

If you have any questions or do not understand this proposal, seek professional advice. Upon acceptance this becomes a binding contract between both parties.

Respectfully submitted,

Able Mann
General Manager

ACCEPTANCE

We the undersigned do hereby agree to and accept all the terms and conditions of this proposal. We fully understand the terms and conditions and hereby consent to enter into this contract.

American Contractors

by _____

Title _____

Date _____

Customer #1

_____

Date _____

Customer #2

_____

Date _____

CHANGE ORDER

This change order, dated this _____th day of _____, 19_____, shall become an integral part of the contract between the two parties below. This change order authorizes the following changes:

_____

_____

_____

_____

_____

_____

_____

_____

_____

_____

Due to these changes, the original contract amount will be adjusted in the following manner:

_____

_____

The above described changes are the only changes allowed and agreed to as of this date. No verbal changes will be recognized and any changes must be signed by all parties.

_____   _____
Customer   Contractor

LIEN WAIVER

The below-mentioned contractor/materialman (vendor) hereby acknowledges payment for all services and materials provided to _____ (customer), for the property located at _____, up to and including this date, this date being _____.

Said vendor is known as _____, and has provided the following services and/or materials:

_____

_____

_____

_____

For these services and/or materials, said vendor has received in payment, the sum of $_____.

With these payments, said vendor releases any lien interest he may hold against the aforementioned property and its owner as of this date.

_____   _____
Customer   Vendor

CONTROLLING YOUR EXPENSES

11

Rehab projects are full of the unexpected and are frequently feared for their reputation of costly unknown factors. Not all of your encounters will be devastating losses. You may begin making planned revisions, only to find the damage is not as bad as you thought. When this happens, the increased profit is a welcome surprise.

Pleasant discoveries are the exception, not the rule. More often, the unanticipated brings expensive adjustments into your plans. The best way to avoid this situation is a thorough inspection of the property and realistic cost forecasting. The amount budgeted for anticipated repairs should be based on standard-grade materials and average labor rates.

Once you have established a reasonable budget for your project, you can work toward reducing those costs. The purpose of this chapter is to show you ways to reduce your expenses without sacrificing the value of your investment.

As with any endeavor, establishing a feasible plan before beginning your project will increase your chances of success. With rehab work, one of your strongest allies is a realistic budget. You cannot seriously consider purchasing a property until you have projected the costs to improve and market it.

Arriving at this renovation figure is essential to projecting your profit and the bottom line. Negotiating for the lowest purchase price on the property is important. You will not know what a good price is, unless you take the cost of repairs into consideration. Building in too much of a safety zone for the rehab costs can cause you to look past a viable property. If you underestimate the repair expenses, your profit can be depleted rapidly.

COST PROJECTIONS

There are several factors affecting your budget projections. Labor and material costs are two of the largest influences. An effective budget should be based on widely accepted and appealing products. Local standard labor rates should be used to build your cost projection estimate. Determining which products to use can be as simple as calling a local building supply company. Describe your needs and ask for recommendations.

If the property is intended for resale, request information on attractive yet inexpensive and easy-to-install products. If the property is meant for your rental portfolio, tell the supplier. Request long-lasting products, with good warranties. Suppliers are accustomed to landlords asking for the cheapest materials on the market, so be sure to specify your requirements.

If you plan to retain the property as your personal rental property, you may desire a better grade of products. As a potential landlord, your rehab budget should be figured on products requiring the least attention and service, rather than cheap, inferior merchandise. The savings from cheap products are short term. If you buy cheap wallpaper for a bathroom, moisture may cause it to peel and fall off in three months. Controlling your expenses is not limited to acquisition and repair of the property. Any long-term expenditures require budgeting considerations as well.

Experienced investors often use broad-based estimates for labor and materials. They know the cost of new bathroom fixtures averages $600. When a project runs into unexpected complications or expenses, many people look for ways to shave the costs. Even veteran investors fall into the trap of bargain buying. An investor can be easily influenced by the least expensive products and lowest trade bids.

ALLOWING FOR PRICE INCREASES

This prejudice can adversely affect the outcome of the project. It can easily cost more than the money saved on the poor quality products. The solution is to refrain from cutting your budget projections to the bare minimum. Add 10% to your improvement cost projections. This lets you allow for price increases and unforeseen problems. The best way to maintain control of your investment is to analyze the work thoroughly before you begin.

MATERIAL DIFFERENCES

Look for opportunities to improve the curb appeal and value of a property. When a property is purchased strictly for resale, many investors believe the less money they spend, the more they will pocket. The truth is, when cheap materials are used, the finished job reflects it. When an investor does inferior work, the entire project can suffer. One of the most common misconceptions with investment properties is that inexpensive is good and cheap is even better. Don't get caught in this trap. Regardless of whether you plan to use a property for resale or rental, you must consider the effect of the materials used on the property's value and appeal.

Some so-called improvements will send tenants and buyers alike running in the opposite directions. The worst thing you can do is spend money on an alteration that detracts from your property. Although this sounds like simple logic, you would be surprised how many investors take the shoddy way out. There are plenty of ways to make money on investment property without cutting crucial corners.

Kitchens

Bathrooms and kitchens will sell or rent your property the fastest, yet these areas are notorious for mediocre improvements. A typical mistake in the kitchen is to leave non-functional space untouched. Another is to avoid cabinet repairs or replacements by painting over the cabinets. Kitchens are not only intended for food preparation, but for eating, working, and storage as well.

When the condition of the kitchen is improved, the desirability of the entire property increases. To be attractive, the kitchen must be both utilitarian and comfortable. Keep this in mind when pricing your intended improvements. If the kitchen is small, you should look for ways to improve the visual appearance and storage space. Add an island countertop and cabinet or pantry unit. Replace badly damaged countertops. Regardless of the work you do, strive to make the kitchen new, clean, open, and functional. Many options exist to contain these expenses.

Slapping a coat of paint over everything, including the cabinets, is seldom the best use of your money. Although you should avoid replacing items unnecessarily, attempt to increase the property's value with every dollar you spend. When adding to existing cabinets and tops, matching materials is a perplexing consideration. If duplicating the pattern or product is not cost effective, don't make do with materials that just come close. You should always think in terms of market appeal.

Would you be inclined to buy a house with mismatched countertops and a bulging vinyl floor? There are two easy ways to consolidate original and current conditions. First, give the new item a reason to look different. Second, divert attention from the difference between the old and new product.

COUNTERTOPS. For example, assume the counter has a large burned area near the sink. When the damage is limited to a specific area, consider replacing it with a built-in cutting board. A cutting block or any number of acrylic materials can be used to convert this ugly eyesore into an attractive, functional work space.

Let's assume you want to add an eat-in bar area to the kitchen. This will make the kitchen more serviceable while adding the value and convenience of the eat-in feature. Maybe the old countertop is in fair condition, but has a faded speckled pattern. Butting a new top directly to the existing top will make the original counter look dull and old. Presented with this scenario, many investors either abandon the bar idea, or go ahead and piece the kitchen together with different tops. The proper procedure requires replacing the existing countertop. To save money, inexperienced investors opt to take the least expensive path to completion. They try to make do with conflicting countertops.

In this case, you need to divert attention from the seam. This can be done by installing a pantry unit against the end of the existing counter. Attach the new bar to the side of the pantry and you have solved several problems at once. The cost of the pantry is comparable to the cost of replacing the old countertop. While you have not saved money, you have gotten more for your money. The pantry adds storage to the kitchen and increases its serviceability.

The bar does not detract from the original counter; moreover, the eat-in area boosts the value of the property. Your cost is contained, and the property's worth increases. Minimizing your investment is effective, as long as it does not detract from the value of the property.

CABINETS. Assume the kitchen has antiquated, scarred cabinets. Rather than incurring the expense to replace them completely, consider installing new cabinet *fronts*.

This process gives a fresh, innovative look to an old kitchen for less than the cost of replacing the existing cabinets. When settling or moisture has caused ceilings and walls to sag out of plumb, cabinet fronts can be the most cost-effective improvement alternative. When the walls or ceiling are not plumb, hanging new cabinets is a technical nightmare. It will be all but impossible to make new cabinets hang properly. Refacing the old cabinets is easier, less expensive, and very effective.

What if the previous owner suffocated the cabinets with numerous coats of paint? Stripping the paint will produce unknown results. Chances are, the cabinets were in rough shape before they were camouflaged with paint. Decorative brass or porcelain hardware and pulls will give these cabinets a simple, economical facelift. The expense is minimal, but the result is impressive. There is a big difference between economical and cheap.

ELECTRICAL. The changes you make can be inexpensive and still enhance the property. Lighting and outlet usage are other items to appraise in rehab properties. If you will be keeping the house as a rental, check the electrical capacity of the kitchen.

To avoid blowing circuits or burning out old wiring, consider having an electrician run separate circuits in the kitchen. An array of small appliances can put heavy demands on a circuit. Something as simple as a coffee maker and toaster will put a strain on an inadequate circuit.

APPLIANCES. Microwave ovens are another load not anticipated with old kitchen wiring. These now common appliances did not exist when many homes were wired. Although you can't increase the rent or raise the sale price because of them, split circuits will eliminate future complaints. To improve the function and appearance of the kitchen, add under-the-cabinet lights. This small improvement increases desirability and will set your property apart from others.

If kitchen appliances need to be replaced, a 16 cubic-foot refrigerator and basic range are acceptable. If the property will be resold, consider giving the buyers an appliance allowance instead of replacing the items. This way, the size, style, and color of the appliances you might have purchased will not deter the home buyer in any way. Impress the buyers with your willingness to allow them to pick the appliances of their choice.

Calculate the allowance amount with builder grade products. Average contractor-discount cost for a refrigerator is about $475, and figure around $325 for a basic range. Given this option, many buyers will accept the old appliances and use the $800 allowance for closing costs or other improvements. This alternative can be the deciding factor in the sale of the property.

Bathrooms

As you assess the work to be done, look for ways to achieve maximum return for your dollar. Some of the worst offenders to this principle are bathrooms. I see more shortcuts in workmanship and cheap products in bathroom improvements than anywhere else. This is particularly alarming because bathrooms are responsible for much of the decision to purchase a home. Artificial tile-board, $12 faucets, peeling wallpaper, and cheap plastic tub surrounds are at the top of the list. Using these products is like trying to put out a fire by throwing gasoline on it. Not only does the original problem still exist, but the remedy has become a complication, rather than a cure.

WALLS. Fake tile panels must have their place, but for the life of me, I don't know where. Usually I see them glued on top of existing tile tub enclosures and bathroom walls. If the tile in your target property is damaged, consider alternatives to the marbleized partitions. Limit your replacement costs by attempting to save as much of the original tile as possible. Many people are discouraged by the difficulty in matching existing tile with a new product. The colors never seem to match, no matter how hard you try. But the supplier of your replacement tile can be the bathroom itself.

Consider your bathroom improvement plans. Will you be replacing a wall-hung sink with a vanity? Will you be installing a new toilet? If so, remove the tile from inside the new vanity and from behind the toilet. This tile may be used to replace the bad tile in the exposed areas of the bathroom. Tile from these locations can be repaired with new tile. If the colors are slightly different, it will not be noticed in these inconspicuous places.

If you need more replacement tile, consider removing a row of tile from the walls. Most walls have a contoured finish tile on the top row. This top row of trim tile is often a different color from the rest of the tile. Removing the next row of regular tile will give you plenty of product to work with. It also provides you with the opportunity to enhance the top row of tile with an additional section of flattering tile. The result is an elegant finished product.

Perhaps the tile walls are buckled from the effects of settling or moisture damage. Don't go out and buy wall panels to hide the problem. A wiser use of your money is to rip out the tile walls completely and replace them with water-resistant drywall. If you keep the property as a rental, you will have circumvented additional disintegration of the walls. When selling the property, you have improved the visual appearance of the bathroom.

Many bathroom walls only need cosmetic attention. A vinyl wallpaper with moisture-proof adhesive is a simple solution. It will repel water and resist mold better than standard wallpaper. If wallpaper is too expensive, paint the walls with a high quality bathroom paint. These special paints are designed for use in moist locations. You can even get paint with a mildew-resisting agent in it.

AVOID OVER-SPENDING

With expensive properties, many investors are tempted to over-invest in improvements. They move away from the problem of underspending by going to the extreme of purchasing extravagant items. Expensive, high fashion colors and unique fixtures are a big risk. High-tech appliances, with all the bells and whistles, do not guarantee a high return of your investment. Standard colors and products, in keeping with the surrounding neighborhood, should be used to maintain an accurate budget.

Don't be coerced by suppliers or contractors into upgrading products. If the other houses on the block all have vanities, don't be talked into buying a signature-grade pedestal sink with gold faucets. Resist the temptation to authorize workmen to upgrade the project. Keep your job on track with your budgeted figures. Center your improvements around reasonable costs and standard, acceptable products.

DON'T UNDERESTIMATE THE NEEDED SKILLS

Many people are intimidated by the concept of hiring a contractor to do work for them. They are convinced contractors will take advantage of them, forcing them to spend more money on repairs than necessary. Others feel it is ridiculous to pay someone else to do work, which they believe anyone with a hammer and half a brain could do. Don't let the apparent simplicity of a job cloud your judgment. Even experienced remodeling contractors are not adept in every phase of home improvement.

Unless you have extensive skills and experience, leave the labor to professionals. Attempting a project yourself may save money initially, but in the end, your rental and resale potential can be adversely affected. Profitable rehab projects rely on quick turnaround and controlled expenses.

Take painting as an example. On a small ranch house, a professional contractor can finish painting the entire interior in a couple of days. The cost will be about $800. Now add up the cost of doing the job yourself. First you need to purchase the materials: paint, thinner, brushes, rollers, tape, scrapers, tarps, ladder (if you don't have one), etc. Next, estimate how long it will take you to finish the job.

Working on the project full-time, it may take you a week to do the job a professional will do in two days. If you don't have a week of free time to paint, you will have to do the job at night. Calculate the cost of your time to do the work. Have you increased your turnaround time? Have you significantly decreased your expenses? Anytime you consider working on the project yourself, analyze these two areas.

You may find aspects of the work that *are* beneficial to do yourself. Phases such as installing decorative shelving and trim, landscaping, weatherstripping, cleanup, and putting in insulation are typical choices. For those areas beyond your skills, hire a professional. Don't let your lack of knowledge discourage you from using contractors. There are many effective ways to negotiate with contractors to get the best job for your money. This is another way of controlling your expenses and preserving your budget estimates.

ESTABLISH PRODUCT REQUIREMENTS

Before you begin contacting contractors, establish what product lines you want included in the work. If you will be using the property for rental, you will want reliable products with strong warranties. If you are improving the house for resale, consider your market and use appropriate products. After speaking with building suppliers to determine what brands to use, create a specifications sheet.

Eventually, you may end up using some other form of materials list, but this will give you a starting point. When you call contractors, you want to look as organized and informed as possible. Refer to the Specifications Sheet at the end of the chapter. It can be used to list your job specifications.

GETTING BIDS

The next step is to assume a dominant position. Contact several contractors to price the same work and let each know you are soliciting bids. This creates a sense of rivalry, and the contractors will usually give more competitive quotes. The key to reliable price quotes is having each contractor bid the job in exactly the same way. Specify exactly what materials and work you want done—don't allow any

substitutions. If a contractor insists there is a more cost-effective way to do the work, have him list the change as a separate bid. If you don't retain consistency in your quotes, you will never be able to determine the best price.

Analyzing the Bids

Once you receive written quotes for the job, you can start to compare them. Scrutinize the following areas:

1. Look at the materials outlined in the various bids. Each quote should include the same list of fixtures, cabinets, products, and materials.

2. Beware of the phrase "or equal," after the specified products. This is an obscure way of saying the contractor will be in control of your product line and may intend to use substitutions.

3. Compare the commencement and completion dates. A low price loses its value if it takes the contractor twice as long to complete the job.

4. Evaluate the description of the work to be done. Credible quotes should detail every aspect of the job. There should be no question in your mind as to the scope of the work or the materials provided. The amount and location of insulation, number of coats of paint, preparation and clean-up responsibilities, and total yards of flooring should all be itemized. If a contractor's price requires you to provide materials or haul trash away, you will need to add that cost to his bid.

5. Analyze the payment schedules. Many trades require a third of the contract price to start the job, a third when the work is half done, and the balance upon completion. Ideally, you should negotiate for a small amount upon commencement, and a 10% or 15% retainage after completion. Contracts specifying large up-front payments should not be accepted.

Choosing a Contractor

Review any recommendations the contractors have made to cut production time or costs. Then make the final decision on exactly how the job will be performed. Finally, be sure to check the contractor's references. Remember, the contractor is going to give you names of satisfied (or possibly bogus) customers. Asking the right questions, in the right way, will provide you with the most unbiased responses. Some examples are:

❑ What kind of work did Mr. Contractor do for you? If you do not describe the work the contractor mentioned, you may discover a discrepancy in the referral's response.

❑ How many substitutions or changes were made on your job? This will give you a feeling for the ability of the contractor to stick to your specifications. If the answer is none, ask the question again. Almost every job encounters at least minor or unforeseen changes.

❑ Please confirm your relationship to Mr. Contractor. This is a trick question and will quickly reveal Mr. Contractor's uncles, girlfriends, and next door neighbors. By asking the question, the referral assumes the contractor has described some sort of relationship. Those with no affiliation to the contractor will answer accordingly.

Negotiating Your Price

Once you have weeded through the proposals and confirmed references, you can begin your bargaining sessions. Of course, the easiest way to lower the price is to ask for the contractor's bottom line. Usually, he will tell you the quote is the lowest price. If so, try to decrease the price by making your job appealing or beneficial to the contractor. An effective way to do this is to ask the contractor some key questions. This is the mediation phase of reducing your expenses. If you can satisfy a need the contractor has, you can negotiate for a better price.

First, find out how long he has been in business. A new company will be looking to build a list of references. Offer to write a letter of recommendation after the job has been satisfactorily completed. This should be worth a slight price drop. Keep in mind that contractors rely on your work to make a living. If you are dealing with an established contractor, point out the benefits of the volume business you can provide as a rehabber.

If you purchase properties for resale, there will be more jobs like this one for the contractor to do

in the future. If you are planning to rent the property, express your interest in using the contractor for impending maintenance and repair work. Describe your relationship with real estate brokers and the volume of work they could provide the contractor. Get the contractor looking beyond this project to the prospect of additional income and referrals. An active investor can easily keep good contractors busy doing rehab work. This should entitle you to a volume discount.

The art of skillful negotiating will serve you well throughout your rehab project. Negotiations start with the initial acquisition. Then your next major negotiations will be with suppliers and contractors. The skills used for each of these bargaining sessions are different. Your dealings with suppliers and contractors carry parallel characteristics, but the methods differ. You learned how to negotiate for the best acquisition price in Chapter 6. Now you are going to get a crash course in professional techniques to find the best labor and material for the lowest price.

Some of these tactics were described earlier in the chapter; this is a consolidation and expansion of negotiating tools to use with suppliers and contractors. The first step of this phase requires you to be organized and well prepared. You must know what you want and how you want it before fishing for the final price. Having a detailed plan and a comprehensive specifications sheet is mandatory. You will want all your vendors and contractors to bid identical products and scopes of work. When you have your information consolidated into bid packages, start the assault for low prices.

Getting to the Meat

Deliver your plans and specifications to at least four suppliers. At the same time, deliver bid packages to four general contractors. If you are acting as the general, distribute the bid packages to appropriate subcontractors. Tell all the bidders there are other bidders and place a deadline on the time for bids to be received. When setting the bid deadline, be reasonable. Allow the competitors adequate time to produce accurate bids. If the deadline is too close, your bids will be thrown together and may omit items or contain mistakes.

While you are waiting for responses to your bid requests, begin interviewing brokers to sell your property. Incorporate their input into your final decisions. Don't simply accept their recommendations, make the broker provide justifiable, indisputable evidence before changing your plans. On most rehab projects, you should begin receiving bid responses in two or three days. Make good use of your time while waiting for the bids to come in.

Once you have a majority of the bids in hand, examine each of them very closely. When going over the bids, don't allow yourself to be distracted. Seek a quiet place to study the bids. If you are answering the phone or doing multiple tasks while reviewing the bids, you may miss a critical component of the bid.

Check each bid for accuracy and compliance with your request. Note the dates on the bids. When were the quotes prepared, and how long are the prices guaranteed? It is not unusual for bidders to delete a costly item intentionally in order to be low bidder. When approached, they will claim a computer error or an oversight is responsible for the omission. This tactic is used to snare the buyer looking only at the bottom line. Most quotes from suppliers are not guaranteed prices. They disclaim this somewhere within the quote.

SELLING A SALESMAN

Everyone you are dealing with is a salesman. Each of them is trying to win your business, and some of them will stoop to trickery to do it. Contractors generally provide their price in the form of a proposal. These proposals are frequently guaranteed for thirty days but may still contain clauses allowing for discrepancies from your bid request. Reviewing the quotes and proposals requires careful attention. You cannot afford to assume anything.

When you are convinced you have arrived at the two best offers from each trade or vendor, the game begins. Beware of exceptionally low prices. Professionals should have bid prices with no more than a 10% variance. If you get a price way below the other three, proceed with extreme caution. It could be an excellent deal, but it is more likely a mistake or a trap.

With your target vendors and contractors selected, contact them and arrange a personal meeting. Start with the higher of the two best bids. This meeting will give you experience without risking your apparent best price. Take copies of your bid package with you to the meeting. Once the social conversation is out of the way, ask the bidder to explain his bid to you. As the bidder explains what is included in his bid, follow his progression with your bid package.

When the supplier says he has included twelve double-hung wood windows, with insulated glass, you must confirm the brand and model number. Do the brand and model number conform to your specifications? If you spec a window with a retail price of $275 and their window is a different brand, you have no concept of the value of their bid. Everyone must, I repeat, must, bid identical products and work requirements. If there are variances in these categories, you will not be able to make a true evaluation of the bids.

Supplier bids are the easiest to decide on. The suppliers are providing identical products for a given price. When you are sure the products are identical, you can base your decision solely on the price. The only variable with suppliers is their ability to meet your delivery date. You have a tangible product to compare each supplier's price with. This is much easi14er than the contractor's bid.

Contractors are providing labor. Workmanship is difficult to standardize. The best you can do is to require all work to comply with local building code requirements. This leaves a lot to the imagination. Finishing drywall to meet local codes is one thing, finishing it to meet your approval is quite another. There are wide-ranging differences in the quality of workmanship.

Craftsmanship is largely intangible and difficult to specify. Knowing the contractor will complete your job in a timely fashion is hard to define. This aspect of the intangibles can be controlled with a strict contract. To satisfy yourself as to the contractor's ability, you must see work he or she has done in the past. Check references and require the contractors to show you work in progress and completed. When you are satisfied that the contractor is capable of providing the type of work you require, begin negotiations.

SHOP IN PHASES

Assuming you know the vendors and contractors you wish to do business with, you are left with negotiating for the best price. With suppliers, you must look deeper than the total price of your materials. Most suppliers will have several items priced higher than their competition. This may not be reflected in the total price. Unless you are determined to deal only with a single supplier, you can save money by shopping phases of the job.

A supplier with the best cabinet prices may be higher than the competition on light fixtures. It is not unusual to find large price differences in different phases of materials. A supplier with great lumber prices may have lousy window and door prices. Shopping for the various phases can save thousands of dollars. It is wise to limit your shopping to specific phases. It is counter-productive to buy some of your cabinets from one vendor and the remainder from another. Your delivery schedules will be hard to coordinate, and the savings will be minimal, if they exist at all.

Don't assume you must accept a subcontractor's price for labor and material. Subcontractors normally mark up the material they provide. You could save hundreds of dollars by supplying the material for the subcontractor. The sub may not like the idea of working with your material, but most will, if it is the only way they can get the job. Some subcontractors increase their labor rate when working with owner-supplied materials. Some of this increase may be justified. If you are inefficient in the material procurement, the sub loses time and money. This is an area you will have to work out with each subcontractor.

Offering to help the workers will not save you much money. In many cases, it will cost you more money. The contractors are professionals. When an inexperienced layman works with them, it slows the professionals down. If you are considering working with the contractor, verify the price with and without your help. You may be surprised how little your time and effort are worth to the contractor.

THE CLINCHERS

In your negotiations, there are several trump cards you can play. You can attempt to convince the bidder you plan to do many more rehabs and are looking to build a long-term relationship. In the case of contractors, you can offer your property as a job reference. You can bargain for a better price in return for allowing the contractor to place a sign on your job. This is cost-effective, quality advertising for the contractor. Allowing the work to be done on a flexible schedule can save money.

Contractors need fill-in jobs to keep their crews busy during odd hours. If they have a scheduled job postponed, your job can mean the difference between productive time and down time. This type of arrangement is risky to the rehabber. It works well for a homeowner, but you are affected by lost time in the completion of your project. Use this strategy sparingly, with subs who don't affect your overall completion date.

The easiest tool to use against suppliers is their competition. Show them their competitor's prices and ask them to give you their best number. Don't abuse this technique. If you make multiple rounds to the suppliers, trying to drive the prices increasingly lower, you may find yourself without a supplier. Doing the show-and-tell routine once is effective; doing it repetitively is dangerous.

Throughout your negotiations, don't allow substitutions in the bids. If you decide to make changes in your plans or specifications, allow all bidders to price the changes. Once your budget and selections are made, stick to them. Wandering between ideas causes confusion and unwarranted expenses. With proper negotiation tactics, you can arrive at desirable prices.

When the best prices have been obtained, you need to lock them in. Require suppliers to make firm commitments on delivery dates and prices. Include a penalty clause in your agreement to discourage the supplier from delaying your job. These same elements are essential in the agreement between you and your contractors. For the contractors, include a start and completion date in your contract. In both cases, use highly detailed specifications, and don't allow substitution clauses. Solid written agreements are your best protection against unexpected price increases.

SAMPLE SPECIFICATIONS SHEET

DEMOLITION: All debris to be removed from the property

SUBFLOOR: $^3/_4$" T&G 4-ply plywood

UNDERLAYMENT: $^1/_4$" lauan

PARTITIONS: 2" x 4", 16" on center, double top plate

WIRING: To code

HEATING: To code

INSULATION: R-19 in walls, R-38 in ceiling

DRYWALL: $^1/_2$", taped and sanded, ready for paint

PAINT: 1 coat of primer, 2 coats of latex white paint

TRIM: Colonial, stain-grade, stained in walnut color

DOORS: Six-panel, pine, stained in walnut color

HARDWARE: Simulated brass

WINDOWS: Wood, double-hung, energy efficient

CARPET: FHA/VA approved material, with pad

(This list could go on for as many items as you may be contracting for. In your specifications, detail name brands and model numbers.)

HIGHEST AND BEST USE 12

The fastest track to becoming a real estate mogul is making the most of what you have. Rehab projects provide exceptional opportunities to create quick cash. Buying, improving, and selling real estate is absolutely one of the most profitable real estate activities. Extending your real estate reach can fill out your money pouch. When you are evaluating properties to rehab, give serious consideration to changing more than the property's appearance.

Rehabbing rundown buildings produces profits in a matter of months. With an added dimension, you can increase these profits by thousands of dollars. The increase can be immediate; as soon as you own the property, these profits can exist. Typically, it will take a little paperwork and time to realize the profits. The time required to reap your reward is decided by many factors. This added dimension is the act of changing the use of the property. It is commonly referred to as obtaining the *highest and best use* of a property.

This endeavor is probably the quickest way to get rich with real estate. When you combine changing a property's use with rehab work, you set the stage for becoming a millionaire. Highest-and-best-use principles apply to single-family homes, as well as commercial buildings. Raw land is also a frequent contender for use conversion. Anything that is real estate has potential for a change of use to create wealth. Whether your forte is single-family homes or apartment buildings, don't overlook the potential for added income from changing the present use.

Favorable conditions for use conversion often exist with no one even noticing. As an investment broker and a consultant, I have used this method to build a stable of happy investors. My activities have primarily concentrated on buildings with twelve apartments or less. In most instances, the most profitable deals involved small multi-family units (four units or less) and single-family homes. Raw land has played a part in my endeavors, but the risks with raw land are much higher.

RAW LAND

Dealing in land is tempting but carries a high risk. Buying a piece of land to convert to a shopping center looks great on paper. The numbers work on the spreadsheet, and your projected earnings promise to make you a millionaire. This is where the good news usually ends. Unless you are an accomplished developer with an enormous net worth, you are buying into bankruptcy. Major land development projects take years to complete. Getting all the required approvals is a science, and carrying the cost of the land is a heavy burden.

Sellers will not want to tie up their property for years with a contingent contract while you seek approval. Unless you can afford to buy the land and carry the holding cost for years, stay away from land developing. Even after years of lobbying for approval, your project may never see success. Land development is best left to the heavyweight pros. If you get stuck with only the land you bought, what will you do with it? You have to pay for it, and it can be hard to sell. Land is difficult to finance and if your development efforts fail, you will not likely see a profit. Land does not appreciate well, and your carry costs and engineering-study fees will be lost.

EXISTING STRUCTURES

The best reason to buy land is to gain the structure on it. Concentrate on existing buildings. Changing the use of an existing building is much easier than grandstanding with flashy land development plans. Keeping a low profile is very advantageous in real estate investing. If others know your plans, they will attempt to beat you to the deal or block the deal out of jealousy. Learning to assess a property's potential for conversion will add thousands to your retained earnings. Depending on others to bring the properties to you increases your risk of buying a dud. Only the most ethical and elite brokers will give you a windfall deal.

Rehab work requires buying property and refurbishing it. Changing the use of a structure often requires a change in the building's physical condition. These two highly rewarding ventures go hand in hand. Why not direct your rehab efforts at making the most of your newly acquired asset? For the remainder of this chapter, you will learn how to blend these two efforts together.

SINGLE-FAMILY HOMES

Single-family homes are where most new investors begin their rehab careers. Changes in the use of single-family homes are difficult to achieve. These homes are commonly situated in subdivisions zoned only for residential use. To capitalize on change-of-use benefits with single-family homes, you must extend the parameters of your search. Homes located along the road in growing towns are a prime target. Single-family residences found in rural settings offer a change-of-use potential, and homes near proposed new developments have possibilities.

In our first example, the subject property is a single-family home on the edge of town. The house has land fronting on a road leading into town. This small town is growing every year, and the demand for office and retail space is increasing. The house is a large two-story home with a spacious lawn surrounding it. There is a two-car garage in the right rear corner of the lot, and the house is in need of substantial repairs.

The house is owned by an out-of-state owner and is being used as residential rental property. Af-ter seeing the house, you pay a visit to the tax assessor's office and the zoning office. You find the name and address of the owner and the tax value of the property. Then you check with the zoning officials to determine the legal uses of the property.

After conferring with the zoning officials, you know the property may be used for professional office space. Ask the zoning officer to give you a brief letter confirming this as a legal use. Ask that the letter clearly state the property may be used for any professional office use, with no conditions. Upon returning to your home or office, you reflect on the potential for the property.

After contemplating all your options, you decide the house is well worth pursuing. The next step requires contacting the out-of-state owner. Draft a letter, on plain writing paper, expressing your interest in purchasing the property. Don't use company letterhead or identify yourself as an investor. Lend the impression of being interested in the property for your personal residence. Explain to the owner that you have seen the exterior of the home and are very interested in buying it. Try to arrange a meeting to view the interior of the property.

An out-of-state owner is a prime pick for this type of buying strategy. She may be tired of being a long-distance landlord and welcome your interest in buying her burden. Since the house is not presently being offered for sale, you may not receive a response from your first letter. If this happens, mail a second letter and wait for a reply. In the meantime, look for other suitable properties in the same zoning area with similar characteristics. When you get an interested owner to respond to your letter, get ready to make major money.

Cashing In

Using the other skills learned in this book, acquire the property at the lowest possible price. Bear in mind that the price you are paying is based on the property's value as a single-family home. Once you own the property and the tenants are out, secure your needed permits. These may include permits for building, mechanical systems, signs, and change-of-use. As soon as the permits are in hand, you can begin to build your fortune.

Using the rehab skills contained in this book, start the conversion of the property. Since this house was in bad shape and was priced accordingly, you can afford a major rehabilitation. When designing the changes, plan on the property being used by professionals. Try to make the changes in a way that residential use is still possible if professional tenants are not available. Obviously, you will need more bathrooms, new plumbing, new wiring, and a new heating system. Arrange these systems so they may be individually metered to serve the professional tenants.

Make a Template

Consider handicap access facilities and clearance requirements. Walk through modern professional offices before rehabbing your property. Make lists of the types of accommodations in these modern buildings and use them as a template for your building. When you have a solid design plan, begin the demo work. Remove the necessary partitions and rebuild the space to your specifications.

Evaluate the garage and determine whether it should be removed or converted into private storage facilities. Since you have a spacious wraparound lawn, private storage may be the highest and best use for the garage. If its presence precludes parking space, remove it and use the area for parking. The exterior of the building should be rehabbed to give it an attractive professional appearance.

Outside Appearance

Your outside renovations should be completed before seeking a buyer or tenant. First impressions are important, and you want your prospect's first look to be a favorable one. When you have reached the construction stage of finished drywall, begin advertising the property for sale or rent, depending upon your preference. It will be much easier for a buyer or tenant to visualize the finished product with the drywall in place. The drywall will also conceal the age of the interior of the structure.

The Results

Starting the advertising at this stage reduces your holding expenses and produces your profits early. When your rehab project is complete, you will have created an astonishing asset from a rundown single-family home. Instead of having a renovated home with a rehab profit of ten or fifteen thousand dollars, you have an office building. The building and change-of-use conversion have made it possible for your profits to exceed $50,000. This is not a bad increase in profits for spending a few hours researching the possible uses of the property.

MULTI CONVERSIONS

The next example is centered on a single-family home in a rural setting just outside of town. This is a rambling two-story farmhouse with several acres of land. The plumbing, heating, and electrical systems are all in need of replacement. The interior of the house is sound but not appealing to the eye. The kitchen and bathroom were added on to the house and form an L-shaped design. There is an old barn with a loft near the house. It is structurally sound and has a pleasant exterior appearance. A couple purchased this home to remodel but are now getting a divorce. They are motivated sellers and willing to sell cheap.

Do you have any ideas of how to maximize the value of this property? Well, the first step is checking the legal uses for the property with the zoning office. In this case, the rural residential zoning allows multi-family dwellings with up to four apartments. Are you starting to get ideas now? Follow similar research steps as explained in the first example. When you have written confirmation on the accepted uses of the property, make your inspection of the home.

This house offers the chance for a conversion into a multi-family building. The conversion will give a positive cash flow from rental income. It will also make the real estate value skyrocket. Looking at design is important with any rehab project, and it is equally important in change-of-use projects. This house has several design bonuses.

Seeing Opportunity

The barn is in good structural condition and can be converted into a two-story duplex. The exterior appearance can be retained to add charm to the overall property. The farmhouse can be split into two apartments. There may be one downstairs apartment and another upstairs, or you may be able to modify the home into two townhouse-style apartments.

Removing the roof from the kitchen and bathroom addition allows you to extend the addition upward to include the second floor. Before doing this, have a professional inspect the foundation and supporting timbers to determine whether it is feasible to add the second story. Extending this addition skyward provides space for another kitchen and bath in the new upstairs apartment. Having the kitchen and bathroom stacked over each other reduces your plumbing costs.

One potential big expense in this conversion is the water and sewer service for the apartments. If the property is using a well and septic system, the cost to expand the systems could be considerable. Take these types of dormant expenses into account before extending yourself too far. The value of a four-unit multi-family building will far exceed that of a single-family farmhouse.

MAKING THE MOST OF EXISTING CONDITIONS

Single-family homes often provide opportunities for interior changes to increase their value. Finding the highest and best use of a home does not have to mean changing its purpose of use. It can be as simple as making the most of existing conditions to increase the home's merit. Locating a home with an expandable attic or an unfinished basement can offer this possibility. Adding two bedrooms and a bathroom in the attic can add thousands of dollars to a home's resale value.

If the home lends itself to attic conversion, it deserves your attention. Pay attention to the appraisal techniques in Chapter 5 and explore your expansion alternatives. If the location, surrounding properties, and existing construction support the improvement, buy the house and add the living space. Attic conversions are a highly cost-effective way to obtain habitable square footage. Your per-square-foot cost is minimal, and the new space will appraise for much more.

An average attic allows enough space for two bedrooms and a bathroom. You may use dormers to add light and head space. Basements offer similar possibilities, but the return on your investment is generally lower. Unless the basement has normal windows and the ability for ground level ingress and

egress, your remodeling money is harder to recover. Basement conversions require extensive thought and research. Before you plan on pouring money into a basement, be sure it will not be buried and irretrievable.

Taking the Roof Off

When zoning laws allow, adding an apartment over an existing garage can be worthwhile. Most two-car garages house adequate space for an apartment to be added over them. Removing the roof and replacing it with a gambrel-style roof provide the space needed. Adding this apartment increases the property value and its desirability. It can be used as income property, an in-law apartment, or a studio. Evaluate your mechanical system costs and the feasibility for a supporting appraisal of the apartment. Some areas will not warrant this type of rehab and change of use. Use discretion, but always look for a way to squeeze more value from your rehab investment.

CREATIVE BUYING WITH MULTI-FAMILY PROPERTIES

This type of creative buying extends into existing multi-family properties. Purchasing a rundown duplex and adding one or two apartments produce tremendous income opportunities. Perhaps you will buy a six-family building and convert it to mixed-use. Highest and best use does not have to involve grandiose modifications. There are many simple changes possible to increase a multi-family building's income.

A few of these exploitable modifications can be done with very little money and still produce large equity gains. In multi-family properties, their value is hugely affected by their gross income. Something as simple as adding a coin-operated laundry can increase a six-unit building's value by thousands of dollars.

Winning with Coins

Using a gross rent multiplier will give you an idea of the effect your minor income improvements will have on a property. To determine a rule-of-thumb gross income multiplier for your building, use the following formula. Divide the property's appraised value by the amount of the past year's gross income. The resulting number will be the gross income multiplier.

If your building is worth $261,000 and your gross income is $29,000, the gross income multiplier for your property is nine. If you install a coin-operated laundry, how much is the improvement likely to be worth? Assume you earn seventy-five cents for every load of clothes washed and a dollar and a quarter for every load dried. This is a total of two dollars for every load of clothes going through your laundry. If you have three-bedroom apartments, it would not be unreasonable to estimate each tenant will do three loads of clothes per week. If all six units produce these results, you have earned thirty-six dollars for the week.

For simplicity of mathematics, assume a gross income of thirty-six dollars per week for fifty-two weeks. Your annual gross income from the laundry is $1,872. Using the gross income multiplier of nine, multiply the added income by nine. The result of this equation is a staggering $16,848 in increased value. The cost of adding and operating the laundry varies with every building, but it is well worth considering.

In reality, you will have to allow for vacancies and reduced annual usage. Not all your tenants will patronize your facilities, and you will have operating expenses, maintenance, and possibly vandalism to ponder. Other factors will affect your building's appraised value, and you will not see a full equity gain of $16,848. Even with these detriments, the improvement is very cost effective. This is a good example of obtaining the highest and best use from minor modifications. There will be more on advantageous improvements in Chapter 14.

Making Space

If you are inclined to larger rehab projects, consider converting residential buildings to mixed-use or adding sleeping space. Many cities offer the opportunity for these conversions. Multi-family buildings with six to twelve units are common fixtures along city streets. These buildings offer many possibilities for making money; let's look at a few of them.

The number of bedrooms in an apartment usually dictates the amount of rent the dwelling will yield. As stated before, the value of rental property is chiefly determined by the amount of income pro-

duced. If you can find a way to expand the number of bedrooms, you will most likely be able to increase the rent. Your rental increase will drive the value of the building upward. Finding unused or improperly used space to convert into a bedroom can be perplexing. Here are a few hints for where to begin your quest for additional bedrooms.

Bedrooms don't have to be large to be profitable. A small room serves well as a nursery for infants. A moderate-sized room with about 75 square feet of space meets the needs of a young child. When looking for a way to add bedrooms, don't prejudice yourself into looking for large rooms. In apartment environments, even a small extra bedroom will give you an edge over the competition.

Look Outside

The first place to look for a hidden bedroom is outside the building. If this statement shocks you, don't feel bad. When I advise investors of this technique, they give me some strange looks. Their first question is how can they find room for a bedroom outside the building. Most large multi-family buildings don't have enough land to construct an addition, and if they did, the cost would be prohibitive. This is true enough, but the outside of the building can provide the space you are searching for.

Many older buildings are equipped with roofed porches and balconies. These exterior appurtenances offer exciting possibilities for bedrooms. Beefing up the supports of these attached floors is not difficult. Roofs are already in place and enclosing the porch or balcony is not a major project. Bedrooms don't require plumbing, and the heating and electrical demands are minimal. This is a prime illustration of taking advantage of the highest and best use of your existing construction.

Closet Capers

If your property does not have porches or balconies, look to storage closets. Numerous older buildings have storage closets recessed into the apartments and accessible from the hall. By sealing the hallway door and installing an interior door, you have an almost instant nursery. Heat and electrical components are the only other elements required to transform these closets into sleeping facilities.

Add a Wall

Some apartments have large kitchens and small dining rooms. When this is the case, convert the dining room into a bedroom. A simple partition wall and door is all it takes to make a dining room a bedroom. The kitchen can become an eat-in kitchen with less trouble and less money. The places you can find for a bedroom are different with every building. The important thing is to look for a way to add an inexpensive bedroom.

MIX THE USE

City buildings may be adaptable to mixed-use. Check with the zoning department and code enforcement office before attempting this rehab project. If everything is in compliance, run the numbers on converting the ground-floor apartments into retail or office space. Commercial and professional space fetches higher rents than residential apartments. Your conversion cost will be moderate, and the building's value should escalate nicely.

Plan on adding glass fronts or large windows on the street side of the ground floor. The interior of the units can be opened up by removing non-bearing partitions. Load-bearing walls can be opened up by using posts at each end and a beam across the top of the posts. Adding the glass and removing selected interior partitions gives the rental unit the appearance of a larger space. Using light colors for walls and floor coverings further adds to the appearance of spaciousness. If you want an even larger illusion, install mirrors on one of the largest walls. The reflections add depth and increase the look of expansiveness.

KNOW YOUR MARKET

Before taking these actions, perform a market study on the area. The study will determine what need exists for additional business space and the types of spaces needed most. Always look below the surface of your potential rehab property. Turn it around in your mind and inspect every entrepreneurial angle. This philosophy will be what makes your venture great instead of good.

Straight commercial properties are another place you can look for a rehab with change-of-use appeal. Avoid large buildings and complexes; they hold too many risks for the average rehabber. Concentrate your search on old motels and gas stations. With today's changing patterns and practices, these old buildings can be revived for a new use.

CONDO A MOTEL

In this example, envision a rundown and failing motel. It is built on a single foundation and is a one-story structure. There is a small house on the property for the owner, an office attached to the motel, and sixteen motel rooms. This motel was doomed to failure when an express highway was installed. The owner tried to maintain the business, but economic support for the motel is absent. When the highway was built, a major lodging chain constructed a new motel near the exit ramp. The owner will be forced into bankruptcy soon, and efforts to sell the business have floundered.

There is no doubt you can buy this rundown antique cheap, but why would you? If the owner can't make money with the motel, why would you buy it? This is where your creative mind takes over and steers you to fertile rewards. The purpose of the new highway was to handle the growing population of the city. There is increased demand for year-round housing as a result of this population boom. Have you figured out how to make the most of the motel yet?

This ignored motel is a perfect property for an apartment complex or small condo project. With the proper zoning (and downgrading from commercial to residential is usually easy), this property can become valuable again. When you purchase it, the owner will undoubtedly think you are stupid or crazy. Don't let the owner or any other potential investor know of your plans until they are in effect. This can be the makings of a very lucrative rehab deal.

Do Your Homework

Before beginning the rehab process, do your homework. Determine where the greatest need for housing in the area lies. The number of bedrooms needed for a successful apartment or condo is your primary consideration. Once your market evaluation is complete and your plans made, you can begin the remodeling. Start with the old owner's house. Keep your improvement cost under control and avoid major investments in the house.

Focus on cosmetic improvements to the exterior and freshen the paint on the inside. Rather than replacing the carpets, have them professionally cleaned. Move through this stage of the renovation as quickly and cost effectively as possible. Your goal is to make the house presentable and desirable to a high-grade tenant. Immediately upon completion, secure a tenant for the house and start collecting rent. This rental income will help defer the financing costs incurred to carry the main project.

After the house is occupied and paying its way, start working on the motel. Your market study and plans will tell you exactly what design approaches to take. You have an office and sixteen motel units to work with. How can you make the most money from this outdated space? Combining two of the motel units will produce a small two-bedroom apartment.

This is the simplest conversion to make. You can discontinue the use of one of the bathrooms and replace it with a kitchenette. The plumbing from the removed bathroom can be used for the kitchen's plumbing needs. Adding interior partitions to one of the motel units will divide it into two acceptable bedrooms. The remainder of the other motel unit will be the living space. The up side of this type of conversion is its low cost requirements. The down side is a small two-bedroom apartment.

These restricted living quarters may have an adverse affect on your ability to rent or sell them. This method will give you eight two-bedroom units, not including the old office. Using this cost-conserving method may hurt you more than it helps. If you want two-bedroom units, consider another approach. (An example of a different approach is discussed shortly, when you reach the three-bedroom principles.) The office is a perfect place to install a laundry room and game room. With the current craze in video games, a coin-operated arcade will add significantly to the income of the property.

Turnover

If one-bedroom apartments or condos are in demand, the above procedure is an excellent choice. The combination of two motel units will make a fine one-bedroom living unit. Using the above rou-tine for one-bedroom units will also give you eight units, excluding the old office. A primary concern for most investors buying rental property is their expected rental turnover. Many investors will not even think about buying a building filled with one-bedroom apartments. They know the term of tenancy will be short and problems will exist with the nature of the tenants. Other investors like this high turnover, as it gives them the chance to raise the rents more often. Before making all one-bedroom units, look at your local market trends and deliberate on your actions carefully.

Three-bedroom units and spacious two-bedroom units require a different rehab method. Assuming you bought the property at the right price, calculate opening the party walls and redefining the interior design. This approach will not yield as many units, but they will be larger and better designed. The rehab expense is higher, but the market demand may increase and allow for higher income. This is certainly worth thinking about and warrants investigating the pros and cons.

If you choose this more extreme rehab method, your costs will be considerably higher. Make certain not to get caught up in the excitement and exceed your budget. Keep your improvements modest and functional. Try to use as much of the existing structure and mechanical systems as possible. With careful planning and design, you should come out of the project with a minimum of four three-bedroom units or five two-bedroom apartments. This may be cutting the profit margin too thin. There is still another alternative.

Mix and Match

Use the mix and match principle. Create efficiency units, one-bedroom units, two-bedroom units, and three-bedroom units. The efficiency units will only require the addition of a kitchenette ensemble. Your rehab cost is almost nothing and you have a rentable apartment. In some towns, efficiencies are in high demand and bring in strong rents. This is primarily true of college towns and areas with contract transient workers. If you can justify doing the whole project in efficiencies, your profit will be unbelievable. Take a moment to add up the rental income from sixteen efficiency apartments, the detached house, and the revenue from the laundry and arcade room. Now pick yourself up off the floor and continue to learn how to reach the highest and best use of a property.

Using the mix and match procedure nets various numbers of units. You can lay out the design to maximize the structure's space. Another advantage to this approach is the wide audience of tenants available. If your property is equipped to handle *any* housing need, you will have a better chance of finding tenants. The quality and consistency of your tenants should be better in the larger units. Evaluate your long-term plans and design the space accordingly. If your motivation is only to sell for a profit, sit down with a real estate broker and check out the recent sales.

Using this type of marketing research will enable you to get a handle on the demands of current buyers. Perhaps efficiencies and one-bedroom apartments are very much desired in your area. You may find only two- and three-bedroom apartments are selling. Use this information to make your final rehab decision. If your tendency is to keep the property, the larger units will give you fewer landlording headaches. Tenants in three-bedroom apartments are traditionally better tenants. They are more stable and responsible than the occupants of small apartments. This is not always the case, but it will prove to be true on most occasions.

FILL 'ER UP

The last type of highest and best use to be discussed here is centered around old gas stations. These buildings, and ones like them, offer unique angles for a change-of-use project. Modern convenience stores have driven the old-fashioned gas stations to their knees. They can't begin to compete with the major oil companies controlling most of the convenience stores. Their loss can be your gain.

Look around you and notice the types of franchises thriving in your area. Look at fast-food businesses, donut shops, and businesses with similar attributes. Check out quick-print shops, express dry cleaners, and video rental stores. What do they all have in common? They are all accessible and offer quick service. Many of these businesses offer drive-through service, and their customers don't stay in their parking lot for long. How does this relate to abandoned gas stations?

Retired filling stations meet many of the requirements for these fast, service-oriented businesses, without major modification. Think about it; they have circle driveways and adequate parking. Gas stations have customarily been easily accessible from major roads and streets. Many of the decrepit dinosaurs have lots of glass and large open spaces once used as garage bays. Converting an unwanted gas station into a desirable business property can be a cinch.

Drive-Through

If the old station was to be used for a video rental business, you could incorporate two approaches. On one side of the building, you could add a drive-through window, for express customers who know what movies they want to rent. In the old service bays, the business owner could display thousands of movies with plenty of space for customers to mingle. The circle driveways associated with old stations make a drive-through conversion ideal.

For a dry cleaning operation, the service bays provide adequate space for the equipment needed to operate the business. A second floor can be easily installed over the service bays for administrative personnel. The office of the antiquated station is used to meet and serve the public. A drive-through pickup for this business could increase sales and reduce lost time for employees.

Box Lunch

A unique idea for an old station could cater to construction workers or anyone looking for a pickup lunch. The products offered by the average fast-food chain lose their appeal after a short time riding around in a truck. Many construction workers start early and despise packing a lunch. They tend to depend on mobile caterers, or "Roach Coaches" as they are called in the trade. For an enterprising entrepreneur, a fast-food operation purveying daily box-lunches could make a fortune.

Old gas stations are a prime candidate for this type of venture. A food preparation area can be installed in the old garage bays, and the drive-through is a great feature. In the appropriate location, this type of business could thrive. The proprietor will cash in on the timeliness of the business, and you will reap the wealth of your change-of-use and rehab skills. The list of potential tenants or purchasers could fill an entire chapter. Give this type of conversion a lot of thought if you are inclined to commercial applications.

By this time, I trust you are beginning to understand the concept of searching for the highest and best use of a property. Undoubtedly, you can see how a little research and paperwork enhances your speculative investment. Learning to recognize a dormant opportunity is an important asset to professional rehab investors. This quality comes naturally to some lucky individuals. Don't despair if you are not one of the gifted investors. You can develop these skills with study and experience.

EXPERIENCE

Experience is the best teacher, but it is an expensive education. My knowledge was gained through this earn-while-you-learn method. If you can learn from other people's mistakes and experience, you will be money ahead. Your decision in buying this book exhibits your intelligence; you are learning inexpensively from my hard knocks. Absorb what has been said here. It may seem simple, but the execution of these tactics requires extreme concentration and attention to detail.

Finding and manipulating buildings for their highest and best use is your quickest way to wealth in real estate. Don't get bogged down with finding no-money-down deals—look for properties with the most profit potential. Leverage is a common tool of real estate entrepreneurs, but too much leverage can break your financial backbone. Securing sound business deals pays off better than the easy-to-get-into, hard-to-get-out-of, high leverage propositions.

SHORTCUTS

There are very few shortcuts to becoming rich in this world. Real estate offers some of the best solid, plausible possibilities for finding financial rewards. It also harbors numerous pitfalls and nightmares. Careful planning and a broad knowledge of the business will keep you out of harm's way. Finding the highest and best use of a property is the quickest way to climb the real estate ladder of success. Your ability to read between the lines can be worth thousands of dollars every time you sign a purchase offer.

Attempting to bypass the learning procedure is likely to cost you everything you own. Bankruptcy is a dirty word and a nasty cloud to have hanging over you. Making the wrong moves early and going bankrupt will retard your investment activity for up to ten years. It is not a jail sentence, and there are ways to overcome the social labeling as a bad credit risk, but why take chances? If you study the habits of successful investors, you can reduce the risks.

One of the biggest mistakes inexperienced investors make is trying to reinvent the wheel. Don't lay all your money on a long shot. Playing for smaller stakes and winning is better than playing for all the marbles and losing. If you gamble for high stakes, there will be hustlers waiting to take advantage of your inexperience.

By controlling your urges to become a millionaire overnight, your likelihood of survival increases dramatically. The keys are not to leverage more than you can handle when things don't go as planned, and to capitalize on hidden treasures. Learning to harness the power of highest-and-best-use techniques will give you the edge to survive in borderline deals. Of everything you learn in rehab principles, identifying the highest and best use is one of the most coveted traits of successful investors.

FREE AND NEARLY FREE IMPROVEMENT MONEY

13

Alert rehab investors can increase their income with special financing and improvement funds. The U.S. Department of Housing and Urban Development (HUD) provides a multitude of programs to encourage and assist rehab investors. These plans can benefit the rehabber planning a quick resale and the investor building a rental portfolio. Learning to make the most of these programs augments your rehab investments.

The list of available programs is extensive. This chapter gives you an overview of most of the programs. It also shows you how the programs can be helpful to your plans. The programs described are the ones most likely to benefit the rehab investor. Descriptions of the programs have been abbreviated but contain the information most pertinent to the rehabber. If you study these programs, you will benefit from higher rehab profits.

COMMUNITY DEVELOPMENT BLOCK GRANTS (ENTITLEMENT)

This is a federal aid program designed to promote sound community development. It provides annual grants to carry out a wide range of development activities. Community Development Block Grants (CDBGs) are issued on a formula basis to entitled comunities. The activities supported by the grants include neighborhood revitalization, economic development, and improved community facilities and services.

The activities produced by these grants must benefit low- and moderate-income persons. This can include preventing and eliminating slum conditions. Communities approved for the grants create their own programs and funding priorities. These communities consult with the local population before making final decisions on the disbursement of funds. Preventing serious and immediate threats to the health and welfare of the community is a prime purpose of the grants.

One of the approved activities of these grants is the purchase or rehabilitation of real estate. At least 60% of the funds must be directed to benefit low- and moderate-income people. The time allowed for the use of funds is established by the grantee but may not exceed three years.

Some of the factors making a location eligible for the grant funding include poverty, population, slow growth, old housing, and general housing overcrowding. Your local housing authority can identify the locations targeted to receive these funds. In fiscal year 1989, about $2,053 billion was appropriated for allocation among 737 cities and 121 urban counties.

This is a lot of potential rehab money. As an active rehab investor, these funds will go a long way in making your plans possible. For complete information on this and the programs described below, contact:

Assistant Secretary for Community Planning
and Development
Department of Housing and Urban Development
Washington, DC 20410-7000

COMMUNITY DEVELOPMENT BLOCK GRANTS FOR STATES AND SMALL CITIES (NON-ENTITLEMENT)

This program is very similar to the one above. The major difference is the method of selection for locations to receive the grants. This program is designed to benefit areas excluded from the above program. All fifty states and Puerto Rico are eligible to apply for funding from this program. Typically, the recipient areas have populations below 50,000.

Every year, states make grants to over 3,000 small communities. Since 1982, more than $6 billion has been disbursed from the program. If your rehab activity is in a small town, these grants can make your day.

URBAN DEVELOPMENT ACTION GRANTS

Urban Development Action Grants (UDAGs) are used to assist distressed cities and urban counties. They are meant as a catalyst to economic recovery. The grants are made to local governments. The local government then loans money to private developers for commercial, residential, and industrial projects. As a rehabber, you can apply for the use of these funds.

To secure the loan, you must obtain approval with a minimum ratio of 2.5 of your dollars for every dollar received from the Action Grant. Factors used to measure the amounts of these grants include old housing, poverty, per capita income, unemployment, and job stability. The rates and terms of these loans can be very attractive.

RENTAL REHABILITATION

This program provides grants to cities and states to encourage rental housing rehabilitation. The funds are also used to subsidize low-income tenants. The goal is to minimize tenant displacement while attracting the private sector for rehab work. The grants are awarded on a formula basis to communities with populations of 50,000 or more.

Funding for a rehab project averages $5,000 to $8,500 per unit, depending on the number of bedrooms contained in the property. The funds may be used to pay for up to one-half the total eligible costs to renovate your property. On average, a minimum of $600 per unit is required to receive any funding participation.

Additional regulations limit the type of improvements the grant money may be used for. The work must correct substandard conditions, make essential improvements, or repair major systems in danger of failure. Energy-related repairs or handicap conversions, approved by the grantee, are also acceptable.

When the improvements are complete, 70% or more of the property's residents must be low-income families. Rents in the completed project must be established in accordance with market rates and not limited by rent controls. The grants are aimed at neighborhoods where the median income does not exceed 80% of the area median. Another location requirement is that rents will not increase more rapidly than rents in the market area.

The distribution of funds is based on a formula with three specific factors considered. These three factors are:

❏ Rental units with households at or below the poverty level.

❏ Rental units constructed prior to 1940, with household incomes at or below poverty level.

❏ Rental units with at least one of four housing problems. These problems are: (1) incomplete plumbing; (2) high rent costs; (3) incomplete kitchen facilities; (4) overcrowding.

In fiscal year 1989, $150 million was allocated for this program. This program is a natural for the residential multi-family rehab professional.

REHABILITATION LOANS

These rehab loans finance the rehabilitation of single-family and multi-family residential properties. They may also be used for mixed-use and non-residential properties. Unnecessary demolition of basically sound structures is not permitted when these funds are used. Insulation and weatherization items are allowed by the program. Steps required to bring the property up to local code requirements and project standards are also acceptable.

The loans may not exceed $33,500 per dwelling, or $100,000 for non-residential properties. You have twenty years to repay the loan, and the interest rates are very attractive. For a low income homeowner, the rate could be as low as 3%. Multi-family properties and moderate income homeowners are charged interest at the Treasury bond rate. In fiscal year 1988, about $102 million was loaned through the program.

URBAN HOMESTEADING

This program is designed to revitalize declining neighborhoods and reduce the inventory of federally owned properties. Its goal is to transfer vacant and rundown properties to new homeowners for rehabilitation. Unless you are rehabbing a home for yourself, this program has limited benefits.

The local government transfers the property for a nominal sum to eligible individuals to rehab. The homesteader can make the repairs or use the services of a contractor. The homesteader must occupy the property as a principal residence for at least five years. Within three years, the homesteader must bring the home up to local code requirements. For the rehab investor, this program is very limited, but you may be able to connect with the homesteaders to turn a rehab profit. Since they may use a contractor to do the work, you could get a piece of the action.

CONDOMINIUM HOUSING

This plan provides federal mortgage insurance to finance the construction and rehab of multi-family housing when the individual units will be sold. For a project to meet the criteria of the program, it must contain at least four residential units. The units may be detached, semi-detached, row, walk-up, or elevator structures. This program had participated in the financing of over 237,792 units through September 1988. The value of these units exceeded $13 billion.

MANUFACTURED HOME PARKS

Don't skip this program, the title is deceiving. This program provides federal mortgage insurance to finance the construction and rehab of manufactured home parks. There is some serious money to be made here.

HUD insures mortgages made by local lenders for these construction and rehab activities. To qualify, the home park must contain a minimum of five lot spaces. Improvement loans have limits from $9,000 to $15,750 per lot, depending on location. The park must be in a HUD-approved area.

Eligibility is open to investors, builders, developers, and others meeting the HUD requirements. The program insured 66,145 spaces through September 1988. Crank up your creative juices and find a way to take advantage of this overlooked program. The profits could put you on a new road to riches.

MULTI-FAMILY RENTAL HOUSING

If commercial-grade multi-family buildings are your forte, this could be your pet program. This program insures the financing for construction and rehabilitation of a broad cross-section of rental housing. If your project contains a minimum of five units, it may qualify. The property should be capable of accommodating families, with or without children, at affordable rents.

EXISTING MULTI-FAMILY RENTAL HOUSING

This program centers around the purchase or refinancing of existing apartment projects. It insures the loans made by local lenders. To qualify, the property must contain a minimum of five units and be at least three years old.

MULTI-FAMILY RENTAL HOUSING FOR MODERATE-INCOME FAMILIES

This program provides mortgage insurance to finance rental or cooperative housing. The housing must be planned for moderate-income residents, including projects for the elderly. Loans made by private lending institutions are insured by HUD. The projects can include new construction or substantial rehabilitation.

The properties must contain a minimum of five

dwellings. They may be detached, semi-detached, row, walk-up, or elevator structures. This is an excellent opportunity for the rehab investor with big plans.

GUIDELINES

Now that you are aware of the types of programs available, all you have to do is take advantage of them. Information on the various programs is available from the Assistant Secretary for Community Planning and Development, Department of Housing and Urban Development, Washington, DC 20410-7000. To give you an idea of one of the programs, the following information is a summary of the requirements for a sample state.

This information is related to efforts for creating new rental units, through new construction and rehab work. The basic requirements of the program dictate a necessity to increase the total number of units available for rent and increase the number of bedrooms without decreasing the total number of units. The following information is a synopsis of the guidelines for this type of program.

Preliminary applications must be complete and signed by each principal of the applicant entity. Before a letter of commitment is issued, the applicant must prove adequate financial strength. Personal financial statements are required before final commitment is made. The progress of the application procedure is detailed below.

The first step is application and proposal submittal. While you are obtaining any required approvals from the zoning board, planning board, or other local agency, your application is being processed. The State Agency reviews your proposal, the site, and your credentials. Then the application is passed to the Finance Committee.

Preliminary designation and an invitation to final approval are next. At this stage, you are required to provide a schematic submission. The appraisal process follows the schematic submission. Your drawings and financial package are reviewed after the appraisal is returned. Then the package is returned to the Finance Committee.

If all goes well, you are issued a letter of commitment. Following commitment, you proceed to your construction loan closing. When the closing is settled, you may begin your construction or rehab

efforts. The general program eligibility requirements are reviewed in the following text.

Units being financed must be in the state and for year-round, non-transient occupancy. They must comply with the State Housing Authority (SHA) and all applicable state and local codes. If tenants will be displaced or relocated, you must comply with the Relocation Policy issued by the state.

Commercial space may be included in the project, but it may not be financed. Each project is subject to review in a public hearing when financing is sought. The public will be apprised of project costs, mortgage amount, location, and the applicant.

To obtain acquisition and rehabilitation financing for existing units, the eligible rehab expenses must equal or exceed 15% of the building's acquisition cost. The rehab work must be non-cosmetic. The expenses must be incurred within two years of the date the building is acquired, or the date a bond is issued. The two-year restriction applies to the later of these two conditions.

To be eligible for the low-income benefit, the applicant must target one of the following areas:

1. A minimum of 20% of the dwellings shall be available to, or occupied by, individuals with incomes at or below 50% of the area's median income. The figures will be adjusted by family size, as determined by IRS regulations.

2. A minimum of 40% of the dwellings shall be available to, or occupied by, individuals with incomes at or below 60% of the area's median income. The figures will be adjusted by family size, as determined by IRS regulations.

Providing multiple bedroom configurations within a project requires a pro-rata portion of each type to be available as a targeted unit. State Housing Authority loans shall be secured by a first lien on the land and improvements. A title search is required prior to financing commitments. Title insurance is required for any loan exceeding $100,000.

Appraisals shall be supplied by an appraiser with the credentials of an MAI or SRPA. The appraisal is required during the final application phase for all projects. Non-profit sponsors may receive 100% financing on eligible costs, if the property's cash flow supports the debt.

Investors planning to make a profit have the option of two types of down payment requirements. If you are personally guaranteeing the loan, you may borrow 95% of the appraised value. If the combined acquisition and improvement cost is less than the appraised value, you can borrow 95% of that amount. The ratio is limited to the lower of the two figures. If you will not be personally guaranteeing the loan, the amount drops to 90%.

Debt service coverage is required to be a minimum of 105%. No more than 95% of the project's net operating income (NOI) may be committed to the total debt service. The applicant's return on equity is not restricted. However, distributions may only be from surplus cash and prior distribution. The applicant must cover all outstanding expenses, and the property must be adequately maintained. Applicants are required to comply with the mortgage and any reporting requirements, such as annual financial statements.

Construction and rehab financing must be obtained before SHA financing is issued. Demand in the market must be demonstrated for the units at their proposed rent levels. Evidence of a professional market analysis may be required prior to commitment. If the SHA feels a first year's operating deficit will exceed 1% of the mortgage, additional security may be required. An operating deficit escrow account may be required under these conditions. The operating deficit escrow account, equal to 2% of the mortgage amount, must be provided by no later than the permanent loan closing. It may be in the form of cash or an irrevocable letter of credit.

All work shall comply with the local building code. An architect, registered in the state, must be retained for design and construction monitoring services. It shall be the responsibility of the applicant and applicant's architect to comply with any and all applicable codes. These codes shall include but are not limited to the following:

❏ local codes

❏ federal codes

❏ federal statutes

❏ state codes

❏ federal regulations

❏ federal ordinances

❏ energy efficiency building standards

At least 10% of the ground level units shall be made accessible to, and usable by, physically handicapped people. This same rule applies to upper story units connected by an elevator. A water quality test must be provided for all units with a private water supply. The test must present results satisfactory to the State Department of Health and Welfare.

There is no fee required to submit a preliminary application. Once your application reaches the stage referred to as "invitation to proceed," a fee is required. This fee is applied to the commitment fee, if the application is approved. The fee is $500 for average investors and $100 for non-profit applicants.

For profit-seeking applicants, an earnest-money deposit is required. The deposit shall be 4% of the loan amount. Half of this deposit will be returned upon the SHA acceptance of a certification of actual costs required to be submitted within sixty days of permanent loan closing. The remaining 2% is held to secure two years of project operations.

The applicant may elect to provide the deposit in the form of cash or two 2% letters of credit. The double letters of credit are required to facilitate processing. Non-profit sponsors are not required to provide an earnest-money deposit. A commitment fee equal to 2% of the loan amount is collected at the construction loan closing. The commitment fee may be financed, but it is not refundable.

The mortgage interest on bond-financed loans can become non-deductible by the borrower. If the project fails to meet low-income targeting requirements, the loss of deductible interest is triggered. The interest will be non-deductible during the period beginning on the first day of the taxable year that the project fails to meet the requirements. The loss of deductions ends on the date the project returns to compliance.

Annual reports to the State Housing Authority are required. These reports will confirm the eligibility of tenants residing in targeted units. They also address the compliance with regards to the number of units to be occupied by qualifying low-income families. In addition, they confirm the project rental requirement. If occupancy is anticipated falling below the minimum requirements, the SHA must be notified.

An annual certification shall be made by you to the U.S. Treasury Department, confirming compliance with low-income targeting and rental requirements. Failing to file this report results in a $100 fine. You may need to file reports relative to the low-income housing tax credit. If you wish to take advantage of the tax credit, consult with your attorney and certified public accountant. The tax credit is complicated and deserves attention from specialized professionals.

PUTTING THE INFORMATION TO WORK

While all this information is very educational, it is a little dry to read. It is hard to translate government programs into enjoyable reading. I apologize if this chapter has been slightly boring, but the facts contained here can make a huge difference in your rehab venture. I think you will find the remainder of the chapter to be more stimulating. It deals with using these programs to line your pockets with some heavy green.

To make the most of these programs, you might want to explore dealing in apartment buildings with at least six or eight units. Buildings of this size are small enough to be approachable and large enough to turn a hefty profit. Some of the programs are perfect for these buildings. When looking through the available programs, don't overlook the possibility of combining programs for maximum earnings.

One of the best programs for mid-range multi-family projects is the program called Rehabilitation Loans. This is a simple name for a dynamite opportunity. This is the program allowing up to $33,500 per unit for improvements. The interest rate on these generous loans is equal to the Treasury bond rate. The term of the loan is twenty years, and the loans are designed for multi-family rehab projects. If you fall into the low-income qualifications, the interest rate may be as low as 3%.

Let's look at how you can profit from this loan. Assume you are a rehabber, about to rehab an eight-unit apartment building. You plan to upgrade the building to meet current code requirements and to improve the energy efficiency of the building. Your plans call for this property to be a cornerstone to your retirement rental portfolio. You could go to the bank for financing, or you could work the rehab through the HUD program.

Securing the loan from a commercial lender is effective, but obtaining your improvement financing from the government program increases your cash flow. The rehab expense is the same, but the payments are much lower with the use of government funds. Even if you only use half of the available funds, the savings can be dramatic.

If you are going to rehab eight units, at $16,750 each, the total improvement cost is $134,000. How will the HUD funding affect your cash flow? It will make it a raging torrent compared to a conventional loan. Your building's income and expenses, except for debt service, are the same with either loan. The original acquisition cost of the building is financed at the same rate with or without the government funding. The only difference is the interest charged on the improvement money.

Assume Treasury bonds are rated at 8%. Assume the conventional lender's loan rate is three points above the bond rate for investment property. How much difference will the 3% in interest charges make on a twenty-year loan? The monthly payment on the conventional loan will be about $743 more than the HUD loan.

Funds from the Rental Rehabilitation program are another excellent source of money for apartment building investors. If you are interested in building a rental portfolio, the grants available under this program are true money-makers. The Rental Rehabilitation program will provide between $5,000 and $8,500 for each of your rental units.

The allowable uses of these funds are wide-ranging and cover most areas you might wish to improve. If your property is in need of a new heating system, it can be supplied and paid for from these funds. When the building contains substandard conditions, you can use the grant money to correct the inferior characteristics. Defective wiring and problem plumbing can both be taken care of with these funds.

In your eight-unit building, the maximum money available can reach $68,000. Two of the targeted areas for this money are baths and kitchens. Of all the improvements you could make to your property, these two rate very high on the list. Updating the kitchen and bathroom allows you to see higher rent and a more profitable building.

Another key element studied in the grant-giving selection is the age of a property. If your units were built prior to 1940, there is a very good chance you can take advantage of the grant program. In selected locations, this could be the type of deal you can structure. Check with the local housing authority to see if a grant program is available for your building.

Working with government programs can make the difference between a profit and a loss. Buildings you would never consider with conventional financing become attractive investments when special programs are available for them. Many investors and rehabbers never explore the federal programs. This oversight on their part is opportunity for you. With an awareness of the programs available for rehab ventures, you can stay a few steps ahead of your competition.

For the single-family rehab investor, the government programs can also produce effective results. The Rehabilitation Loans program mentioned in the multi-family example can also be used on single-family residences. The ceiling for improvements on a single-family home is $33,500. This kind of money goes a very long way in renovating a house. This same program can be utilized with mixed-use and commercial properties. The limit of the loan for these properties is $100,000.

When your interest is in developing a string of single-family rental properties, low-rate financing on the improvement cost can make the plan work. It is difficult to make an average single-family home a profitable rental investment. The cost to acquire and refurbish a home is often more than the income will carry. With the use of low-interest loans, the numbers work and your cash flow is positive. Check with the current regulations to see if there are any restrictions to this program to deter your interest in it.

As noted earlier, you should not turn your nose up at the thought of the manufactured home parks program. Being a rehab investor allows you to work many angles. Don't confine yourself to the obvious

selections of common real estate investors. Under the proper conditions, you can make a small fortune working with manufactured home parks.

Most high-rolling rehabbers have made their money by taking chances and being different. While you should not try to revolutionize the industry, you should explore all aspects of the business. As affordable housing continues to become a memory, manufactured home parks could offer an exclusive alternative. As an entrepreneur, you owe it to yourself to gather the facts on any legitimate money-making venture.

Another consideration to keep in mind is resale. When you are planning the improvements for your single-family project, keep the sale price in mind. There are many agency programs aimed at helping low-income individuals obtain a home of their own. These programs place maximum sale prices on the homes eligible for the funding. They also limit the amenities a property may possess. Investigate these facts before making your improvements. Minor revisions in your rehab plans could keep the house in the targeted range of attractive programs. These special programs can provide you with a broader base of potential purchasers.

One of these programs is the Joint Venture for Affordable Housing plan. It allows contractors to create affordable housing through regulatory reform and the elimination of red tape. It is directed at controllable factors contributing to housing costs. With the lenient permissions offered by this program, you may be able to hit an untapped market.

With the many possibilities available, there is no reason you cannot elevate your earnings in the rehab business. Your rehab effort will be unchanged, only your profits will increase. This is an avenue you cannot afford to ignore. These programs are provided to encourage investors to take an active interest in housing for lower income tenants. Some of the programs cater to first-time home buyers. In either case, the program is meant to stimulate the economy and help disadvantaged people. If you are thinking of feeling guilty for using the system, don't. The system was established to be used, and you will be helping to provide housing for a mass of people.

How Much Improvement is too Much?

14

New rehab investors commonly make a serious mistake. This mistake causes inexperienced rehabbers to become disenchanted with the business. Losing money is only part of the effects felt from the miscalculation. Wide-ranging and long-term negative consequences surround the nucleus of this common error. The looming fault is created when investors put their rehab dollars to the wrong use.

The key to making money in the rehab business is knowing how much money to spend and what to spend it on. When poor decisions are made on what improvements to invest in, the investor feels the sting of the mistake. Making the wrong improvements may affect you in many ways.

Poor improvement selection can make a property nearly impossible to sell. It can also keep the sale from being profitable, if the sale happens at all. Making the wrong moves may alienate prospective tenants and kill a property's cash flow. There is no golden rule on what improvements to make on a property. Each individual building requires and supports its own type of improvements.

While there is no template for guaranteed success, there are ways to improve your odds. History has proven certain improvements to be universally acceptable in the rehab business. By the same token, it has pointed out the blunders to avoid. Taking the time to make solid improvement selections will improve your income and your rollover time.

ROLLOVER TIME

Rollover time is very important in this business. The longer you have to market the property, the more money you are losing. Most rehab projects are financed, and every day the property goes unsold, you are paying interest on the loan. On a large project, this can amount to several hundred dollars each month. Making payments on a vacant property while it is being marketed can deplete your savings and profit quickly.

The time needed to sell the building is heavily affected by your rehab efforts. If you have made the property desirable while keeping it affordable, you should see a fast sale. If you used bad judgment in your improvements, the property could sit on the market until your profit is nonexistent.

To avoid losing money and confidence in the rehab business, you must learn to evaluate improvements. As you gain experience, this will come naturally. You will not consciously have to scrutinize each and every improvement. Experience will teach you the difference between winners and losers. Experience will reduce your risks, but how do you evade losses while gaining experience?

MAKE CHANGE CAUTIOUSLY

Market research and common sense will help you dodge most of the serious infractions of the rehab rules. Identifying the red flags of inopportune improvements takes time and training. You can train yourself by watching others and reading quality books. Watching contractors, investors, and market trends is the best way to protect yourself. If a program is successful for others, it should have the potential to be successful for you.

Renegade rehabbers come into the business and promise to change rehab procedures as the world knows them. This aggressive attempt to reinvent the wheel usually results in devastating failure. Radical new approaches seldom work. The public is resistant to abrupt change, and the enterprising entrepreneurs are under-capitalized to make their mark. Their day in the paper is frequently in the form of a bankruptcy notice.

TEST THE WATERS

Progress and innovative change are good and needed. Knowing how to temper and meld the new with the old is the secret to success. Before you jump into deep water, test the market. Run test advertisements to see if your ideas are valid. If you believe a roof-top sauna and tanning salon will go over big, ask the public before you invest in the project. When you are sure adding an in-ground pool to your recently purchased rehab house will make it irresistible, run a test ad.

Installing the pool will cost many thousands of dollars. There is no return policy on in-ground pools, so you can't afford to be wrong. Before installing the pool, run two advertisements in the same paper, at the same time. Make the two ads very similar, except for the pool. Leave the pool out of the first ad and incorporate it in the second ad. Even though the pool is not installed, you can test the market with your advertising. The ads might read like the following.

Both advertisements say the same thing, except for playing up the pool in the second ad. Run both ads simultaneously and see which ad pulls the most qualified buyers. The ad with the pool will probably not generate any more serious calls than the first ad. When the phone response begins, ask the callers what features of the home they are most interested in. This type of test marketing could prevent you from making a $12,000 mistake.

Test Ad (Without Mention of Pool)

STUNNING CATHEDRAL CEILINGS WITH EXPOSED-BEAM CONSTRUCTION. Outstanding views, through walls of energy-efficient glass, facing the mountains and capturing every warm sunset. Spacious loft for work or play and skylights to brighten your day. Three spacious bedrooms and two and a half baths make this contemporary home very livable. Fieldstone fireplace warms the family room, and elegant features adorn the formal dining room. This unique custom home meets the expectations of the most demanding professional. Situated on a large two-acre lot, this home combines privacy with convenience, only minutes from shopping and the workplace. If you have dreamed of the perfect home, this is it. Call 555-5563 today for your personal inspection of an architectural masterpiece.

Test Ad (Incorporating the Proposed In-Ground Pool)

STUNNING CATHEDRAL CEILINGS WITH EXPOSED-BEAM CONSTRUCTION. Outstanding views, through walls of energy-efficient glass, facing the mountains and capturing every warm sunset. Spacious loft for work or play and skylights to brighten your day. Three spacious bedrooms and two and a half baths make this contemporary home very livable. Fieldstone fireplace warms the family room, and elegant features adorn the formal dining room. This unique custom home meets the expectations of the most demanding professional. Situated on a large two-acre lot, this home combines privacy with convenience, only minutes from shopping and the workplace. In addition to comfortable and enviable living, you can have the pool you have always wanted. Full-size in-ground pool is planned to enhance this already perfect home. If you have dreamed of the ideal home, this is it. Call 555-5563 today for your personal inspection of an architectural masterpiece.

Swimming pools are a fantasy for most people considering them. While these potential buyers may want a pool, few of them will be willing to pay the price for the luxury. A test advertisement will tell you whether an in-ground pool will enhance the value of your property. Chances are, you will get more calls on the ad with the pool, but you may receive fewer calls from qualified buyers. This is the type of market research you must conduct before investing in specialty improvements.

Installing a pool without testing the market can result in several problems. You may make the house less desirable to qualified purchasers. Why would anyone prefer *not* to have a pool? Pools require maintenance and money to maintain. They present a hazard to children and a liability to their owners. Fences are frequently required around pools. Fences are expensive to construct and require routine upkeep. For many people, a fence detracts from the appearance of a home.

These negative factors can influence the buying public to pass your home by. Can you imagine your disgust at spending $12,000 on an improvement that repels qualified buyers? This example shows how easily a costly improvement can put your rehab profits in the loss column.

If you are inundated with people interested in the house *because* of the pool, you have made a wise move. The ad identifies the pool as a proposed improvement, so you can confirm the sale of the property before installing the expensive option. By accepting a contract contingent on the installation of the pool, you are assured of recovering your investment. Using this strategy, you cannot lose. Test ads allow you to have the best of both worlds without risking your rehab investment.

PLAYING ON PRETTY IMPROVEMENTS

Many of the most effective improvements are relatively inexpensive. When you are dressing a property up for sale, you must work on the buyer's desires and emotions. It is often the pretty improvement that sells more homes than the practical investment. Installing automatic foundation vents and a ground cover to act as a vapor barrier will reduce moisture damage. This improvement saves the homeowner money in painting expenses and extends the life of the home. Providing attractive mini-blinds for the windows and painting a stenciled border around the kitchen ceiling do nothing to prolong the home's useful life. Yet these cos-

metic improvements will fetch a higher sale price than the logical investment in moisture control. Not only will it yield a higher price, it will spawn a quicker sale.

People buy homes because they like them and because they appreciate the home's location. Houses are sold on emotions, and logic plays a minor role in the sale. Apartment buildings are typically purchased by cost-conscious investors. These investors will not be easily swayed by stenciled borders and mini-blinds. They will be concentrating on the hard physical aspects of the investment.

The value of commercial and retail space is based on location and performance potential. The business investor is focused on numbers, not pretty embellishments. You must use judgment in your improvement decisions. Direct the improvements to meet the desires of your potential customers. Having the ability to recognize and separate the various types of improvements is critical to your prosperity.

WINNING PROJECTS

Rewarding rehab projects should be placed in at least three categories. Single-family homes head the list, followed by multi-family income properties. Commercial business property completes the category. You can expand on the dissection of these categories. For the sake of simplicity, the examples here are limited to the three primary types of rehab projects.

Business Property

Commercial property is not a common project for most investors. The cost of acquiring, rehabbing, and selling these properties prohibits many investors from participating in this type of job. Most of this chapter is devoted to residential and small to medium multi-family properties.

Trying to identify the best improvements for commercial property is difficult. So much of the impetus is related to the type and use of the commercial property. If you are venturing into commercial rehab projects, the most profit will be derived from upgrading the use of the property.

Converting ineffective business property into a profitable enterprise is the principal path to rehab profits. Your improvements should produce a definite financial advantage and be recoverable in your sales price. Buying business property to make minor cosmetic improvements carries more risk than reward. It is much safer to make improvements that can increase the property's income potential.

Business property is bought based on performance results and projections. If your improvements do not promise to increase the building's rate of return, you are wasting your time. Here are a few examples to consider.

Buying a beauty salon and converting it to a real estate office will probably not make you wealthy. Buying a fix-it shop and converting it to a convenience store could be a winning idea. Location is a prime consideration with all commercial property. You must assess the market demand and voids before making a commitment to a commercial project.

Does the location you are considering need another convenience store? Could the area support a new fast-food restaurant? Can the rundown realty office be divided into lucrative professional space? Inspect the past performance of the property. Obtain a traffic-count survey, and evaluate the need and support for the changes you are planning.

Most commercial rehab mistakes are made because of ineffective planning and research. Your opinions and beliefs are not enough, you must deal with facts. Gathering supporting evidence for the viability of your project is essential. You will not be able to sell for a profit without a comprehensive business study.

Your decision to create the perfect spot for a service business may result in extreme disappointment. If you remodel the property for a service building and find no demand for the space, you stand to lose a lot of money. It may be that the need for service space is nonexistent, while the demand for retail space is ballooning. Making these determinations prior to commitment is mandatory.

Commercial rehab is a complicated and expensive procedure. Unless you have past experience in the business, you should not get involved with commercial properties. Until you have broad-based experience, the residential market is much safer. The money-making potential may be lower with residential buildings, but the risk is also lower. In your developing stage, concentrate on residential deals. Residential mistakes are not as costly, and

they are easier to compensate for.

There is another drawback to commercial renovations. Commercial projects offer lucrative income for investors with the right abilities. The presence of big money draws a specialized crowd. These people are experts in the field and make their living dealing with business rehabs. Many of these players are well-funded and very competitive. If you attempt to compete with these professionals, the odds are high that you will not win.

Your chances of winning are much improved with residential properties. The demand for residential property is easier to identify. Residential investors are more numerous but less intimidating. With residential projects, the average rehabber is better qualified to make sound decisions. Your experience as a tenant or homeowner can be used in this side of the rehab business.

Residential Income Property

Residential income property still requires a business approach but not on the same level as commercial projects. While buildings with over four apartments require a commercial loan, they can still be looked at with a residential eye. These commercial properties make money by providing housing. You cannot treat them as you would a single-family home, but they can be rehabbed with similar results.

Investor demand for buildings with six or eight units is steady and dependable. These buildings are large enough to be profitable without overpowering the owner. An experienced owner can personally manage these moderate multi-family buildings. As a multi-family rehabber, you can make large returns on your improvement investments.

To see the most profit, spend your money on improvements to increase the property's cash flow. These improvements could be cosmetic, structural, or mechanical, or they could create a change of use. They could also include adding features with income potential to the property. When you are trying to sell a six-unit building, you may encounter two types of buyers.

The first buyer may be impressed with physical appearance and location. The second buyer may be interested only in the net income of the property. To satisfy the needs of both types of investors, you will have to plan your improvements carefully. The value of a moderate multi-family building is directly related to the property's income.

Every improvement made to an income property should be targeted to increase the building's earning potential. Painting the exterior of the apartment building could meet this goal. Adding attractive landscaping might enhance the building and produce a higher caliber of tenants. Creating clean, personal, secure storage allows an apartment to pull higher rent. Expanding the parking area for tenants could justify a rental income increase.

Installing energy-efficient mechanical systems may reduce operating expenses. Reducing expenses is increasing net income and the property's value. New energy-efficient windows can have the same effect and improve the building's appearance. Exterior appearance is instrumental in lowering vacancy rates and increasing income. If prospective tenants don't like the looks of the property, they won't rent one of the apartments.

Rental Renovation Rules

While all these improvements are worth serious consideration, there are many improvements that are not worth their expense. Multi-family properties should be attractive, but they need not be lavish. Rental property sees a lot of abuse, and fancy finishes are generally a waste of money. Investors will not pay extra for flamboyant renovations. Starting with exterior improvements, what are the rules of rental renovation?

LANDSCAPING. Simple landscaping is a good investment. It will increase the curb appeal of the property and encourage tenants to call the complex home. Don't invest in exotic or fragile plants and shrubbery. Spend your money on hearty shrubs requiring little attention. Unless you have the time and temperament to pamper your plantings, rugged, independent shrubs are the best investment.

Acquire plants with a long season of green color. Any competent landscaper or nurseryman can advise you on the best plants for your geographical area and climate. If the lawn has bare spots, consider filling them with sod. Sod is more expensive than seed, but the eye-pleasing results are instantaneous. This visual advantage will help to increase your sales activity.

Don't be talked into an outrageous landscaping expense. Adequate results can be achieved with minimal expense. If your property is in an area that gets a lot of abuse, landscaping may not be a good investment. Evaluate the area and surrounding properties before making the move to landscape. If you feel the area will support the improvement, it will amplify the property's eye appeal. While this improvement does not directly produce extra income, it can increase the demand for the building. Tenants may rent your apartments because of the attractive exterior. Filling the building with good tenants increases the property's value.

PARKING AREA. Should you pave the parking area? Unless a majority of the competitive buildings have paved parking, don't pave yours. This is an expensive project and the return on the investment is seldom justified.

ROOFING. Is a new roof a worthwhile investment? If the existing roof is not leaking or an eyesore, don't bother to replace it. When the shingles are curling, cracking, or ugly, replacement is a viable consideration. If the roof looks aged but is in good condition and isn't leaking, don't spend money on it.

SIDING. Would new siding improve the complex's value? Unless the siding is rotted, cracked, or filled with asbestos, replacement is a mistake. The type of siding is not very important, it is the condition of the siding you should be concerned with. Will a coat of paint make the siding fresh and pleasant? Painting is relatively inexpensive and can produce a noticeable difference in the value of the property.

Installing a maintenance-free vinyl siding may be worthwhile, but the occasions are limited. If the entire building needs siding repair and painting, covering the existing siding with a vinyl product could be a good deal. Price the jobs and compare the expense. If you can install new vinyl siding without a drastic price increase, it will pay for itself in the appraised value. When the cost is steep, weigh the variables and make a decision with which you are comfortable. In general, vinyl siding is desirable. If minor repairs and paint will make the property presentable and save thousands of dollars, they are more practical than new siding.

WINDOWS AND DOORS. Should the windows and doors be replaced? In most buildings, these replacements are not worth their expense for a strictly cosmetic effect. If the building is designed for the landlord to pay heating and cooling expenses, the improvement may be worthwhile. Windows and doors are very expensive. The high product cost is a deterrent to providing this improvement. Unless the operating expenses will be lowered with the improved efficiency of the windows and doors, avoid this costly improvement.

HALLWAYS. Moving inside the building, assess the hallways. This area has tremendous influence on investors and potential tenants. The halls should be clean and in good condition. If the walls are damaged and dark, change them. Fix the holes and paint the walls a bright, cheerful color. Giving a pleasing hallway impression will add to the value and influence appraisers, investors, and tenants.

The halls should be well-lighted with acceptable fixtures. Don't ignore light fixtures equipped with nothing more than a light bulb. If globes or covers are missing, replace them. Make sure the halls are equipped with working smoke detectors before the property is shown. Never allow garbage cans or bags to be left in the hallways. The halls prejudice the opinion of anyone evaluating the property. Hallways are a critical element in the marketing and appraisal of residential income properties.

If the hall flooring is heavily worn, replace it. Do not buy top-of-the-line flooring, but purchase a product that will complement the building. New floor coverings in the halls can invoke an overall upgraded opinion of the property. Vinyl flooring is a good choice in tough neighborhoods. Carpet is the flooring of choice in upper-class rental areas. Walk through neighboring properties and make yours better without going overboard.

If the entrance doors to the apartments are unsightly, repair or replace them. Hallway improvements are some of the first noticed and longest remembered. Impressions made from the hall will have an influence on the entire building's desirability and value.

BASEMENTS. With the exterior and hallways taken care of, move your improvement planning into the basement. The basement should be clean and free of fire hazards. If the basement is filled with boxes, get them out of there. When the basement lights don't work, fix them. Inspect the basement for water problems and other visual problems.

If you find water problems, investigate the cost to eliminate them. With outdated wiring and plumbing, get estimates to update the systems. On any expensive project, such as these, get estimates from several sources and evaluate the cost of improvements. If the plumbing works properly, there is no justification in replacing it. The cost of replacing the plumbing is difficult to recover in the sale or rental of the property.

In general, if the plumbing, heating, and electrical systems are safe and operational, don't replace them. The increase in property value will not offset the cost of these improvements. Once the basement is presentable, move your planning into the apartments.

INSIDE THE APARTMENTS. Most apartments contain bedrooms, a bathroom, a kitchen, and a living room. Some larger apartments will have separate dining areas and multi-use rooms. When you are planning the reconditioning of the apartments, break your plans down into rooms. With most apartments, the first room entered is the living room.

LIVING ROOM. Rental living rooms are not expected to be finished in grand scale. The important items are the floor covering, the walls, and the ceiling. Window treatments are another aspect of the living room to keep in mind. Landlords should provide window treatments to discourage the use of bed sheets as curtains. Landlord-supplied window treatments also make the apartments appear occupied when they are vacant. This can reduce vandalism and burglary.

Carpet is fine for the living room floor. Hardwood floors in rental property are a costly waste of money. They simply are not needed, and they are too easily damaged. Freshly painted walls and ceilings are acceptable. There is no need for wallpaper or fancy wall coverings. Provide a clean, bright room with an attractive floor, but don't spend too much money on the improvements.

KITCHEN. The next space to consider is the kitchen. Kitchens play a major role in all residential properties. With rental property you should be conservative, but don't overlook the need for a desirable kitchen. Kitchen appliances do not need to be new, but they must be clean and functional. When you are rehabbing the property, used appliances can save money without ruining your rehab efforts.

Countertops should be clean and free of defects. If the counters are broken or chipped, consider replacing them. Take a look at the kitchen sink. If it is permanently stained, replace it. The sink is associated with personal health and hygiene. If it looks dirty, it needs to be replaced.

Cabinets are another prime consideration in the kitchen. If cabinets are rundown or nonexistent, you should investigate the cost to upgrade the kitchen cabinets. Cabinets are not cheap, but they do have an impact on acceptance of a kitchen. Kitchens should be well-lighted. If there is no light over the sink, plan to install one. Lights placed under the cabinets are an appealing feature with the ability to influence appraisers and tenants.

The floor should be clean and in good condition. Vinyl sheet goods are a wise flooring choice. Individual vinyl tiles are frequently unsatisfactory because of their tendency to curl and become loose. The walls and ceilings should be degreased and painted. Improvements in the kitchen do not need to be extravagant, but they should be attractive. With rental property, avoid expensive selections and evaluate each dollar you invest. Typically, the money spent on kitchen remodeling will be returned in full.

BATHROOMS. Bathrooms are as important as the kitchen. The same rules apply for walls, ceilings, and floor coverings. Inspect the tub, toilet, and lavatory. Wall-hung lavatories are okay, if they are clean and operational. Bathtubs do not need to be new, but they must look nice. The same is true of the toilet. If the fixtures are functional but ugly, you have some choices.

You can replace the fixtures or have them resurfaced. Replacing bathroom fixtures gets expensive fast. Adding a new look to the existing fixtures is not cheap, but it is much less expensive than replacing them. There are many firms available to recondition the surface of the fixtures. This procedure can be applied to fiberglass and enameled fixtures.

Leaking faucets should be repaired or replaced. If you replace a wall-hung lavatory with a vanity and top, you will change the look of the bathroom. There are even some very inexpensive pedestal lavatories available to dress up a dull bathroom. Bathrooms are associated with personal hygiene, so they must be clean and functional.

Linen closets are nice, but they are not a requirement. Replacing the medicine cabinet can change the look of the room. Substituting a new oak cabinet for an old metal medicine cabinet makes a big difference. Re-grouting old ceramic tile protects walls from water damage and provides an eye-catching improvement.

Bathrooms deserve a large share of your improvement money. The bathroom and kitchen are the two best places to target your improvements. Of all the rooms in the apartment, these two have the most effect on your success. Bedrooms are the next area to evaluate.

BEDROOMS. Bedrooms can be treated like the living room. It is not necessary to provide special effects in the bedrooms. Size is the most important asset possessed by a bedroom. Normally, this is difficult and expensive to change. If the rooms are of adequate size, all you should do is the walls, ceiling, and floor covering. If the bedrooms are too small, don't buy the property for your rehab project.

If your building has a separate dining area, keep it simple. Provide an attractive overhead light, but don't invest in a high-dollar chandelier. The walls, ceiling, and floor covering should be fresh, but they don't have to be elaborate. Painted walls and ceilings are suitable for rental dining areas. The floor can be carpeted; hardwood flooring is too expensive and too fragile for heavy traffic. Keep it clean and simple.

THE OVERVIEW

As an overview for apartments, concentrate on the kitchens and bathrooms. Spend your money on these two rooms and on freshening the painted areas of the apartment. Next, upgrade the floor coverings, if your budget allows. Keep your improvements conservative in quality. Rental property is expected to be repaired after each rental period. When tenants move, landlords anticipate cleaning and painting the apartments. It would be senseless to install luxury carpet and hand-painted wallpaper in the average apartment.

The last consideration for multi-family buildings is the attic. When you are rehabbing, evaluate increasing the insulation in the attic. This improvement won't be readily seen, but it will improve the efficiency of the heating and cooling of the building. This translates into lower utility bills and reduced operating expenses. Anytime you reduce operating expenses, you increase net income and property values.

DIFFERENT TACTICS

Small multi-family properties sometimes require a different approach. These small buildings contain two to four apartments and may be occupied by the owner. Since the owner may live on site, improvements may need to be of a better quality. The investors buying these small income properties may act on emotion, rather than using business principles.

When the owner lives in the property, he frequently wants the property to be above average. A working strategy for these properties can involve creating one extra-nice apartment. This upgraded unit is planned for the owner. The remaining units can be done along the same lines as the apartments in larger buildings. You must be cautious in upgrading the intended owner's apartment.

Off-site investors account for many of the sales involving small residential income properties. If you are too lavish in the upgraded apartment, your money may not be recovered. Possible upgrades should be selected with care. Installing an expensive carpet will not make a noticeable difference in the property's appraised value. Consider other types of upgrades.

A dishwasher might be something to include in the best apartment. A bathroom vanity is also a wise choice. It gives a more elegant appearance than a wall-hung lavatory, without extreme expense. Again, concentrate on the kitchen and bathroom. These are the best places to spend your money.

SINGLE-FAMILY VARIANCES

Single-family homes present a completely different scenario. These are most frequently purchased by individuals planning to live in them. This fact sets a stage with different guidelines from income properties. Your buyers will not be looking at spreadsheets; they will be looking at the features and benefits of the property. They will also be examining the sale price.

Price is always a consideration in a rehab project. The price of income property is derived from the performance of the property. The price of a home is determined by comparable sale comparisons and features. In any rehab deal, the surrounding properties contribute to the property's value. This is especially true of single-family residences. Before making any improvement, be sure the property will support the financial investment.

Curb Appeal

When you make plans for renovating a home, start with the exterior. Curb appeal is critical in making a first impression on buyers. Houses should be landscaped to meet, or slightly exceed, the standards of the surrounding homes. The landscaping does not have to include exotic trees and plants. As long as the trees and shrubs are attractive and healthy, your goal is met.

The lawn should be well-maintained at all times. If the grass is growing, keep it mowed to an acceptable height. Inspect the walkway. If it is cracked or otherwise in poor repair, invest in correcting its problems. If there is no walkway, plan to provide an inexpensive but distinctive path to the door.

Are the front steps in good shape? Concrete stoops sometimes pull away from the home. Wooden landings rot and discolor. Railings can become loose or deteriorated. When these conditions exist, make arrangements to repair them. Adding a covered porch or landing can change the whole complexion of a house. This isn't an extremely expensive option, but it can increase the home's appeal and value.

Follow the multi-family guidelines for the siding and roof. Windows and doors are quickly noticed in a home. If the existing windows and doors are outdated, consider replacing them. Paving a gravel driveway adds class and value but is not a good investment unless a majority of the surrounding homes have paved driveways. Shutters are another sensible improvement. They are not too expensive and they add charm to many styles of homes.

Gutters are negotiable. Follow the neighborhood trend with gutters. They are not a necessary improvement and usually will not play a significant role in the sale of the home. On the other hand, if the house has gutters, they should be in good repair. Don't leave rusted gutters or gutters filled with pine needles and leaves ignored. Ugly and neglected gutters are worse than no gutters.

The Interior

Once inside, similar rules to those used in apartments apply. The quality of the improvements can be higher, but the principles are basically the same. Take care of the needs before adding desires. Once the interior meets the minimum requirements, you can contemplate adding special touches.

Much of your decision on what improvements to add will come from your appraisal research. Adding a fireplace is expensive and may be ludicrous. It could also be an excellent selling point and a profitable upgrade. This type of improvement must be justified with supporting appraisal documentation. You should never make capital improvements without knowing the appraisal will support such improvements.

Replacing carpet with hardwood floors is a sure way to lose money. Modern buyers don't expect wood floors, and many don't even like them. The work required to maintain these floors is not appreciated in today's fast-paced lifestyle. Installing an expensive quarry tile floor in the kitchen could be a financial loss. Most houses are equipped with vinyl floors in the kitchen. Your tile upgrade will be appreciated but will probably not pay for itself.

Unless the home is functionally obsolete, don't invest the money to do major interior remodeling. Moving walls, windows, and doors is very expensive. You never know if a prospective buyer will concur with your opinion on what rooms to restructure. Replacing bathroom fixtures is debatable when doing speculative rehab work. The cost is high and the returns are unknown. You could spend $300 on a pedestal sink, only to find the buyer would prefer an oak vanity and cultured marble top.

Stay in Line

Keep your improvements in line with the other local homes. Try to keep your sale price lower than the higher-priced homes in the subdivision. Trying to sell the best house on the street can be a time-consuming process. The money spent on renovations will be reflected in your sale price.

When dealing with residential rehabs, there is no blanket answer on what improvements should be excluded. It may be necessary for your project to include a large deck and sunroom. If these are standard equipment on neighboring homes, you may have to provide similar modifications. Reading comparable sale reports will expose the features expected in your project.

Rehab projects should include all the necessary improvements and none of the frivolous ones. This is a simple statement, but knowing which improvements fall into each category is not so simple. As a rule of thumb, follow the lead of other homes that are selling quickly. A real estate broker can provide information on the recent home sales around your property.

Avoid spending money on improvements that will not expedite the sale of the property. Installing wainscoting and wallpaper will make the home more elegant, but will doing so help it sell faster? Selling for a profit is your goal. If the house sits vacant for an extended time, you are losing money.

Get the Public's Opinion

To make money in the rehab business, you must learn to pick the improvements with the most profit potential. This can only be accomplished by research and experience. If you have doubts, don't invest in the refinement. Many improvements can be made later without undue hardship. Try selling the property and pay attention to the market reaction. If the home is constantly rejected for not having a fireplace, consider building one.

Pre-marketing the home will save you risk and money. By advertising early, you will learn what the public is looking for. Beware of advertising before the basic improvements are made. If you allow your potential purchasers to see the property in its raw stage, they may be repulsed. Get the home into good condition before advertising it. Once the basic repairs are made, offer the property for sale.

When your prospects inspect the property, inquire about their likes and dislikes. Ask them to complete an evaluation form on the property. There is a form below titled Property Evaluation Report. The feedback from the types of comments included in the report will prove invaluable in the marketing of your property. It will also steer you to the final touches you should add to your project.

PROPERTY EVALUATION REPORT

Item	Poor	Fair	Good	Excell.	Item	Poor	Fair	Good	Excell.
Foyer					Closet Space				
Hall					Floor Coverings				
Kitchen					Interior Paint				
Living Room					Plumbing System				
Dining Room					Heating System				
Master Bedroom					Electrical System				
Family Room					Basement				
Bedroom 2					Attic				
Bedroom 3					Insulation				
Bedroom 4					Garage				
Bedroom 5					Deck				
Master Bathroom					Siding				
Bathroom 2					Exterior Paint				
Bathroom 3					Lawn				
Half Bath					Roof				

COMMENTS:

THE SELL OR KEEP OPTION 15

When you consider becoming a rehab investor, are you thinking of doing the rehab and selling as quickly as possible? A majority of the people involved with rehabs are. They plan to buy cheap, renovate, and sell for a fast profit. There is nothing wrong with their plan, but you should explore all your options to maximize your profits. Generating fast sales is good for cash flow, but you may be losing out on potential profit.

As a one-dimensional rehab investor, you are subject to the ever-changing real estate market. When you buy a property to rehab, you must base your income on projections. You can assume the market will remain stable and allow you to make your projected profit. What will you do if the market takes a temporary downturn? You will have a completed rehab project and a bad market in which to try and sell it.

If selling is your only option, you may lose much of your projected income. If you must sell cheap just to get rid of the place, your rehab efforts may not be rewarded. At best, you could only break even. At worst, you could ultimately lose the property in foreclosure proceedings. Real estate runs in cycles, and you must be prepared for the surges and recessions in the market.

CONSIDERING ALTERNATIVES

To be successful for more than a year or two, you must be prepared to accept bad market conditions. At some point, you are going to get caught in the middle of a project, with a declining economy. If you do not have a contingency plan, your rehab days

are numbered. This reason alone is enough to make responsible rehabbers consider their alternatives.

Another reason to look beyond the quick-flip deal is the extra money you can make with a well-rounded approach. With proper planning, you can increase your rehab earnings dramatically. This increased income is the result of a broad range of options. To take advantage of these options, you will have to consider holding your properties a little longer.

Some investors are convinced the only way to make serious money in real estate is to hold it. Historically, real estate does show annual gains in value. It stands to reason that the longer you hold a property, the more it will be worth. As an investor, these holdings must not drain your financial resources during the holding period. The property must pay its own way or provide offsetting qualities to justify holding it.

Being in the rehab business makes it possible to create some very lucrative deals. If you went out and purchased an average single-family home for rental income, you would not show much return, if any, on your investment. If you refurbish a rundown home, it may make an excellent rental investment. Multi-family buildings offer even higher incentives to the rehabber with rental portfolio plans.

Experienced rehabbers frequently concentrate their efforts on renovating properties to include in a personal rental portfolio. When they get an excellent offer they sell, but selling is not their primary motivation. Owning rental property can be addictive and the more you own, the easier it is to acquire more. Professional builders often build property with the sole intent of using it for rental income.

The rental income industry has changed substantially since the tax reform laws were put in place. The changes in the tax laws removed some of the most alluring aspects of landlording. While these changes have made landlording less attractive, owning rental property can still be quite lucrative.

Some rehabbers cringe at the thought of being a landlord. They have heard the horror stories associated with tenants and rental property. In some few cases, being involved with rental property may not suit you. There are aspects of landlording that conflict with certain personalities. Unless you have extreme sensitivity to the thought of holding rental property, you owe it to yourself to explore long-term real estate investments. By long-term, I am referring to a time frame of at least three years.

If you hold a property for three to five years, you may be amazed at the difference in your rehab profit. Even holding the property for a year can create a noticeable increase in your income. As you proceed through the chapter, you will see examples of how you can expand your income with rental holdings.

By converting your rehab to an income-producing property, you can derive several benefits. The equity in your rental portfolio will make your net worth grow. Increased net worth translates into stronger borrowing power. Stronger borrowing power can be directly related to a higher volume of activity. Increased rehab activity should provide increased earnings. This is only the beginning of what rental property can do for your financial statement.

The proper creative rent-with-option-to-buy plans are capable of increasing your monthly cash flow and the profits from your sales. When you put together the right package, your income will explode into a new tax bracket. To avoid the heavy bite of taxes, cultivating property can provide a shelter. With the right sequence of properties, you can enjoy the best of both worlds. You will hold some, sell some, and enjoy every available tax advantage.

REHABBING FOR RETIREMENT

Rehabbing properties to hold until retirement can be a very logical investment. Your rehab profit is present in the equity, and you can leverage each completed property to acquire new ones. With staggered payoff dates, when you retire your income will be very satisfying. Unlike fixed investments, such as certificates of deposit, rents escalate with the cost of living. When your certificate's return is being consumed by inflation, your rental income is keeping stride with rising costs. By retirement, your rental income will be in step with current economic values. The fixed certificate's value will be heavily devalued by inflation. Which would you prefer to have?

Today's dollars will not be worth much in twenty or thirty years. Inflation will reduce the effective amount of today's dollar to a ridiculous figure. There is no way a cash investment can keep up with the fast pace of inflation. Rental property can not only keep up, it can overtake inflation. As the old saying goes, "They are not making any more land." When the land is developed to its limits, those holding real estate will be in control. Let's look at how some of these deals work in the real world.

Since many rehabbers start with single-family homes, the first example is based on this type of property. In the first example, the rehab investor is operating with a plan to sell his completed project. There are several possible outcomes to this investor's rehab plans. The following examples detail some of them.

EXAMPLE ONE

The rehab investor has purchased a home for $52,000. It needs major updating to reach its potential in the open real estate market. Other homes in the neighborhood are selling for $100,000 to $123,000. The projected cost to get the house suitable for competition is $33,000. With a combined investment of $85,000, the resale value of the property, in today's market, will be between $105,000 and $110,000. There is strong evidence to support an acceptable profit.

The rehabber buys the property and completes the prescribed work. The investor acted as his own general contractor in this deal. In the example, the house is sold by a real estate broker for $107,800. The broker's commission is 6% of the sale price or $6,468. This leaves the rehabber with a gross profit, before taxes, of $16,332. This is certainly a very acceptable and lucrative profit. The investor has a state tax consequence of 5%. His federal tax bite is

28%. The combined tax on the property is 33%. This equals a tax payment of about $5,389. The investor's compensation for his efforts is around $10,943. There is no doubt this deal was worth doing and the rehab investor did well.

How could the rehabber have done better? Selling the property himself would have saved a percentage of the broker's commission. There would have been advertising expenses and demands on the investor's time to factor into the savings. For the sake of simplicity in the examples, assume the broker is a necessary cost of sale.

In this example, the net income was nearly $11,000. If you are turning over this kind of money in a few months by general contracting your own rehab deals, you are doing well. Accepting this profit is reasonable, but you are leaving a lot of money on the table. The broker's commission was $6,468 and the tax payment was about $5,389. These two expenses total $11,857. You could be making good use of this money. If the property was held as rental property, these expenses would not be incurred at this time. Your net worth would be stronger by the $11,857 figure.

EXAMPLE TWO

In this scenario, the investor starts with the same plans the investor had in Example One. During the rehab process, many previously undiscovered structural problems are found. The rehab cost exceeds the projected costs by $4,300. These are not optional repairs; they are essential to meet local code requirements. With the same circumstances as found in Example One, these extra costs reduce the investor's profit to less than $6,700. Admittedly, this is still a profit, but it is much smaller than the targeted profit.

With a straight-sell plan, the investor will have to settle for the reduced earnings. If the investor was willing to hold the property, his profit could be recovered over time. Having the ability to retain your rehab projects allows a safety net for miscalculated figures and unforeseen expenses.

EXAMPLE THREE

This example is based on the same projections as in Example One. The investor starts the job anticipating a very comfortable profit. During the rehab process, the real estate market declines rapidly. By the time his rehab project is complete, the market is dead. Buyers are scarce and offers to purchase are well below the market values of only a few months ago. This investor is stuck in a declining market with a vacant property. The interest is adding up on the rehab and acquisition loan.

Every week the property sits idle, the investor loses money. There is no money coming in, but the loan payments must continue to go out. If the loan requirements are not met, the investor will lose the improved property to foreclosure. This rehabber is in a very difficult position. He cannot afford to absorb the carry cost of his loan for very long. His options as a have-to-sell rehabber are extremely limited. To get out of the property, he will forfeit most, if not all, of his rehab profit.

This solution is not palatable, but it looks better than foreclosure and possible bankruptcy. The pressed investor gives in and sells the property to the first qualified buyer making an offer. His net profit from the deal is only $1,800. This isn't enough profit to offset his time in the deal, not to mention his loss of profit. It could have been worse — he could have lost the property and his credit.

If this rehabber was able to hold the property, he could have waited for better times. Since he had placed himself in a box, he escaped, but without a realistic profit. Under the circumstances, he did well to get out with his credit intact. To avoid this type of trap, conceive a contingency plan in advance. To see how having a secondary plan could have helped each of these investors, refer to the following examples. They will show you the benefit of having alternate plans available.

ALTERNATE PLAN FOR EXAMPLE ONE

As mentioned in Example One, the rehab investor saw a pocket profit of just under $11,000. The investor did very well on the deal but could have done better. If the home had been kept for rental property, the broker's commission and the taxes would not have been paid at this time. These two expenses amounted to nearly $12,000. By selling the home, the investor received about $11,000 in cash. If he had held the property, his net worth would have increased by $12,000.

The rehabber's total investment was $85,000. The home was valued at $107,800. The rehabber could have obtained an 80% loan-to-value (LTV) permanent mortgage on the property, with no down payment. On a $107,800 home, the bank would have loaned the investor $86,240. By working with the appraiser to stretch the appraised value, the investor could have placed the permanent loan on the home without using any of his cash. Loan fees and closing costs could have been paid with the additional proceeds from the stronger appraisal.

By doing this deal, the investor would not have received any of his profit in the form of cash. All profit would be invested as equity. The rental income on this sample property would cover the expenses of ownership, but provide no monthly profit. Why would the investor decide to do such a deal? Let's assume the investor was able to obtain a strong appraisal of $110,000. Also assume an annual real estate appreciation rate of 7%; this is a very believable figure. What will the house be worth in five years?

At the end of five years, assuming a steady 7% appreciation rate, the home would be worth over $154,000. This means the home has gained $44,000 in value in just five years. Now, assume the investor had taken the cash from his quick sale and invested it in a certificate of deposit (CD) with an interest rate of 8.5%. What would his cash investment amount to in five years? The original $11,000 investment would have grown to $16,800.

Some quick math will show you which investment strategy provided the highest rate of return. This is strong evidence to support the theory that selling fast is not always best. To be fair in this example, we should factor the cost of sale for the property at the end of five years. Assuming a 6% commission, the broker will take $9,240 of the $44,000. This is only a factor if a broker sells the property.

The tax consequences are too complicated to figure in a simple example. Taxes will affect each of these deals. There will be taxes required for the interest earned on the CD and taxes will be assessed against the profits from a sale. Many factors come into play with the tax angle. Perhaps, at the end of five years, the investor is in a lower tax bracket. This could make a big difference in the tax effects. The investor may have benefited from tax shelter with the property for the last five years. You will have to work the tax computations for your own situation.

If we assume a broker sold the house, the net profit before taxes is reduced to $34,760. This is still double the money earned on the cash investment. You should see the reasoning behind holding your rehabs until they mature. Annual appreciation rates rarely go below 5% and they sometimes go to 15% or more. If you want to really make your eyes blink, run this deal with a 15% appreciation rate.

There is another angle to this same deal. At the end of five years, the house is worth $154,000. The investor has $85,000 invested in it. If the owner refinanced the property with a 20% LTV loan, he could receive $38,200 in cash. There would be no taxes to pay on this cash—it is a loan, not profit. There are no broker's fees to pay with the refinance. The cash taken out of the home's equity is more than double the amount that would be available from the original CD investment.

If rental rates have moved upward with inflation, the new loan could be paid by the increased rental income. The investor still has a break-even rental investment and $38,200 in untaxed dollars to work with. How could it get any better? Well, it gets better because the rents and property value should continue to increase, but the mortgage remains stable. This is an extremely profitable way to do business. Being in the rehab business allows you these extra perks in your retirement planning.

ALTERNATE PLAN FOR EXAMPLE TWO

The rehabber in Example Two would benefit from holding the property. By following the guidelines in the alternate plan for Example One, this investor could increase his profits in a year or two. He could adhere to the advice in the alternate plan for Example One to bring his earnings back on track.

ALTERNATE PLAN FOR EXAMPLE THREE

This investor would have done well to have conceived a backup plan. By following the steps in the alternate for Example One, the investor would be on top of the deal, instead of dodging foreclosure. Even if you never want to be a landlord, developing a contingency plan protects you from financial failure.

These single-family examples should have impressed you. They are very realistic and logical. There are no gimmicks and the money is not made with smoke and mirrors. The earning potential is real and obtainable by the average rehabber. While these examples are producing lucrative compensation, they cannot compare with multi-family properties.

In the next set of examples, the property discussed is a six-unit apartment building. Six-unit buildings are the ideal size for a semi-experienced investor to work with. They are large enough to produce positive cash flow and small enough to manage yourself. In the following examples, the building being rehabbed is a structurally sound six-unit apartment building. It needs updating of the mechanical systems and cosmetic improvements.

The building allows for some increased use of available space. It is also located in an area targeted for renovation incentive programs. All the apartments contain three bedrooms, providing a base for stable tenants and maximum improvement assistance from the targeted funds.

MULTI-FAMILY EXAMPLE

The rehab investor buys a six-unit building with strong rehab potential. The work needed on the building is largely cosmetic. A few upgrades in the mechanical system, some cosmetic work, and the building will be a very attractive income property. The building is purchased for $180,000. The planned improvements are estimated to cost $60,000. The per-plans appraisal indicates a completed value of $300,000. This investor is seeking to make some heavy profit.

The needed work is performed, and the building's value grows to $300,000. Since these are new improvements, the income and expense figures for the newly renovated building are projected. They are not verifiable from a determined history. Trying to sell the building with projected numbers is difficult. The highest offer made on the building is $280,000. Since this is classed as a commercial property, the broker's commission is 10%.

Time is a factor to this rehabber. She has planned to do a quick-flip from the beginning. Since the best offer she has received is $280,000, she accepts it. Her total investment in the property is $240,000.

The real estate commission is $28,000. The investor's profit before taxes is $12,000. In her case, after paying the tax on the profit, she will net $8,400.

The rehab process took three months, and she used the services of a construction management firm. Considering her time investment, this is a satisfactory profit. The investor sells the building and is happy with her financial gains. Being happy with your results is important, but she left a lot of money on the table. The alternate example shows how she could have done much better.

ALTERNATE PLAN FOR THE MULTI-FAMILY EXAMPLE

In the first example, the investor only paid attention to the obvious means of improving the property. She overlooked the potential for adding a coin-operated laundry. The additional cost to add the laundry would have been $2,300. The extra income from the coin-operated machines would have increased the building's worth by $5,600. She essentially threw away $3,300 by not making this one change.

Since she was going to sell the building upon completion, she did not take advantage of the funds targeted to improve the area. In a quick-sale situation, these low-interest loans are not as important as they would be to the investor with long-range holding plans. Because she sold the building through a broker, her cost of sale was $28,000. All these are areas she would have been wise to evaluate before making a decision on the disposition of the property.

Since each apartment contained three bedrooms, the property was capable of attracting long-term tenants. The location was good, and the improvements to the property made it a desirable rental choice. How could she have done better? There were numerous options open to this investor. If she had taken advantage of them, her deal would have looked like this.

For her best deal, she would have made use of all available resources and held the building as a profitable rental property. In the following scenario, the investor is going to hold the building for five years. In addition to the $60,000 improvement costs, she should have included the $2,300 to add the laundry facilities. The acquisition cost is the same—$180,000. The combined investment in the property is $242,300.

Instead of selling the building, the investor rents the units for a high market rent. This is possible due to the three-bedroom units and new improvements. The lender will loan $240,000 on the property; this is an 80% LTV loan. The interest rate from the commercial lender is 11.5%. The loan has a twenty-year term with a fixed rate. The monthly payment is $2,559.43. At this payment, the building shows a slight negative cash flow. The negative cash flow could be offset by tax advantages. This is not a bad deal, but there is a better option available.

The investor could borrow the acquisition cost from a commercial lender and the improvement money from targeted rehab funds available for neighborhood revitalization. If she did this, the commercial loan would be for $180,000. The payment on this loan is $1,919.57. The rehab loan is in the amount of $62,300. The term is twenty years, with a fixed rate of 9%. The payment on the rehab loan is $560.52.

The total monthly payment on the property is $2,480.09. This represents a savings of $79.34 per month when compared to using straight commercial loan money. This savings is enough to make the property pay for itself. The investor has financed the entire property, except for loan fees and closing costs. She has almost no cash investment in the property. In the first example, her after-sale, before-tax profit was $12,000.

First, let's see what her $12,000 would be worth in five years. If the entire $12,000 could be invested in a CD at 8.5%, what would it yield? Remember, the $12,000 profit was before taxes, so there would be less than $12,000 to invest after taxes were paid. I am doing the example in this manner to make the figures easy to understand. The $12,000 cash investment would be worth $18,327.61 at the end of five years. Now, examine the return of investment from the building.

Multi-family property does not always appreciate as rapidly as single-family homes do. For this example, assume a stable 5% annual appreciation rate. The building's beginning value, including the laundry, is $305,600. The total money invested in the property is $242,300. A key factor is that none of this money belonged to the investor. It was all leverage equity, not cash. At the end of five years,

the building is worth a whopping $392,194.41.

If the building is sold for this price, with a 10% brokerage fee, the gross earnings are $110,674.96. When you compare the value of both efforts before taxes, holding the building grosses a profit of $92,347.36 more than the quick-sell deal. With this kind of money to be made, landlording is a tolerable business. You can afford to hire someone else to deal with the rental details and still walk away with staggering profits.

These are not exaggerated examples; these results are very possible in the average real estate market. Changing the way you look at your rehab endeavors can mean more money in the bank. Consider the results of refinancing the building at the end of five years. With an 80% LTV loan, the refinance would give you $71,455.52 in untaxed dollars to play with. There would be minor refinancing fees for the new loan, but they would be insignificant compared to the advantages.

This type of rehab strategy is what makes millionaires. Instead of being shortsighted, look to the future. When you are fortunate enough to acquire a good building, strongly consider keeping it. These "keepers" are worth their weight in advantages and increased income.

DON'T TRAP YOURSELF

As you gain experience, you will learn to increase the compensation for your rehab work. There are many ways to expand the profit potential in real estate ventures. Reading and paying attention to other investors' activities will help you identify strong opportunities. When building a no-money-down rental portfolio, there are risks involved. You must be responsible enough to avoid tying yourself into a financial knot.

The ease of this type of fast money-making deal is addictive. The more you do, the more you want to do. In addition, the more you do, the stronger your net worth becomes. These two factors place you at risk. Without careful planning, you can get leveraged beyond your abilities. On paper, these deals show a no-lose potential. In reality, you could be stranded with vacant apartments and negative cash flow. Before putting everything on the line, be sure you can deal with the worst case scenario.

LIQUIDITY COUNTS

Building your real estate empire is both fun and lucrative; losing it is devastating. To ensure longevity in the business, develop a liquid investment fund to protect your real estate. This is easy to do in the rehab business. Keep the best properties and sell the marginal ones. The proceeds from your sales can be placed in safe liquid investments. These liquid assets can be used to bridge the gap during tough rental conditions.

Real estate investment always requires some level of risk. The risk factor is why many investors enjoy playing the market. Smart investors never risk more than they can afford to lose. If you get consumed in the get-rich-quick crowd, you may find yourself in the bankruptcy courts before your investments mature. With logic and well-founded research, you can get rich with real estate. The safe route will take a little longer, but the rewards will last much longer.

As a multi-family broker, I have put many investors on the path to financial freedom. Some of these investors balked at my advice and tried to become high rollers. Many of this group did not have sufficient reserve capital and ultimately lost everything. All I could do was relate my experiences to them. They felt they could beat the odds and continued to buy with abandon. In time, often in less than two years, these fast-paced investors no longer owned apartments, they were renting them. I want to stress the risk involved with the lure of such large sums of money. The money is real and achievable, but the risks are just as real. Take the time to calculate your exposure and protect yourself from financial failure.

RENTAL REPERCUSSIONS AND REWARDS 16

Becoming a landlord is a natural progression for the real estate investor with rehab experience. Occasionally, a property comes along that offers too much long-term potential to sell quickly. The rehabber chooses to hold the property while its value appreciates. He turns to the rental market. Using the property for rental purposes provides income and allows the profit to build. Although there are many pitfalls to landlording, foresight and careful planning can reduce the risks.

Many investors buy with the sole intent of creating a retirement income and high net worth. Income property meets both of these goals and allows the rehab profits to escalate each year. When a property is sold immediately upon completion of rehabilitation efforts, the profit is good. When this same property is sold five years later, after being used to produce monthly cash flow, the profits are great. Building a strong rental portfolio deserves every rehabber's attention.

Rehab property can be placed in two groups. The first group is known as *flippers*. The second group is called *keepers*. Flippers are properties offering little long-term, high-gain potential. They are best suited for buying, rehabbing quickly, and selling immediately upon completion. Keepers have underlying features providing strong evidence of fast appreciation in just a few years. These buildings beg to be rehabbed, used as income property, and sold a few years later.

QUICK SALES

Flippers may be in stagnant locations. This quality suggests holding the property will not significantly increase its value. Buying the building at the right price allows for instant rehab profits but little hope for large future gains. These quick-turn investments may have overall deteriorating construction conditions. With this situation, an experienced rehabber will give the unit a facelift and roll it quickly for a profit. Keeping the real estate requires continual maintenance and offers little hope for high appreciation. While this type of property may be acceptable for a personal residence, it is not a good long-term investment.

A KEEPER

Buying a home requiring only minor cosmetic work to create instant equity is always a good deal. If this home is located near a site proposed for future development, it can be a gold mine. Depending on the type of development, the home's value can build in astounding increments. Consider this example. You purchase a home in need of new paint, floor coverings, bath fixtures, and kitchen cabinets. These are all minor rehab jobs, but they will increase the value of the home overnight. Assume your rehab work will produce enough equity to allow you to own the house with no out-of-pocket cash investment.

If the home can be financed to reimburse you for your rehab expenses and cover the acquisition cost, you own it without putting your cash into it. Instead of selling the home to reduce your mortgage debt, you lease the home to negate the loan payments. In addition to having your invested money returned through financing, you also enjoy the benefit of the remaining equity. You don't have your cash profit yet, but you do have a paper profit.

Your financial statement shows the remaining equity as a part of your net worth. The increased net worth and rental income allow you to continue to buy more properties. The more you buy under these conditions, the more your net worth grows. This can be addictive and will be discussed a little later. For now, concentrate on the example. You have bought a house without investing any of your cash. The house is rented for enough to pay the mortgage payments, and you have increased your net worth.

The house has cost you nothing in terms of cash outlay. Real estate traditionally appreciates every year. Appreciation rates average 5% and in some areas approach 15%. This factor alone is enough to make you think about building a stable of rental properties. The real advantage to this particular house is its speculation value. If the future development plans of the city proceed as planned, this house will become a true treasure. It is located near the proposed site of a new school and shopping center. These proposed developments are scheduled for completion in four years.

When the new school and shopping center are built, this home's value could increase by 30% or more. As the years between now and then recede, the value steadily grows. Short-term investors will be looking for property in this development zone. They will seek housing in good condition for a quick profit. Their intent is to buy the house in year three and sell it in year four, when the projects are completed.

THE SLY SLEUTH

After the new school and shopping center are finished, home buyers will flock to the area. They want a home close to the convenience of the shopping center and near the school. Having done your preliminary research for highest and best use, you know of this potential now. Most home buyers and many investors will not be buying in the area until construction starts on the new projects. At the earliest, they won't concentrate on this area until the media begins playing up the coming development. Your early detective work has put you in a power position.

If you sell the house as soon as the remodeling is complete, you will make a $12,000 profit. By holding the property, you stand to see a profit in excess of $40,000. All you have to do to earn this additional profit is keep the house and maintain its physical condition. Using the home for rental property gives you the ability to wait. By becoming a part-time landlord, you are more than tripling your rehab profits. Can you see the advantages offered from income-producing profits?

THE TAX ANGLE

Other advantages can include some tax breaks and possibly additional profits from the rental income. Many of the tax advantages were stripped from landlording with the tax reform changes. But there are still tax savings to be had with investment property. The rules for these savings are complex and should be discussed with a certified public accountant. Obtaining a positive cash flow from a single-family home is difficult. In this case, it would be worth feeding a small negative cash flow to get to the final windfall profit. Run the numbers and evaluate your personal situation. Talking with a CPA will clear up questions you may have on tax advantages, and cash flow is a subject you are qualified to make the decision on.

THE TRAP

In this example, I spoke of building net worth as being addictive. It is and can be dangerous. Highly leveraging yourself into multiple properties can place you in jeopardy. The no-money-down approach is popular and sought by thousands of investors. In limited use, or for special properties, this approach is fine. Using the no-money-down method for marginal properties may force you into bankruptcy. An investment property must be able to appreciate faster than normal to warrant a no-money-down approach.

When investors learn how to buy real estate without using their own cash, they become greedy. Their objectivity is distorted by the ease with which their holdings grow. At first glance, this newfound way to wealth appears unstoppable. When the investor's primary reason for buying a property is the availability of creative financing, he sets himself up for a fall. The fall will be hard and can come fast. Experienced investors know *you must buy real estate because it is a good investment, not because you can buy it without a down payment*.

Engrave this advice into your brain. When you get on the fast track, it is easy to be blinded by racking up large numbers on your financial statement. Remember, it is not the quantity of your assets that counts. The most important number on your financial statement is the net worth number. Buying numerous properties with extreme leverage will do little to increase your net worth. This policy results in a modest net worth increase and a massive increase in risk. Take it from an investor who learned the hard way—buy solid investments, not creatively financed deals.

LANDLORDING

Now, with the lecture behind us, let's look ahead to landlording. If you are going to build a rental portfolio, you will become a landlord. Knowing the ins and outs of landlording means the difference between happiness and despair. Even if you engage a property management firm, you should learn the basics of landlording. Whether you own one single-family home or dozens of apartment buildings, these principles will keep your cash flow and your attitude positive.

Professional Property Management

Hiring a property management firm is the easiest way to be a landlord. You give them 10% of your gross rental income, and they handle the everyday problems of tenants and the building. The amount charged varies, but 10% is the accepted average. In addition to the fixed percentage, many companies charge extra for services you might think are included in the set percentage. Some property management firms charge you for all advertisements placed to secure tenants. You may be charged a showing fee every time they show your rental unit. They may charge another fee, known as a rent-up fee, when they find a tenant to lease your space.

Other charges may be applied if repairs to the property are needed. Some firms charge a fee for supervising the repairs. This fee is typically 10% of the total cost of the authorized repair. The company doing the repairs may be owned by the property management firm. This creates a circumstance for conflict of interest and unreasonable repair charges. Depending on your contract with the management firm, you could be spending upwards of 20% of your gross income for their service.

The advantage to a good management firm is your lack of contact with tenants and their experience with rental properties. This benefit may be worth a percentage of your gross, but be sure what you are getting for your money. The amount charged by management companies can turn a positive cash flow into a loss. As with most things in life, few people take as much interest in your money as you do. Learning to run your own rentals will save you money, and you will know where every dime is being spent.

If a management firm offers enough benefits to warrant your business, investigate the company thoroughly. Don't sign a contract with the first company you interview. Shop management firms for the best prices and services. Approach a management contract with the same caution you exercise in a general or subcontractor contract. If you prefer doing things yourself, the following information will be indispensable in your tenure as a landlord.

The Do-It-Yourself Approach

If you are acquiring a property already containing tenants, you may be able to raise the rents. Tenants expect a new owner to increase the rent and will be expecting you to do so upon possession. But immediate rent increases can cause your newly acquired property to become vacant fast. There is a much safer way to raise the rents without losing the tenants.

Write each tenant a letter explaining their building has been sold and as the new owner, you would like to meet with them. When you meet for the first time, tenants will barrage you with questions. The question of rent increases will be high on most tenants' list. When confronted with this question, be diplomatic. Explain to the tenant that you want to complete some research before making a determination on the rental charges. This first meeting should not be used to discuss raising the rent directly. This is a fact-finding mission, designed to provide information to base your landlording decisions on.

Interview the tenants and make notes from what is said. Decide whether the tenant is the type of tenant you want in the property. If they meet your preliminary approval, move into the paperwork stage. This is when you leave a handful of forms for the tenant to complete. These should include a Rental Policy Form and Tenant Rental Application Form. Examples of these forms are provided at the end of the chapter. Make arrangements for the tenant to mail the forms to you within five days. Don't meet with the tenant personally to pick up the forms. The tenant would have an opportunity to read your reactions and probe you for information. This is your fact-finding mission, not his.

I have included numerous landlording forms in this chapter. By obtaining the information requested on these forms, you will be able to make informed decisions on the tenants and rental conditions. If you decide to keep a tenant, it is necessary to plow through more paperwork. Keep your rehab activities in mind before making commitments to tenants. If they will be living in the property during the renovations, set the ground rules now.

Making the Rules

Draft an agreement with the tenant allowing you access to the rental unit. Establish the acceptable working hours and how the remodeling will be done. Coordinating your refurbishing with a tenant's schedule can be tedious. All this should be decided before you agree to keep the tenant in the building. Put everything in writing and have the tenant sign the agreement. If the tenant's presence will not impede your rehab work, try to keep the property occupied. The rental income is welcome and reduces the cost of your construction financing.

When you decide to maintain existing tenants, you should have them complete a new rental agreement or lease. You will find a Sample Lease at the end of the chapter. If rental deposits did not exist when you purchased the property, obtain deposits with the new leases. Check the laws in your area, but you will most likely need a new bank account. This account should be an escrow account for holding the tenants' deposits. At this same time, you may want to raise the rent. Before picking a new rent rate, do some market research on comparable rents.

Check Your Rent Figures

Keep your new rents in line with other rents in the area. Settled tenants will be prone to pay the additional rent without a ruckus. Their option to move is not the most workable one. A new apartment will cost as much as the one they are in, and they will incur moving expenses. The inconvenience of moving is another motivator for the tenant to accept the rental increase. If your improvements will be completed quickly, you might wait until then to raise the rents. Tenants have no trouble understanding a rent increase if they are getting improved living conditions.

Tenant Acquisition

When you are ready to find new tenants, be selective. Finding good tenants is time consuming but not nearly as difficult as removing a bad tenant. There are a few tricks of the trade that can reduce your time spent renting your property. The first deals with advertising. I have found you will get a better quality tenant with highly descriptive advertisements. The more information an ad contains, the fewer curiosity calls you will receive. Having the phone ringing constantly is annoying and a waste of time. You should only be interested in talking with qualified tenants.

If you are not going to allow pets, put it in the ad. State the amount of the monthly rent and the security deposit. Having the rental rates in the ad reduces the number of calls from people unable to afford your dwelling. Include the number of bedrooms, as this is always a concern of prospective tenants. Describe relevant amenities such as laundry facilities, a fenced yard, and off-street parking. You can expand on these ideas, but the point is to include all pertinent details in the ad. The added expense of the larger ad will be recovered in the lack of wasted time handling worthless phone calls. Avoid wasting words on overly descriptive explanations of hardwood floors, sunny kitchens, or nice neighborhoods. You can relate these features to prospective tenants once the phone starts ringing.

When you are going to show the rental property, schedule as many showings as possible for the same day. Schedule them about fifteen minutes apart. This is another time management maneuver. Some people will not show up for the scheduled appointment. Using this stacked showing principle, you will only lose fifteen minutes of your time before the next prospect arrives. This is much better than driving across town to show a property to a single prospect who never shows up. The mental effect of this continuous string of prospective tenants also has value. If a prospect is interested in the rental and sees a long line of other interested parties, he or she may be driven to a quick decision.

Take blank Tenant Rental Application Forms with you for each showing. An example is given at the end of the chapter. Have all prospective tenants complete the application. Verify references, employment, and credit history. Don't fall for the old trick of giving friends and relatives as previous landlord references. Bad tenants are resourceful and know how to deceive you. Avoid this with thorough investigation of all information on the application.

Here is one suggestion for weeding through a possible deception. When calling the references, avoid identifying yourself and the specific reason for your call. One approach is as follows:

"Hello, this is Bob Roberts. I'm calling as a follow-up on some information provided to us by Dave Farrel. Dave said we could give you a call and you would tell us a little bit about your relationship with Dave. Could you tell me how long you and Dave have been friends?"

Wording of this nature throws co-conspirators off track. They may forget who they are supposed to be, or not realize you are Dave's prospective landlord. Many times you will get some interesting candid answers to this line of questioning.

If everything checks out, arrange another meeting with the prospective tenant. Meeting him in his present home is the ideal place for this rendezvous. If you can meet in his home, you will be able to see how he lives. Don't give him enough time to alter his living habits. Make the meeting time first and then set the meeting for his residence. Go to the ap-

pointment with all your pre-rental forms. These should include a rental policy form, a property description, and even change of address forms, which are often available free from the post office and utility companies. Bring a copy of your lease, but keep it separate from the other forms. If you don't like what you see of his housekeeping, ask him to review the rental policy form and mail it back to you. This gives you a reason for being there without committing you to signing a lease on the spot.

If the tenant meets with your approval, have him fill out the lease as well. You can do this on the spot or allow him to mail the forms back to you. These forms lay down the law and make your intentions known. They save frustration for you and the tenant. If the conditions of the rental cannot be agreed to, you can part company before having the tenant in your property. This is an integral step to building a solid rental relationship.

Keeping Good Tenants

Once you find a good tenant, it is imperative to keep the tenant. Good tenants make landlording easy, and they are worth extra effort to keep. If the terms of the tenancy are clearly understood, you should not have major problems with responsible tenants. When small problems arise, respond to the tenant's requests. If the faucet is dripping, fix it. You will save money on your water bill, and the tenant will be happy.

While it is important to respect good tenants, it is also important to maintain an arms-length relationship. Don't get involved with the tenant on a personal level. Follow standard social protocol, but don't become buddies with your tenants. You must maintain control at all times. Never engage in activities with the tenants that are not related to the rental property. If you get too friendly, you will not be able to enforce your rules as effectively.

When Tenants Turn Bad

Even with extensive investigation and judgment calls, you may find yourself cursed with unsavory tenants. Typically, these occupants fall into two classes. The first is the late-pay group; the second is the rules-don't-matter type. Beware of tenants who no longer pay their rent on time. Often, due to financial distress or lack of concern, this group will gradually pay the rent later and later. It starts a week in arrears, then two, and before you know it they are a month behind. Yes, your lease is a legal document that binds them to pay in accordance with the lease terms, but when those terms are ignored additional steps must be taken. You may find it necessary to issue a Notice to Pay Rent or Quit as a preliminary step towards eviction. See the example at the end of the chapter. Eviction laws vary from state to state and should be discussed with an attorney.

A late-paying tenant may be undergoing a temporary financial hardship or may see withholding rent as the only solution to a problem with the property. The group that blatantly ignores stipulations in the lease or rental policy is much more difficult to deal with. Often, you will not even be aware of their infractions unless you visit the property for some reason. Suddenly, you discover they have dogs, cats, or even pigs on the property, not to mention junked cars and a trash pile the size of Mt. Everest. A Thirty-Day Notice to Perform Covenant should be delivered to them immediately (see the end of the chapter).

One way to avoid unpleasant surprises is to visit the property regularly. Many landlords include trash pickup or grass-cutting services as part of the lease. This allows them to catch many infringements on rental policies before they become extreme.

Eviction

Removing problem tenants is aggravating and costly. The best approach to this problem is to avoid it. Eviction is the ugliest word in landlording. Following the above advice should limit your exposure to the bad guys, but you may still get stuck with one now and then. If you find yourself in a combat position, maintain your composure. Threatening to take the tenant to court is not your first course of action. Talking is a much more sensible solution to the problem.

Before taking any action, consult an attorney. Tenants have long lists of rights, and you don't want to be the one being sued. Follow your attorney's advice and try to negotiate a friendly departure. The cost of a full-blown eviction is considerable. If you can buy the tenant out of the building, you may be money ahead. I know this goes against the grain.

You are paying a tenant to leave who probably owes you money. Put these emotions aside and look at the situation with a business person's eye.

Evictions can take months to perform. During this time, you have a bad tenant and probably no rental income. If the unit rents for $600, the rental loss from a four-month eviction is $2,400. Add to this attorney's fees, possible countersuit fees, and lost time from work. Your cost to remove a renegade tenant could easily top $5,000. Do you really want to stand up for what's right and proceed this way?

An Alternative Option

Consider this option. Let's say the tenant owes you $600 and refuses to leave. You can offer to forgive the debt and not take legal action as a motivation for the tenant to vacate. If this doesn't work, give the tenant $500 as "moving money." The tenant who accepts this proposal is saving you money. You lose up to $1,100, instead of up to $5,000. With diplomatic skills, you might be able to talk the tenant out of the building.

Listen to the tenant's grievance and consider removing his objections. Sometimes a small compromise is all that is needed to change a horrible situation. Do whatever you legally can to avoid going through an extended eviction. When the tenant leaves you with no other options, depend on your attorney for the removal of the hardnose. Walk carefully around the eviction issue; it can get out of hand quickly.

Moving Out

Whether with good lessees or bad, when the time comes for a tenant to move, be involved in the process. Being present to inspect the property promptly benefits you and the tenant. A thorough rental policy form requires the tenants to provide you with a punch-list when they first move in. You can refer to this list now and note any specific damages caused since that time. Disagreements over damages are reduced. The tenants receive their refundable security deposit faster, and you notice problems sooner. If the decision to move is not shared by you and the tenant, you are in for a bad time.

INSURANCE

Insurance—this word may chill your spine with resentment, and the premiums may be high, but you cannot afford to operate without it. Insurance is a cost of doing business and a necessity of the rental profession. What type of insurance do you need? Well, in this litigious world, the more coverage you have, the safer you are. Today's tenants may try to make their fortune by taking yours in a lawsuit. Let's review the various types of insurance and their place in a landlording enterprise.

Fire Insurance

Fire insurance is pretty self-explanatory. It protects you from losses incurred from fire damage. If your property is financed, the lender requires fire insurance. They insist on coverage in an amount at least equal to the loan amount. The lender will stipulate themselves as the beneficiary of benefits until the loan is satisfied. If the proceeds from the insurance claim exceed the payoff amount of the loan, you will be entitled to the remaining money.

In addition to the minimum required coverage, you should have coverage to protect your equity. Don't try to over-insure your building. If you have replacement cost insurance, you will only be awarded money to replace the building. You cannot insure the building for an extra $50,000 and put the additional money in your pocket. When determining how much fire insurance is needed, don't include the land value in your cost estimates. Land is not a factor in fire insurance; it will still be there when the smoke clears.

Extended Coverage

Investigate extended coverage for your insurance policy. For small additional premiums, you can benefit from a variety of protection. Some of these additional coverage items might include:

❑ falling trees

❑ hail

❑ glass breakage

❑ vandalism

❑ freeze damage

❑ explosion

❑ ruptured plumbing

❑ high winds

These and other additional rider coverage are worth looking into. Their cost may be minimal when combined with your fire insurance policy.

Flood Insurance

Flood insurance is rarely purchased unless the property is situated in a flood zone or flood plain. The same applies to earthquake insurance. It is an uncommon purchase for investors in average areas. These two types of insurance are specialized and are not normally needed. If you feel your investment is at risk from flooding or earthquakes, consult your insurance agent.

Loss-of-Rents Insurance

Loss-of-rents insurance could benefit any landlord. These policies vary in content and conditions, but they are desirable. If your rental units become uninhabitable, you will have some retribution from the insurance company. In a serious case, such as a fire, these policies can save your property and your credit rating. Investigate the types of coverage available and evaluate their benefits to you.

Personal Property Insurance

A policy for your belongings housed in the property may be in order. If you keep lawn care equipment or tools on site, get a policy to cover them. Your homeowner's insurance may not cover the personal property under these conditions. Premiums for this coverage will not amount to much, and if something happens, you will be glad you have it.

Mortgage Insurance

Mortgage insurance is mostly a thing of the past. The purpose behind this insurance is to satisfy the loan upon your demise. These policies carry steep premiums and are often cost-prohibitive. The same result can be achieved with an inexpensive decreasing-term life insurance policy. If you die, the proceeds from the policy can be used to satisfy the property's mortgage. This method leaves your heirs with a choice. They can pay off the mortgage or make some other use of the payoff.

Title Insurance

Title insurance is a requirement of lenders in most locations. This insurance protects against claims from unidentified alleged owners of the property. Title inspections are required before this insurance is issued. The person checking the title performs an extensive search of the title. He or she looks for liens, attachments, old and outstanding loans, and a chain of title. These searches are very effective, and problems rarely arise after title insurance is issued. In a worst case scenario, you could lose the property, but the title company would reimburse you financially for your loss.

If an old and undiscovered heir claimed ownership of your property, he or she could be granted possession. The same is true of old but perfected liens, judgment attachments, and related clouds of title. The title insurance cannot guarantee you will not lose possession of the property. It is designed to protect you financially if the property is lost. When the property is financed, the lender is the first beneficiary. After the loan is satisfied, you receive the residual money.

Liability Insurance

Liability insurance falls into the must-have category. You cannot afford to own property without liability insurance. Liability insurance protects your assets from a multitude of lawsuits. People falling on your icy sidewalk will not take your personal residence. Loose shingles blowing off the building onto a classic Corvette will not put you in debtor's prison. You need to protect yourself and your assets from any conceivable eventuality.

When shopping liability insurance, look for quality coverage. Demand the best and buy enough of it. With most insurance carriers, a million dollar policy will not be much more than a policy with a quarter-million dollar cap. You may have trouble envisioning being sued for more than a few hundred thousand dollars. This is a common response, but it is not rational. Today's legal system encourages people to exploit the smallest liability claim. If someone is permanently crippled or killed, you could be faced with a massive lawsuit. Don't gamble everything you have worked for to save a few bucks.

KEEP GOOD RECORDS

Keeping good records is required to get the most from your time as a landlord. You should endeavor to make a strong paper trail on all your landlord-related expenses. These expense files need to be organized and accurate. They are worth money to you at tax time. To obtain maximum benefits from your rental property, your records must be precise. Talk with tax professionals to determine what tax advantages apply to your personal status. Don't treat your rental endeavor as a hobby. Even if you enjoy being a landlord, income property should be treated as a business. Without this approach, you will not realize the profits you deserve.

SUBSIDIZED HOUSING FUNDS

The last key factor affecting your landlording business may be subsidized housing money. In the rental business, this is called "Section 8 money." This program was established in or about 1974. It is a federal program encompassing billions of dollars. The program is designed to help ill-fortuned people live acceptable lives. As a landlord, you have a choice; you can participate in the program, but you are not required to.

On a local level, the players in the program are the landlord, the tenant, and a housing authority. Tenants must meet defined criteria to qualify for rental assistance. Landlords' buildings must meet certain specifications to house Section 8 tenants. Tenants may qualify for a number of reasons. They may be elderly, financially restricted, single, married, or meet one of many mandated requirements.

Qualification incomes vary from region to region. Typically, the income requirements are aimed at people with below average incomes. In most cases, your property will have to have certain physical characteristics to qualify for the program. These restrictions are liberal and not difficult to comply with. If your building is considered in compliance with local building codes, it will probably qualify for Section 8 funding. The local housing authority acts as a liaison with the Housing and Urban Development agency.

How It Works

Tenants apply to the housing authority for help.

The housing authority inspects all facilities offered for subsidized housing. Then the matchmaking begins. When a tenant finds a suitable property, he requests a lease. If you, as the landlord, agree to accept the tenant, you must request a property inspection. If you, the tenant, and the housing authority have a meeting of the minds, you sign a lease. The lease has a term of one year. If your property fails the inspection test, you are given the chance to bring it into compliance with housing authority rules.

The landlord receives a modest portion of the monthly rent from the tenant. The remainder and bulk of the rent comes directly from the housing authority. This is guaranteed money, and it can do a lot for your cash flow. You can apply to the housing authority to have your building placed on their rental list. While this is guaranteed money, it is not a free ride. Section 8 tenancies require effort and can go bad.

The program is mixed with advantages and disadvantages. You have Uncle Sam on your side when it comes to collecting the lion's share of your rent. If the tenants default and are evicted, the government meets their end of the obligation. The program enables you to reduce your potential vacancy rate. Typically, there is an abundant source of qualified tenants waiting to rent your empty units.

Paperwork can pile up with the Section 8 program, but any government interaction requires reams of paper. You must commit to a one-year lease. This is good when things go well but may become a hassle under some circumstances. You are dealing with a tenant who is not paying the total rental expense. This could result in a lack of responsibility on the tenant's part. Normally, these disadvantages are overcome by the advantages.

You enjoy stable one-year leases, guaranteed income, and controlled rental conditions. In many instances, you obtain a higher income from subsidized tenants. The housing authority has maximum rental values for different areas. Many investors exploit this procedure and increase their rental income accordingly. Obviously, if you plan to sell, increased income means increased value. The housing authority representative may negotiate rental amounts with you. You are not assured of receiving the maximum rent, but the odds favor the landlord.

There is a common resistance to subsidized housing by investors. Prejudiced landlords believe everyone on subsidized housing is a deadbeat. This is not true! Many of the recipients are disadvantaged, responsible people. These people can make model tenants. Many of them are elderly or physically disabled. They are not all lazy good-for-nothing jerks looking for a pleasure ride on our tax dollars. If you can't get past this impression, forget Section 8 funding.

Treat a Section 8 tenant just as you would any other tenant. Have him follow your pre-rental guidelines, and you perform your responsibilities as a landlord. If you do this, you may be pleasantly surprised. For further information on this program, contact your local housing authority. Proceed on this path with an open mind, but don't close your eyes. There are bad tenants in any program, and you must evaluate each tenant for yourself. These tenants do not pose any more risk than an open-market tenant does. If anything, you have some additional assurances because of the structured program.

Learning these landlording procedures expands your profit potential. You can take advantage of larger profits through annual appreciation. Consider this facet of real estate for your plans. You will probably become a landlord at some time in your rehab career. If you stay in the business, there will be deals too tempting to part with. When this happens, you should be prepared to make property management decisions.

RENTAL POLICY FORM

GENERAL RULES AND REGULATIONS FOR TENANTS

1. Keep all areas clean.

2. Do not disturb other people's peace and quiet.

3. Do not alter the dwelling.

4. Park only in assigned parking spaces.

5. Keep the parking area clean and free of oil drippings.

6. Do not repair motor vehicles on the premises.

7. Owners may inspect the dwelling with 24 hours' verbal notice.

8. Owners may have reasonable access to have work done on the dwelling.

9. Owners or their agent may show the dwelling to prospective tenants or purchasers at reasonable times, with 24 hours' verbal notice.

10. Use of a water bed requires written permission from the landlord.

11. Tenant is required to pay all costs of repairs or damage, including drain stoppages they or their guests cause.

12. Tenants shall maintain adequate heat in their dwelling at all times to prevent plumbing from freezing.

13. Tenants shall provide Owners with a punch-list of any existing items that are damaged, missing, or

    in need of repair within five days of taking possession of the property.

14. Tenants shall inform the Owners of any defects or material problems that may cause damage to the property.

15. Pets are allowed only by written permission of the landlord.

16. Violation of any part of these requirements, or the conditions of the lease or nonpayment of rent as agreed, shall be cause for eviction and all legal action allowed by law.

LEASE

This agreement is between _____, Owners, and _____, Tenants, for a dwelling located at:
_____, unit number _____.

Tenants agree to lease this dwelling for a term of _____, beginning _____, and ending _____, for $_____, per _____, payable in advance on the first day of every _____. Rent shall be paid to _____. Payments shall be mailed to _____, at _____.

The first _____ rent for this dwelling is $ _____. The entire sum of this lease is $ _____. The security deposit on this dwelling is $ _____. This deposit is refundable if Tenants comply with this lease and leave the dwelling clean and undamaged. If Tenants intend to move at the end of this lease, they agree to give Owners notice, in writing, at least thirty days before the lease expires. A deposit of $ _____ will be required for two keys. It will be refunded to the Tenants when both keys are returned to the Owners. Owners will refund all deposits due within ten days after Tenants have moved out completely and returned the keys. Only the following persons are to live in the above-mentioned dwelling:

_____

_____

_____

Without Owners' prior written permission, no other persons may live in the dwelling and no pets shall be admitted to the dwelling, even temporarily. The dwelling may not be sublet or used for business purposes.

Use of the following is included in the rent, at Tenants' own risk: _____.

Tenants agree: (1) to keep all areas clean; (2) not to disturb other people's peace and quiet; (3) not to alter the dwelling without first obtaining the Owners' written permission; (4) to park in an assigned parking space; (5) to keep the parking area clean and free of oil drippings; (6) not to repair motor vehicles on the premises; (7) to allow Owners to inspect the dwelling with twenty-four hours' verbal notice; (8) to allow the Owners reasonable access to have work done on the dwelling; (9) to allow the Owners, or their agent, to show the dwelling to prospective tenants or purchasers at reasonable times, with twenty-four hours' verbal notice; (10) not to use a water bed without written permission from the owner. (11) to pay all costs of repairs or damage, including drain stoppages, which they or their guests cause; (12) to maintain adequate heat in their dwelling at all times to prevent plumbing from freezing; (13) to inform the Owners of any defects or material problems that may cause damage to the property. Violation of any part of this agreement, or nonpayment of rent as agreed, shall be cause for eviction and all legal action allowed by law. The Owners reserve the right to seek any legal means to collect monies owed to them. The prevailing party shall recover reasonable attorney's fees incurred to settle disputes.

SPECIAL TERMS OR CONDITIONS

_____

_____

_____

_____

_____

_____

Tenants hereby acknowledge that they have read this agreement, understand the entire agreement, agree to the entire agreement, and have been given a copy of the agreement.

IF YOU DO NOT UNDERSTAND THIS DOCUMENT, CONSULT AN ATTORNEY.
THIS IS A LEGAL, BINDING DOCUMENT.

Owner	Date	Tenant	Date
Owner	Date	Tenant	Date
Witness	Date	Witness	Date

TENANT RENTAL APPLICATION FORM

Name _____

Social security # _____ Home phone _____

Current address _____

How long at present address _____

Landlord's name _____ Phone _____

Reason for leaving _____

PREVIOUS ADDRESSES FOR THE LAST THREE YEARS

Address _____ From _____ to _____

Landlord's name _____ Phone _____

Reason for moving _____

Address _____ From _____ to _____

Landlord's name _____ Phone _____

Reason for moving _____

Address _____ From _____ to _____

Landlord's name _____ Phone _____

Reason for moving _____

Driver's license # _____ State _____

Vehicle license # _____ State _____

Car make _____ Model _____ Year _____

CREDIT REFERENCES

Name _____ Account # _____

Address _____

Name _____ Account # _____

Address _____

Name _____ Account # _____

Address _____

Name, address, and phone number of nearest relative not living with you:

_____

Name, address, and phone number of two personal references not related to you:

_____

_____

Names of all people planning to reside in your rental unit:

_____

_____

OTHER PERTINENT INFORMATION

_____

_____

NOTICE TO PAY RENT OR QUIT

To _____, tenant in possession:

Please be advised, your rent is now due and payable on the premises held and occupied by you, being those premises situated in the city of _____, county of _____, state of _____, commonly known as _____.

Your account is delinquent in the amount of $ _____, being the rent for the period from _____ to _____.

You are required to pay said rent in full within _____ days or remove yourself from and deliver up possession of the above-mentioned premises. If this order is not complied with, legal proceedings will be instituted against you to recover possession of said premises, to declare the forfeiture of all agreements between us, and to recover rents and damages, including court costs and attorney's fees, according to the terms of our agreement.

Dated this _____ day of _____, 19_____.

_____
Owner

PROOF OF SERVICE

I, the undersigned, being of legal age, declare under penalty of perjury that I served the thirty-day notice to pay or quit, of which this is a true copy, on the above-mentioned tenant in possession as follows:

_____

_____

_____

Executed on _____, 19_____, at _____.
By: _____
Title: _____

THIRTY-DAY NOTICE TO PERFORM COVENANT

To _____, tenant in possession:
Please be advised, you have violated the following covenant(s) in our agreement:

_____

_____

You are hereby required within _____ days to perform the aforesaid covenant or deliver possession of the premises now held by you, being those premises situated in the city of _____, county of _____, state of _____, commonly known as _____.

If you fail to do so, legal proceedings will be brought against you to recover said premises and all restitution allowed by law.

This notice is intended to require performance of the aforementioned covenant. It is not intended to terminate or forfeit the agreement under which you occupy said premises.

Dated this _____ day of _____, 19_____.

_____
Owner

PROOF OF SERVICE

I, the undersigned, being of legal age, declare under penalty of perjury that I served the thirty-day notice to perform covenant, of which this is a true copy, on the above-mentioned tenant in possession in the following manner:

_____

_____

_____

Executed on _____, 19_____, at _____.

By: _____

Title: _____

THIRTY-DAY NOTICE TO TERMINATE TENANCY

To _____, tenant in possession:

Please be advised, you are hereby required within thirty days from this date to vacate and deliver possession of the premises now held by you, being those premises situated in the city of _____, county of _____, state of _____, commonly known as _____.

This notice is intended for the purpose of terminating the agreement by which you now hold possession of the above-described property. Should you fail to comply with this order, legal proceedings will be levied against you to recover possession of the property. In addition, the agreement by which you presently hold the property will be forfeited. It will be the intent to recover rents and damages for the period of the unlawful detention.

Please be advised that your rent on said premises is due and payable up to and including the date of termination of your tenancy under this notice.

Dated this _____ day of _____, 19_____.

_____
Owner

PROOF OF SERVICE

I, the undersigned, being of legal age, declare under penalty of perjury that I served the thirty-day notice to perform covenant, of which this is a true copy, on the above-mentioned tenant in possession in the following manner:

_____

_____

_____

Executed on _____, 19_____, at _____.

By: _____

Title: _____

SELLING FOR A PROFIT 17

Making a profit is what it is all about, and selling is the quickest way to collect your reward. When you buy your first rehab property, you may have concerns about selling it. There will always be some doubt about liquidating the property to recover your investment and pocket your profits. These concerns are natural and a part of the business. Nothing is guaranteed in life, and rehab deals are no different. There are no assurances of a profit until it is in your bank account. This logical apprehension is no reason to lose sleep.

Prepared with the proper knowledge, you can almost assume success. By following the advice in this book, you are well equipped to rehab your way to riches. The road will have humps and bumps, but there is a pot of gold at the end. Getting the property rehabbed is a substantial accomplishment; selling it for maximum profit is fantastic.

The methods employed in selling real estate are as diverse as the properties being sold. Techniques for single-family homes are completely different from the tactics used in selling income properties. Small multi-family properties present their own challenges and require yet another approach. All in all, use the methods that work best for you.

This chapter provides detailed information on selling single-family homes, small multi-family dwellings, and commercial grade multi-family buildings. Each of these types of properties requires a different strategy. By the end of the chapter, you will know more than many real estate agents. The odds are good you will know more than many seasoned investors. I have enjoyed the challenges involved with real estate sales. Such battles of wits have spurred me to explore many unique methods. I am going to share these diverse experiences with you. Settle in and get ready to learn how to make the most of your real estate investment.

SELLING SINGLE-FAMILY HOMES

The first type of property to be examined is the single-family home. This group includes detached homes, townhomes, and condos. The emphasis will be on detached homes and townhouses since these are the most common single-family residences. In every case, I will assume your property is complete and ready to sell. The examples are based on selling the property in six months or less. If you have to sell fast, refer to the section near the end of the chapter. It gives you ideas for selling fast with minimal lost income.

Single-family homes are marketed to people planning to live in them. This is their highest and best use and will net the most profit. As a rehabber, you must step out of your contractor's boots and into your salesman's shoes. Don't look at the property as an investment, view it as a home. There are big differences between these two perspectives. Selling to a happy home buyer requires the use of politics and flash.

Preparing the Property

When your rehab work is complete, you will need to prepare the home for sale. This won't require large sums of cash, but the effort is necessary to see a high return on your investment. Little things mean a lot to prospective home buyers. Allot money in your rehab estimate to dress up the home. You don't have to furnish the home, but you should make it homey. The goal is to separate your property from others on the market. This separation can be accomplished with small embellishments. Something as simple as cut flowers in the window sill can make a difference.

Selling a home is a matter of developing a marketing plan and implementing it. The first chore is to make the home appealing to the buying public. With a newly renovated home, this only requires making the house into a home. Assuming the house is unfurnished, these accents may test your creativity. Start with the exterior, as these improvements will be the same with a furnished or an unfurnished home.

Invest in attractive landscaping. You don't have to buy exotic shrubbery, any alluring greenery is suitable. Landscaping is an often overlooked enhancement. Pleasing landscaping adds much to the first impression of a home. These first impressions are decisive in capturing and holding a prospective buyer's attention. If a buyer is turned off by the exterior appearance of a home, it is very difficult to generate an interest in the interior of the property. Creating an attractive lawn and landscaping is pivotal in the sale of a home.

The next major factor in exterior attraction is a neat and orderly look. If the property has a disheveled appearance, it will bias the prospective buyer. An unkempt exterior instigates the impression of an equally unkempt interior. Be certain the grounds are neat and orderly. Trim the hedges, edge the walkways, and dress up the flower beds. Don't leave garden hoses stretched across the lawn. Close garage doors and keep garbage cans out of sight.

Placing a wreath on the front door makes the house appear inviting. Curtains in the window provide good curb appeal and a measure of security. Vandals are less likely to target the home if it looks lived in. Gutters should be in good repair and clear of debris. Fences need to be painted and window panes should be clean. Remember, the exterior of the home is the first view observed by a prospective purchaser.

Interior preparations should include clean floors

and as many amenities as you can provide. A basket of potpourri in the bathroom provides a pleasant fragrance. If the home has a fireplace, put logs on the andirons. When appliances are present, have them in working order. This removes any doubt about the working condition of conveying appliances. Have the home's heating, cooling, and plumbing facilities functional. Buyers like to test the plumbing and heating systems. Don't neglect to have the electrical service active. There is nothing worse than trying to tour a home by flashlight.

These tips will give you an edge over much of the competition. Any advantage you can gain is money in your pocket. When the house is ready to be shown, you must make a decision. Will you attempt to sell the property yourself, or will you engage the services of a real estate broker? This is a vital decision with many consequences.

Should You Sell It Yourself?

By selling the home yourself, you will save between five and seven percent of the selling price. This isn't pocket change, but can you sell the property quickly and efficiently? Every month the home is on the market, you are losing money. If a broker can sell the property quickly, her commission is a small price to pay. The question is, can a broker sell the home any faster than you can? There is no clear-cut answer for this question. Every investor you pose the question to will have a different opinion.

Again, I have been on both sides of this question. As a builder and rehabber, I have weighed the advantage of brokers. As a broker, I have tried to convince sellers of my advantages in the sale of their real estate. What are my conclusions? I have concluded the question cannot be answered with a blanket statement. Good brokers are indispensable and bad brokers are a disaster. The trick is finding an excellent broker with your best interests at heart. This is no easy task.

Broker Advantages

Brokers have many advantages on their side. Most of them are members of multiple listing services. This exposes your property to hundreds or thousands of brokers. Each of these brokers could be working with eight buyers at any given time. This is a lot of exposure. The odds dictate the numbers should prevail. Brokers are trained salespeople; this not often a rehabber's strength. When using a broker, you don't have to pay for advertising directly. Real estate firms enjoy walk-in traffic and the interest of a wide range of clients. As a rehabber, you do not have access to these potential buyers.

When a broker sells a home, it is rarely the one advertised and called on by the buyer. Most brokers use these ad calls to sell another property. They don't plan this strategy, but the numbers prove the statistic to be accurate. As a rehabber, you probably only have the one house to sell. You don't have access to other properties to spin a buyer into. Brokers are also in tune with financing and lending institutions. This single fact can mean the difference in a sale and a serious looker.

Real estate brokerages are designed to sell homes. They have every sales tool at their disposal. Brokers save you time and frustration, if they do their job efficiently. A good broker will work with the buyer from start to finish. She will show the property and obtain a signed offer. Then she should assist in the loan application process. Next, she will perform the necessary follow-up on the loan processing. During this time, she will soothe the nerves of anxious buyers. The seasoned broker will attend the closing. Experienced brokers have seen too many deals die at the closing table not to attend. There are many good reasons to list your property with a known brokerage.

Making a Decision

The decision to list with a broker is something only you can make. If you have a highly desirable property, you may not need professional sales help. Maybe you are as qualified as anyone else to find a buyer. You might look at paying the advertising cost as being minimal when compared to a broker's commission. Time is another factor. Do you have the time to return phone calls and show the property at inconvenient times? Buyers are noted for wanting to see a property at their convenience, not yours.

Attitude and personality play a part in your decision. Acting as your own salesperson can be very frustrating. If you don't enjoy working with people, your performance in sales is very ineffective. The steps to reaching a successful closing are much more involved than they appear. Without almost constant follow-up and baby-sitting of the potential buyers and others involved in the process, you will not see a completed transaction. Whichever choice you make, insist on selling smart.

If you list with a broker, push her to sell your property. You have more to gain from the sale than anyone else. A broker gets paid for any house sold; she does not care whether it is yours or your neighbor's. Keep tight reins on the broker and offer bonus incentives for the quick sale of your home. Making the decision to sell your own property means taking full responsibility for your success or failure. Follow the advice in this chapter to reduce your holding time and increase your profits.

SUCCESSFUL SELLING

In a competitive market, you will need a hook to sell your property fast. There are dozens of possibilities for making your property the first on the block to sell. In addition to selling fast, your goal is to obtain the highest price possible. When you are able to combine these two qualities, you will be one happy rehabber. Let's look at some ways to do just that.

Pre-Arrange Financing

If you take an active interest in the sale, pre-arrange financing for your prospective purchaser. Even if you list with a broker, you can structure a financing plan for the buyer. If this is done in advance, with attractive features, your sale should come together much quicker. Talk with the lender holding the note on your property. Frequently, they will be open to putting together a competitive loan package for new owners. There are ways you can participate in making your financing alluring.

Buy-Downs

Buy-downs are one way to give your house an edge in the financing arena. By paying discount points, you can lower the interest rate your buyer will receive on a new loan. Different lenders offer sundry forms of buy-downs. They are all similar but may have different terms and caps. Check this option out—a loan with a below-market interest rate can push a buyer over the edge. The money paid in discount points should be saved due to a quick sale. Holding the property will cause you to incur carry costs on your rehab loan. Selling fast eliminates this expense and pays for the discount points.

Rebates

Rebates are usually an effective incentive for a fast sale. Offer the buyer a cash rebate of $2,000 when the closing is complete. Call it anything you want. It might be money for moving, drapes, or a vacation. In fact, offer the buyer a free vacation to a selected travel hotspot. Travel agencies may offer a great deal on some vacation packages. This tactic can be especially effective in winter. When the weather is inclement and the temperature is hugging zero, a vacation to a tropical paradise can be very tempting. This temptation becomes stronger when the trip is a bonus for buying a home you already like.

Rebates and vacations won't be the single deciding factor in a buyer's decision to act. It may, however, be the pressure point on the decision to buy your home instead of the competition's. The expense of providing these incentives is returned in the form of reduced carry costs. If you get a good offer fast, take it. A closed sale, with the proceeds in the bank, is better than the gamble of waiting for a higher price. The real estate market is volatile; waiting another month could mean seeing the market take a dive.

Option to Buy

This next approach is one I had great success with. When your home is finished, advertise it as a lease-with-option-to-buy property. You have to be willing to become a landlord, but this procedure can produce great income. If comparable houses are renting for $800, lease yours for $975. Why would people pay $175 more for your house than one just like it down the road? Because, you are going to apply $300 of their monthly rent to the closing costs for the purchase of the home. Don't get all upset about giving away your money. In fact, you are giving much less than you are getting.

Before showing the rest of my cards, let me tell you the early advantages of this deal. By charging $175 more than current market rents, you should get a better grade of tenant. This reduces landlording headaches and preserves your property. Preser-

vation of your home should be a prime objective. You don't want to rehab the home twice in one year. By having tenants planning to buy your home, they will treat it as their own. They won't view the house as a rental. Their focus will be on buying the house. These tenants are golden—the chances are good they will improve the property.

The higher rent allows for a positive cash flow. At market rents, the cash flow would probably be negative. The tax advantages of owning rental property add up to increase your overall profit. By signing a year's lease as a tenant, the buyer won't purchase the home for at least a year. This is a key element of your money-making strategy; I will go into this more in a moment. To summarize, you get an excellent tenant, tax advantages, above market rent, and the potential for a much higher sale price. Now, let's continue with the structure of the deal.

The Deal

If you sold the house today, you would get $75,000 for it. Following the lease-option approach, your contract amount will be based on the home's projected value a year into the future. Using a 7% rate of appreciation, the appraised value then will be $80,250. This is a $5,250 gain in appraised value. Don't confuse appraised value with sale value. You can sell your home for any amount agreed to between you and the buyer.

Selling on lease-option terms gives you leverage for a higher price. These buyers are limited in what they can do to obtain their own home. I would not hesitate to increase my cash sale price by 10% on a lease-option deal. Your justification for this increase is the lock-in you are making on the sale price. How much will the house be worth in a year? No one knows how much the property value will increase or decrease in a year. You are guaranteeing the price a year in advance.

Adding 10% for the option and assuming a 7% appreciation increase, your final sale price will be $87,750. Giving a cash rebate equal to $300 per month will cost you $3,600. Be careful how you design the rebate. Most loans have a due-on-sale clause prohibiting you from entering into an installment contract of sale. Directly applying a portion of the monthly rent to the purchase can trigger this clause. If that happens, you may have to pay the entire loan off immediately. If you are not able to do this, you could lose your property to the lender.

The way to work this deal involves two agreements. The first agreement is a standard rental lease. The other document is an option to purchase. In the option, you agree to pay $3,600 of the buyer's closing costs at closing. You could negotiate your sale price of $87,750 and offer to discount it by $3,600 if the optionee signs the option today. In either case, you are achieving the same result, without violating the due-on-sale clause. Never allow the rebate to apply to the down payment, which I will explain later.

By doing this deal you have enjoyed monthly income, tax advantages, and an increased sale profit of $9,150. In the beginning, you thought you were giving $300 a month away. Now, you can see you got more than you gave. This is the outcome if the house is actually purchased. In the majority of my deals, the homes were never bought by the optionee. I never planned on their buying the property, I just wanted the rental advantages associated with this plan. This is where the rebate for down payment comes into the deal.

In the option agreement, you agree to pay closing costs or reduce the sale price. The optionee must still accumulate a down payment. He or she is rarely able to do this and either renegotiates the option or moves. If you renegotiate, the sale price and rent are increased. You continue this year after year until they buy or move. Each year you are building equity and net worth. When they do buy, you make more money than selling with a standard deal. The only way you lose is if they trash the house. Due to the quality of the tenant and the intent to purchase, the risk of destruction is greatly reduced.

DON'T OVER-IMPROVE

When you rehab a home for sale, don't get carried away. Making too many improvements will place the home in a higher price range. Improving the home should be done in a way to make it appealing and affordable. Many rehabbers think like quality contractors, not like salespeople. You must learn to assume both positions when making your rehab decisions. Here are a few examples.

Roofs

The house you are remodeling has an old roof. The roof doesn't leak; the shingles are not curling or missing. Should you replace the shingles? Most contractors will say they would install a new roof. This could be a mistake. If the roof isn't leaking and doesn't look bad from the ground, don't replace it. Home buyers are not likely to crawl up on the roof to inspect it. Most buyers will not even consider a roof's condition.

Replacing the roof adds enough to the price of the house that it may disqualify an interested buyer. If the purchaser has a professional inspect the home, the roof may become an issue. This is not a problem. You have two options. You can replace the roof as a contingency in the contract, or you may offer a cash rebate for the home buyer to have the roof replaced later. The advantage to this approach is one of choices.

You are giving the buyer an opportunity to buy for a lower price. If he wants and can afford a new roof, you will provide it or allow a rebate for the expense. You have kept the sale price low to attract a broader share of the market. This gives you more action and a better chance for a fast sale. In addition, you are prepared to remove the objection to the roof with two options. This is the smart approach to marginal improvements.

Windows

The windows in the house may be out of plumb and drafty. As a rehabber, you might automatically plan on replacing the windows. Doing this will add thousands of dollars to the sale price of the home. It is a salable feature, but the cost may blow out your buyer. Consider these factors with every improvement you plan. Look at the effect your improvement will have on the finished price and determine whether it is recoverable and profitable.

GETTING THE WORD OUT

If you decide to sell your own property, how will you let the world know it is for sale? Newspaper advertisement is the first place most for-sale-by-owners (FSBOs) turn. It is a common medium for finding buyers, but it is not the only way to attract buyers. Posting property data sheets, with photos, on community bulletin boards may produce good results. The alcoves in food stores are a good place to post your notices. These bulletin boards are seen by thousands of people each day.

Sending property data sheets to large corporations may generate some interest in your property. These corporations often help their transferring employees find suitable housing. Military bases are another place you can mail your information to. They have a large influx of people with housing needs. Many of these corporations and bases will post your listing on their bulletin boards. There is a sample Property Data Sheet at the end of this chapter.

The fact that you don't want to list your home with a broker doesn't mean you can't work with brokers. Send brokerages an information package on your property. Include a letter stressing the fact that you have no interest in signing an exclusive right to sell listing. Invite their participation on an open listing basis. If the average commission for your property would be 6%, offer a 3% commission to the brokerages. When brokerages co-broker with another agency, they normally receive one-half of the total commission. You are basically acting as the listing broker and inviting the brokers to co-broker with you.

This is a fair deal for the brokers, and if they sell the house their effort will be worth the commission. Be prepared to be hounded by brokers. As soon as your ad hits the paper, you will be called by numerous brokers. They target FSBOs for listings. Good brokers will be persistent in their attempt to list your property. The smart ones will keep after you without becoming pests. The longer your house goes unsold, the more they will move on you. They hope your confidence is broken and you will list with them.

Brokerage assaults are part of the business. As a FSBO, you will have to endure it. If a particular broker is hassling you repetitively, call the brokerage's owner. Let the owner know your next call will be to the state authorities to complain of harassment. Your bothersome calls from that brokerage will stop immediately. Real estate brokerages are heavily monitored by the governing bodies of their state. As a consumer, you have rights and leverage to send brokers looking for a less aggressive FSBO.

Signs Sell Houses

When you decide to sell your property, don't be shy about it. People cannot buy it if they don't know it is for sale. Look for exposure in every conceivable place. Placing a sign on the property is an obvious step. Ride-by buyers will have seen the exterior of the home before calling you. These are good prospects—they like the outside and want to see more. Advertising costs are the single most expensive part of selling a home. Anytime you engage in advertising, you are taking a risk. There is no guarantee an ad will produce buyers. But you can be assured buyers will not call you if they don't know the property is for sale.

Playing Out Your Hand

You must advertise and gamble to sell your property. You have established your ranking as a gambler by rehabbing the property. Continue your speculation with advertising. If you feel unqualified to sell your own property, list it with a successful broker. Don't list with the first broker you talk to. Investigate the success ratios for the broker and the brokerage. Ask yourself if you have noticed heavy advertising from this firm in the past. Do your homework and choose a broker carefully.

Make the Most of Your Advertising Money

As a FSBO, once your phone starts ringing, you will want to make the most of your prospect's interest. Advertising is expensive; knowing how to handle inquiries maximizes your advertising investment. Keep a prospect log beside your phone and enter information on every serious prospect in it. The first entry should include the prospect's name, phone number, address (when possible), and initial comments. Have a copy of your specification sheet near the phone. Relying on memory can be the beginning of costly mistakes. Have all your facts and figures readily available to present to the inquirer. There is a Prospect Log at the end of this chapter.

Answer the caller's questions and take the opportunity to ask some of your own. This question-and-answer period is a crucial step in the sale of your property. You may use the Phone Query Form at the end of the chapter as a guide.

The information gained by both parties sets the pace for the next encounter. Keeping notes of your conversation assists you in qualifying the prospect. It is a waste of time running around showing your property to unqualified buyers. Asking questions concerning the prospect's likes and dislikes about their current home shows you aspects of your property to emphasize.

Setting Appointments

If the prospective purchaser meets your qualifying criteria, set an appointment to show the property. When possible, arrange multiple showings for the same day. They should be set about thirty minutes apart. It saves wasted time with broken appointments and puts pressure on the potential buyer. When they see a steady stream of lookers, they will feel compelled to make a quick decision.

The First Meeting

When you meet the prospects, give them a well-prepared specification sheet. The sheet should include all pertinent data on the property. Most property data sheets include a photo of the home and a listing of the home's features. To make your specification sheet more effective, include some extras. Pro-vide a floor plan of the house. It should include accurate dimensions for rooms, windows, and doors. These plans help a serious buyer assess furniture placement and drapery needs. The floor plan also reduces your time showing the property. Serious lookers often want a second tour to collect measurements. Your data sheet provides this information and eliminates the need for a trip to gather measurements. You may also want to include a copy of the plat.

Look for comparable sales in your area with closed sale prices higher than your asking price. Provide this information to your buyer. It reinforces the value of your home. As you show the house, probe the prospects for comments. Let them look around on their own and get comfortable with the property. When they are ready to leave, ask more questions. Even if the people don't buy, their comments are valuable to your marketing plan.

Considering Their Comments

Reviewing the comments collected each week will give you insight to your property and your marketing plan. If you receive multiple complaints on

the price, take a closer look at comparable properties on the market. See if you are overpriced or if the people are out of touch with going prices. If the complaints revolve around small cosmetic items, change the items to comply with public demand.

MULTI-FAMILY SALES

Multi-family properties are sold differently than single-family homes. Many of the techniques are the same, but you will need to put some additional information in your sales package. Income property buyers have a keen interest in the income history of the property. With a rehabbed building, you will probably have to use projected income and expense figures. Numbers from past years give you a starting point, but they will not be accurate.

Many aspects of remodeling can change the income potential for a multi-family property. If you install a new energy-efficient heating system, the heating expenses should be less than in previous years. Installing water-saver toilets and shower head flow restriction devices and replacing dripping faucets will reduce your water and sewer bill. Increasing the value of the property with improvements may increase the property taxes. Insulation or new windows and doors may decrease the heating and cooling expenses.

Improving or enlarging apartments may allow for higher rents. Adding a coin-operated laundry boosts the building's income and value. All this activity has an effect on the value of the property. In single-family homes, these types of improvements only increase the value of the home based on the cost of the improvement. With multi-family units, the value is increased because of the improvement and the effect on the income.

Catch an Investor's Interest

When preparing an income property for sale, address your attention to areas of interest to investors. Remove all debris from the hallways, grounds, attic, and basement. You should do this for fire reasons, but definitely do it for sale purposes. Make sure the building is in compliance with all building and fire codes. Let the tenants, if there are any, know the property is for sale. Loudmouth tenants can kill your deal before it starts. If they start bad-mouthing the building, prospective investors will quickly look elsewhere for their investment. Talk with the tenants and remove their fears of ejection.

Provide good lighting in and around the property. This adds to the security of the property and makes it easier for an investor to see the property. Have the mechanical systems inspected and serviced before showing the property. Save your receipts to show the buyers; doing so will remove fears and lost time for duplicate inspections.

Make sure the hallways and common areas are clean and neat. Investors draw conclusions about the tenants and the neighborhood from these public areas. Be sure all lights are in working condition. If an investor sees missing light bulbs and smoke detectors, he assumes thieves are in the building. The parking area will be closely scrutinized. Have any junk cars removed and make certain the parking area is clean and well-lighted.

Put a Package Together

Have past years' expenses available for review by the investors. When you forecast your future income projections, include substantiating documentation. This type of information can be supplied by the local housing authority and your market research. Talk with your banker and have facts and figures on available financing plans. The more information you provide the investors, the better your chances are of getting a quick offer to purchase.

When selling to multi-family investors, you must appeal to their bank account. They are not nearly as concerned about your ornate trimwork as they are about your net operating income. Remember to step out of your contractor's boots and into salesman's shoes. Most investors could not care less about your craftsmanship. Their interest is in positive cash flow, creative financing, and minimal rental headaches.

Creative financing, with commercial grade multi-family buildings, is frequently a deciding factor in a sale. Every investor is going to want to keep as much of his cash as possible. The new breed of investor is focused on finding no-money-down deals. This desire is fueled by books and seminars preaching the power of leveraged buying. Much of the meat from these deals was lost in tax reform. Even so, novice investors will try to buy the prop-

erty with little to no down payment. These guys will pay more than a building is worth if they can keep their cash.

Hold Your Ground

Most of these armchair investors are a pain to deal with. If you deal with them at all, do so on your terms. Never hold paper on a second or third mortgage for more than you are willing to lose. The odds of these OPM (other people's money) investors going belly up are good. You may never see the payoff for any paper you are holding. The redeeming quality to these investors is your potential ability to sell for an inflated price. The disciples of the no-money-down crowd will tell you all about it.

They claim you simply increase the sale price and hold a second mortgage for the down payment amount. This allows the investor to buy into the building with minimal cash. There is usually a major flaw in this plan. Most buildings are financed, and the lender requires a certified appraisal of the property. The lender is going to base the loan on a percentage of the property's appraised value or contract amount, whichever is lower. For investment property, this amount ranges between 70% and 80% on average.

Professional appraisals are expected to be accurate within about 5% of a property's value. How do you inflate the other 15% to 25% to cover the down payment? You can't do it unless you get very creative and flirt with fraud. Certainly, in big deals unique arrangements are made, but for most deals, it cannot be done. The paper you are holding is part of your legitimate earnings. Don't jump into this without a safety net. Whenever you hold a junior mortgage, you are at risk.

If you are buying, insist on junior mortgages; when you are selling, refuse them. Get your cash up front and don't leave yourself hanging on a weak limb. Highly leveraged deals usually break, and the guy holding a junior position loses. There are some ways to improve your odds if you insist on holding paper. Require a blanket second mortgage on all the investor's real estate. At the least, place your junior mortgage against their personal residence. Most investors will resist these two suggestions. When they do, you have your out for not accepting their demands for a second against your property.

Look them in the eye and ask why you should have confidence in them if they don't have confidence in themselves. You will get some blank stares with this question, but it is a valid question. If they are afraid to secure the loan with their other property, they must be afraid of default. Sure, they won't want to tie up their other equity. It reduces their ability to leverage other properties. Turning this question on them will flush out some of their intentions.

As a long-time multi-family investor and broker, I know how buyers and sellers think. As an investment consultant, my advice is the exact opposite for buyers and sellers when it comes to alternative financing. This same advice applies to you, the rehabber. It may be tempting to take your profit in the form of a note. This willingness may make you an extra ten grand on paper, but if you never get paid, you lose it all. Be very selective in your decision to hold a junior mortgage. As a seller, the risks are high and the returns are rarely seen.

Appraisal Manipulation

One way to gain extra profits from multi-family properties is through legal appraisal manipulation. As a broker and an investor, this is how I arranged most of my leveraged deals. This tactic is easy to do with rehab buildings. When you substantially change the physical features of a building, you alter the income potential. This is your power in the appraisal manipulation.

Most lenders and appraisers are willing to work with projected income and expense figures. They are particularly willing to take this course with refurbished buildings. The type of improvements discussed earlier gives you justification to request an appraisal based on projected numbers. Your appraisal results may be more favorable if you help the appraiser. I'm not suggesting you do the appraiser's job for him, but it never hurts to provide factual information.

Create a spreadsheet with historical rents for the last two or three years. Average out the annual rental increases and current market rents on comparable properties. Document all your sources of information for the appraiser. Do an extensive market survey on present rental incomes in the area for comparable properties. Have your contractors participate in your information gathering.

If you are installing a new heating system, ask the contractor to provide estimated annual cost savings derived from the new system. Have your plumber estimate the number of gallons you will save with your water conservation improvements. Compile information on potential money-saving improvements from every contractor. Obtain information on the maximum amount allowed by the Section 8 program for one of your units. Build a comprehensive report containing all this information. Keep it simple; bankers and appraisers may have short attention spans regarding your proposal.

With documented figures, show the appraiser how much your annual expenses will be reduced by your improvements. Stress the potential for much higher rents due to the improved living conditions. Punch every button the appraiser has to raise the value of the property. If you added a coin-operated laundry, include a projection for its income. When you create personal storage facilities, underscore their value to a tenant. Play up every angle you can think of. Keep the projections realistic and feasible. Summarize the complete report in column form or in a simple graph.

This procedure will undoubtedly produce favorable results. You can count on appraisers and lenders being impressed with your market knowledge. The end result of this effort will be an appraisal based on future projections. Following this approach practically guarantees a higher appraisal for your income property. This will translate into more profit for you. The work involved will take several hours, but the results will be worth thousands of dollars.

In Closing

The type of property you are selling is not the issue. The main objective is to sell smart for the highest profit possible. The biggest mistake most rehabbers make is doing too good a job on the remodel. If you plan to sell, keep the improvements on a builder-grade level for most properties. You need to be competitively priced in a crowded real estate market. It may go against the grain to leave some items as is, but you will make more money when you sell.

PROPERTY DATA SHEET

Address _____

Style _____   Price _____

Exterior Dimensions _____

Road Frontage _____   Water Frontage _____

Land Area _____   Zoning _____

Number of Rooms _____   Number of Bedrooms _____

Number of Bathrooms _____   Annual Taxes _____

Deed Book and Page _____   Map/Lot/Blk _____

County _____   School District _____

Siding Type _____   Color _____

Electric Service _____   Heat Type _____

Type of Hot Water _____   Water (Public/private) _____

Attic (Yes/no) _____   Sewer (Public/private) _____

Basement (Yes/no) _____   Assumable Loan (Yes/no) _____

FLOOR PLAN

	1st	2nd	3rd	Basement
Living Room				
Dining Room				
Family Room				
Bedrooms				
Bathrooms				
Kitchen				

COMMENTS

PROSPECT LOG

Name	Address	Phone	Date

PHONE QUERY FORM

1. How many bedrooms do you need?_____

2. How many bathrooms are needed?_____

3. Will this be your first home?_____

4. Do you have a house to sell?_____

5. Have you talked with a loan officer?_____

6. What type of financing will you seek? _____

7. Have you been pre-qualified for financing?_____

8. Have you been looking for a home long?_____

9. When do you plan to move into your new home? _____

10. Do you work in this area?_____

11. When would you like to see the property? _____

12. Will you and your spouse be attending the showing?_____

13. What is the biggest complaint you have about your existing home? _____
    _____

14. May I have your name and phone number, in case I need to change the appointment for some reason? _____

15. Do you have any other questions at this time?_____
    _____
    _____

PLEASE CALL IF YOU CANNOT KEEP OUR APPOINTMENT.

GLOSSARY OF REHAB AND REAL ESTATE TERMS

ACCRUED INTEREST—Earned but unpaid interest. Example: A loan is designed to have accrued interest to be paid at maturity. Interest builds throughout the term of the loan and is paid in a lump sum on the date the loan becomes due in full.

ACQUISITION COST—The sale price and all associated fees incurred to obtain a property.

ADDENDUM—A document added or attached to a contract, becoming a part of the contract.

ADJUSTABLE RATE MORTGAGE (ARM)—A mortgage loan allowing the interest rate to change at specific intervals for a determined period of time.

AMENITIES—In appraisal terms, amenities are benefits derived from property ownership without a monetary value.

AMORTIZATION—The act of repaying a debt gradually with periodic installments.

AMORTIZATION SCHEDULE—A table identifying periodic payment amounts for principal and interest requirements. The table may show the unpaid balance of the loan being profiled.

ANNUAL DEBT SERVICE — The amount of principal and interest required to be paid for a loan.

ANNUAL PERCENTAGE RATE—The effective rate of interest charged over the year for a loan.

APARTMENT—A residential dwelling contained in a multi-family building, usually rented to a tenant.

APARTMENT BUILDING—A property containing multiple residential dwellings with a common entrance and hallway.

APPRAISAL—An estimated value of a property.

APPRAISER — A person qualified to estimate a property's value.

APPURTENANCE—An item outside the property but considered a part of the realty.

ARM'S LENGTH TRANSACTION — A transaction between parties seeking their personal best interest. Not a transaction between husband and wife, parent and child, or corporate divisions.

AS IS—A term meaning the property is accepted in its present condition, with no warranty or guarantee.

ASKING PRICE—The listed sale price of a property.

ASSESSED VALUE — A value established by an assessor for property tax purposes.

ASSESSMENT—The amount of tax charged by a municipality or local authority for property tax.

ASSESSMENT RATIO — A formula used to determine a property's assessed value, based on the property's market value. Example: If the assessment ratio is 50% and a property has a market value of $100,000, the assessed value of the property is $50,000.

ASSESSOR—An individual who is responsible for determining the assessed value of real property.

ASSIGNEE—A person or an entity to whom a contract is sold or transferred.

ASSIGNMENT—A method used to transfer rights or interest in a contract to another party.

ASSIGNOR—A person or an entity who assigns rights or a contractual interest to another party.

ASSUMABLE MORTGAGE—A mortgage loan that may be assumed from the present mortgagor by another party. Note: When a mortgage is assumed, the person assuming the mortgage accepts responsibility for the debt, but the seller of the property is responsible for the loan if the new buyer defaults on the loan. The seller can be relieved of liability if the lender will grant a novation.

ATTACHMENT—A legal act to seize property to secure or force payment of a debt.

ATTORNEY-IN-FACT—A person or an entity authorized to act for another in the capacity of a power of attorney. The authorization may be limited to certain aspects, or it may be general in scope with all aspects included.

BACKUP CONTRACT—A binding real estate contract that becomes effective when a prior contract is void.

BALANCE SHEET—A financial sheet showing assets, equity, and liabilities in two columns where the totals of each column balance.

BALLOON MORTGAGE—A mortgage loan with a balloon payment.

BALLOON PAYMENT—A lump sum loan payment due at a specific time.

BANKRUPTCY — A court action to protect debtors who have become insolvent.

BILATERAL CONTRACT — A contractual agreement requiring both parties of the contract to promise performance.

BLANKET MORTGAGE—A mortgage covering more than one real property.

BLENDED RATE LOAN—A loan mixing the interest rate of an existing loan with the current market interest rate to arrive at an attractive interest rate for the blended rate loan.

BLIND POOL—A term used to describe a group of investors placing funds in a program to buy unknown properties.

BROKER — A state-licensed individual acting on behalf of others for a fee.

BROKERAGE—A business utilizing brokers.

BUILDING CODES — Rules and regulations adopted by the local jurisdiction to maintain an established minimum level of consistency in building practices.

BUILDING PERMIT—A license to build.

CASH FLOW — Used to describe the amount of money received during the life of an investment.

CERTIFICATE OF INSURANCE — Evidence from an insurer proving the type and amount of coverage on the insured.

CERTIFICATE OF OCCUPANCY—A certificate issued by the code enforcement office allowing a property to be occupied.

CERTIFICATE OF TITLE—An opinion of title provided by an attorney to address the status of a property's title, based on recorded public records.

CHAIN OF TITLE—The history of all acts affecting the title of a property.

CHATTEL—Personal property. Example: A range or refrigerator may be found in a house, but they are chattel, or personal property, not real property.

CHATTEL MORTGAGE—A mortgage loan secured by personal property. Example: An investor buying a furnished apartment building might pledge the furniture as a chattel mortgage.

CLEAR TITLE—A title free of clouds or liens that may be considered marketable.

CLOSING—The procedure in which real property is transferred from seller to buyer, and the time when the change of ownership is official.

CLOSING COSTS — Fees incurred during the closing of a real estate transaction. These fees include such items as commissions, discount points, and legal fees.

CLOSING STATEMENT—A sheet detailing a full accounting of all sources and uses of funds in a real estate transaction.

CLOUD OF TITLE—A dispute, an encumbrance, or a pending lawsuit that if valid or perfected will affect the value of the title.

COLLATERAL—Property or goods pledged to secure a loan.

COMMON AREA—The area of a property used by all tenants or owners. Examples: hallways, parking areas.

CONSIDERATION — An object of value given when entering into a contract. Examples: earnest-money deposit, love and affection, a promise for a promise.

CONTRACTOR—A person or an entity contracting to provide goods or services for an agreed upon fee.

CONVEY—To transfer to another.

CONVEYANCE—The act of conveying rights or a deed to another.

COUNTER-OFFER—A rebuttal offer to a previous offer to purchase real property.

COVENANTS — Promises or rules written into deeds, or placed on public record, to require or prohibit certain items or acts. Example: A deed may have covenants preventing the use of a home for business purposes.

CREATIVE FINANCING — Any financing deviating from traditional term mortgages.

DEED—A properly signed and delivered written instrument, conveying title to real property.

DEED IN LIEU OF FORECLOSURE—The voluntary return of a property to the lender without requiring the foreclosure process.

DEED RESTRICTION—Similar to a covenant, a restriction placed in a property's deed.

DEFAULT—Breaching agreed-upon terms.

DEFECT OF TITLE—A recorded encumbrance prohibiting the transfer of a free and clear title.

DEFERRED PAYMENT—Payments to be made at a later date.

DEFICIENCY JUDGMENT—A court action requiring a debtor to repay the difference between a defaulted debt and the value of the security pledged to the debt.

DEMOGRAPHIC STUDY—Research to establish characteristics of the population of an area, such as sex, age, size of families, and occupations.

DEPOSIT OF EARNEST MONEY — Money placed with an offer to purchase real estate to assure good faith and performance of the contract.

DISCOUNT POINTS—Fees paid to a lender at the time of loan origination, to offset the difference between the note rate of the loan and the true annual percentage rate.

DISCRIMINATION — Showing special treatment (good or bad) to an individual based on the person's race, religion, or sex.

DOWN PAYMENT—Money paid as equity and security to cover the amount of purchase not financed.

DRAW—An advance of money from a construction loan, to reimburse the contractor for labor and materials put in place.

DUE-ON-SALE CLAUSE — A clause found in modern loans forbidding the owner from financing the sale of the property until the existing loan is paid in full. These clauses can be triggered by some lease-purchase agreements. The clause gives a lender the right to demand the existing mortgage be paid in full, upon demand. Failure to comply can result in the loss of the property to the lender.

DUPLEX — A residential property housing two residential dwellings.

DWELLING—A place of residency in a residential property.

EARNEST MONEY—Money placed with an offer to purchase real estate to assure good faith and performance of the contract.

EASEMENT—A license, a right, a privilege, or an interest that one party has in another party's property.

EQUITABLE TITLE — An interest held by the purchaser of a property placed under contract but not yet closed upon.

EQUITY — The difference between the market value of a property and the outstanding liens against it.

ESCROW—The act of placing certain money or documents in the hands of a neutral third party for safekeeping until the transaction can be completed.

ESCROW AGENT—A person or an entity receiving escrows for deposit and disbursement.

ESTATE FOR LIFE—An interest in real property that ends with the death of a particular person.

ESTOPPEL CERTIFICATE—A document proving the amount of lien or mortgage levied against a property.

EVICTION—A legal method for a property owner to regain possession of real property.

FAIR MARKET RENT—The amount of money a rental property may command in the present economy.

FAIR MARKET VALUE—The amount of money a property may be sold for in the present economy.

FEASIBILITY STUDY — A study used to determine whether a venture is viable.

FIRST MORTGAGE — A mortgage with priority over all other mortgages as a lien.

HYPOTHECATE—The act of pledging an item as security without relinquishing possession of the item.

INCOME PROPERTY—Real property generating rental income.

INSURABLE TITLE—A title to property that is capable of being insured by a title insurance company.

INTEREST-ONLY LOAN—A loan with terms requiring only the payment of interest at regular intervals until the note reaches maturity.

LANDLORD—A person who leases property to another.

LEASEHOLD — The interest a tenant holds in rental property.

LESSEE—A person renting property from a landlord.

LESSOR—A landlord renting property to a tenant.

LETTER OF CREDIT — A document acknowledging a lender's promise to provide credit for a customer.

LEVERAGE—The act of using borrowed money to increase buying power.

LIEN—A notice against property to secure a debt or other financial obligations.

LIFE ESTATE—An interest in real property that terminates upon the death of the holder or other designated individual.

LIFE TENANT—An individual allowed to use a property until the death of a designated individual.

LIMITED PARTNERSHIP — A partnership in which there is a general partner and limited partners. The limited partners are limited in their risk of liability.

LINE OF CREDIT—An agreement from a lender to loan a specified sum of money upon demand without further loan application.

MAI—An appraisal designation meaning Member, Appraisal Institute.

MARKETABLE TITLE—A title to real property free from defects and enforceable by a court decision.

MORTGAGE BANKER — Someone who originates, sells, and services mortgage loans.

MORTGAGE BROKER—Someone who arranges financing for a fee.

MORTGAGEE—An entity holding a lien against real property.

MORTGAGOR—An entity pledging property as security for a loan.

NET INCOME—The amount of money remaining after all expenses are paid.

NET WORTH—The amount of equity remaining when all liabilities are subtracted from all assets.

NET YIELD—The return on an investment after all fees and expenses of the deal are subtracted.

NOVATION—An agreement in which one individual is released from an obligation through the substitution of another party.

PASSIVE INVESTOR—An investor who provides money but does not provide personal services in a business endeavor.

PRO-FORMA STATEMENT — A spreadsheet projecting the outcome of an investment.

SECONDARY MORTGAGE MARKET—A system in which mortgages are bought and sold by investors.

SRPA—Senior Real Property Appraiser.

WARRANTY DEED — A deed in which the grantor protects the grantee against any and all claims.

ZONING—The legal regulation of the use of private land.

INDEX